Crisis, Recovery and War

Crisis, Recovery and War

An Economic History of Continental Europe, 1918–1945

Roger Munting and B.A. Holderness

PHILIP ALLAN

New York · London · Toronto · Sydney · Tokyo · Singapore

First published 1991 by
Philip Allan
66 Wood Lane End, Hemel Hempstead
Hertfordshire HP2 4RG
A division of
Simon & Schuster International Group

Typeset in 10/12pt Times
by Inforum Typesetting, Portsmouth.

Printed and bound in Great Britain
by BPCC Wheatons Ltd, Exeter.

British Library Cataloguing in Publication Data

Munting, Roger
  Crisis recovery and war: An economic history of
  continental Europe 1918–1945.
  I. Title   II. Holderness, B.A.
  338.94

ISBN 0–86003–805–X (Cloth)
ISBN 0–86003–904–8

---

1 2 3 4 5   95 94 93 92 91

In memory of Anne Holderness

Contents

Tables

Part 3

Part 4

Units of measurement

Metric measures are used throughout. Thus, for example, tons are 1000 kilograms; quintals, a less frequently found unit, are 100 kilograms. The word 'billion' is used for one thousand million, to accord with the increasing practice in Britain. In Germany and much of continental Europe (and, indeed, properly in English) this figure is referred to as a 'milliard' and 'billion' means one million million. We have avoided this usage except where necessary for clarification (e.g. when referring to the German '*Billmark*' in 1923), and indicated this clearly in the text.

Exchange rates

Country	1913	1932	1938
UK	486.6	350.6	489.0
Germany	23.8	23.8	40.2
France	19.3	3.9	2.9
Italy	19.3	5.1	5.3
Belgium	19.3	2.8	3.4
Netherlands	40.2	40.3	55.0
Switzerland	19.3	19.4	22.9
Sweden	26.8	18.5	25.2
Denmark	26.8	18.8	21.8
Norway	26.8	18.0	24.6
Finland	19.3	1.5	2.2
Austria	20.3*	14.0	18.9
Hungary	20.3*	17.4	19.7
Czechoslovakia	20.3*	3.9	3.5
Poland	23.8†	11.2	18.9
Romania	19.3	0.6	0.7
Bulgaria	19.3	0.7	1.2
Spain	19.3	8.0	5.6
Portugal	–	3.2	4.4
Yugoslavia	–	1.6	2.3

Expressed as US cents per unit of currency

* Pre-war Austro–Hungarian Empire
† Pre-war Germany

From I. Svennilson (1954) *Growth and Stagnation in the European Economy* (Geneva: United Nations), pp. 318–19

Preface

Our purpose in writing this book is to provide a reasonably concise survey of the main economic developments in continental Europe in the years from the end of the First World War to the end of the Second. This is an area well covered in specialist literature but there are few general works which attempt an international comparison. Notable exceptions include the survey by Derek Aldcroft (1980) *The European Economy 1914–1980*, and more recently the two volume book by F. Tipton and R. Aldrich (1987) *An Economic and Social History of Europe, 1890–1939 and 1939–1980*. Both of these are wide ranging in time and space. We hope in this volume to offer more detail, especially on national experiences, while at the same time allowing comparative and international surveys of cyclical and structural change.

The period chosen covers the major turning points of the twentieth century: the great economic Depression and two world wars. Both wars resulted in the redrawing of the map of Europe and profound economic change both within the continent and in terms of Europe's standing in the world. The geography, the concept of 'Europe', is less straightforward. Practicality dictates our focus. Works on the economic history of Britain in the English language are legion. Although Britain is clearly part of Europe in many respects her economic experience has differed from that of the continent. Thus we have chosen not to include particular treatment of Britain, though where British experience has a bearing on the general we make appropriate reference to this. There is a similar, indeed stronger, case for excluding the USSR. Throughout the period the Soviet economy was to a large extent separate if not insulated from the economic forces which influenced the rest of the continent. There is in addition a large and specialised literature on the USSR.

In preparing this book we have called on a large number of works by authors more expert than ourselves. Although we eschew footnote references in the text, we include a guide for further reading with each chapter. In most cases we confine these to works in English, except where suitable references are not available. This cannot constitute a comprehensive bibliography, however. We therefore wish to acknowledge the expertise of a great many authors who remain nameless.

Many people have helped us more directly, however. First we must thank Philip Allan for his early encouragement, our editor, Peter Johns of Simon and Schuster, and the anonymous referees for their comments and helpful suggestions. We are particularly indebted to Professor Martin Vogt of the Institute of European History, Mainz, for his assistance with German material. Similarly, we acknowledge, with gratitude, the advice and information from Professor Akos Paulinyi of the Technische Hochschule, Darmstadt, and Dr Shaun Hargreaves-Heap of the University of East Anglia. We thank also Hazel Taylor and Judith Sparks for assistance with typing. Needless to say we alone are responsible for the shortcomings.

Introduction

The First World War was a major historical turning point. At the time poet and politician alike saw the Great War, as it came to be called, as the war to end all wars, the end of an era. The war brought a social trauma. Although it was not a 'total war', in the sense that all society was involved, in the way that they were in the Second World War, the experience affected people far more profoundly than previous conflicts had done. At the start of hostilities no combatants expected the war to last very long. Just as in Britain, life in most of Europe not directly affected by fighting went on under the initial expectation that the troops would be home by Christmas, and that in the meantime there would be 'business as usual'. Such expectations were to be disappointed and as the war dragged on the initial enthusiasm, which many ordinary people had expressed, waned. Although the fighting was limited in space it was more prolonged and bloody than previously experienced. In various parts of Europe civilian populations became directly involved, suffering shortages of food and other goods.

Thus in the post-war years there was an expectation that the world would be made better. The statesmen who met at Versailles to determine the fate of Europe, with the best of intentions, set out to create a better Europe. As we shall see many of their expectations were to be disappointed. There were also some contradictions. There was a widespread belief in Europe and the USA that the clock could be turned back to re-establish the pre-war status quo. This was not nostalgia so much as a desire to dismantle the paraphernalia of the war years, to get back to peacetime normality. This can only have been to accord with the experiences before 1914. But it went further than this. The peacetime economy before 1914 had been successful and attractive and it was understandable that the peacemakers sought to retrieve these virtues. What were the features that were being re-established?

Undoubtedly the years before the First World War had seen an expansion of international economic exchange and interdependence. Trade had grown at a faster rate than total production; there was free movement of capital and, for many, of peoples as well. In the generation before 1914 great waves of migrants, including refugees from poverty and discrimination, flooded into North and South America, Australia, New Zealand and South Africa. International capital movements increased also. Huge investments from outside funded capital construction in the Americas, Russia and the European empires overseas. Within Europe Britain and France above all were the great international creditors; Russia and south eastern Europe the great debtors. Trade, too, increased. Western Europe (again largely Britain) provided the largest market for food and raw materials. Manufacturers in Britain, Germany, France and Belgium depended on the world markets to absorb their production. Thus the markets of the world became more interdependent. All this was aided by improved technology of communication – steamships, railways, telegraphy. Above all exchange was facilitated by a financial system of fixed exchange rates, based on the Gold Standard, which provided security and stability in dealings.

However, all was not sweetness and light. The free flow of goods in trade was severely restricted by tariffs and other protective measures. Indeed these had increased in the late nineteenth century, particularly for agricultural products. In response to falling world prices, European governments raised tariffs to protect their own producers. In Germany food tariffs were increased in 1879, 1885, 1887 and 1902; in France in 1881, 1885, 1887 and 1892. Russia had the highest food tariffs in Europe – at over 96 per cent on grain – after 1891, as well as a massive general tariff on all goods. Of the major European producers only Britain clung to free trade (Denmark and the Netherlands were also free food importers).

The Gold Standard appeared to operate smoothly before 1914. At its heart was a system of fixed international exchange rates with the value of each currency being determined by its gold content. In many places gold coin circulated as currency alongside bank notes and other metals. In principle, the amount of money in circulation was regulated by the amount of gold holdings of each national bank. In practice, however, the ideals were not always followed, as each national exchequer followed national interests rather than some international 'rules'. In reality the most important factor was confidence, in steady rates of exchange and in the international banking functions of the City of London. British banks and finance houses provided loans for the shipment of goods and very often a note issued by a major London bank was readily accepted as secure payment and could easily be rediscounted. The 'system' was not put to the crucial test before 1914 as it was in later years. The City of London also provided the major insurance centre and Britain also had the world's largest shipping fleet. Britain's role as an open market was vital also, though never the function of any great design. Britain had a trade deficit with most manufacturing economies which enabled them to finance their own deficits with primary producers. Britain, in turn, funded her trading deficit with invisible earnings (though she had a trade surplus with some primary exporters as well). International trade and payments were balanced multilaterally, with the British economy playing a pivotal role. Thus in several ways Britain provided a fulcrum to the world economy even though in industrial output Britain had been eclipsed by Germany and the USA.

The current account surpluses earned by the major economies of western Europe funded a large amount of the capital invested abroad, particularly in Russia, the Balkans, Scandinavia and beyond Europe. Britain and France in particular, but also Germany, the Netherlands and Belgium, funded foreign investments in this way. The major European economies accounted for the greater part of the world's production before 1913. The Great War brought not only conflict and destruction on an unprecedented scale but also the destruction of much of the international 'system' that had developed before 1914.

In the short run, the break up of trading relations was obvious. Before 1914 Germany had been Russia's major trading partner, Britain had been Germany's. In the longer run other changes could never be reversed. Not only were there profound changes in Europe, Europe as a whole was weakened compared to the USA (and others) in terms of production. In financial terms also there was a major change. Britain and France were plunged into debt; for the first time the USA became a major creditor nation. The international economic balance of power changed. Thus to attempt to re-establish the features of the pre-war world economy was a lost cause; Europe was never able to recover its previous position in the world economy.

On the other hand it is important not to exaggerate the extent of change. Empires within Europe were destroyed: the Habsburg Empire was broken up, the Russian Empire overthrown by revolution, imperial Germany defeated in war and further weakened at the peace conference; and the residual Ottoman Empire was finally destroyed. However, the British and French imperial possessions remained and were consolidated. In later years they were to increase in economic importance. Indeed British and French overseas interests were enhanced and extended as imperial rivals were weakened. In particular, Britain and France became active and politically responsible in the Middle East.

Domestically, radical political changes in much of Europe were not universal. There was no social revolution in western Europe. The social fabric of Britain was not altered fundamentally; Third Republic France remained. Notwithstanding the march of industrialisation and the demonstration in the war of the power of heavy industry, agriculture remained a major employer and producer of income and the agricultural interest remained politically powerful.

Thus changes in social fabric and economic organisation were more often gradual than radical. Yet the First World War opened a period which saw profound changes within and beyond Europe.

The war itself, most commentators would agree, was largely the result of German expansionism and aggrandisement. The major objective in Germany's war aims was to form a huge economic area within Europe. It was conceived that this could become an economic empire to match the might of British and French possessions overseas. Arguably, therefore, the war can be seen as a search for markets and secure sources of supply. This might explain the great irony that the major European powers went to war with their principal trading partners. The conflict gave the lie to the liberal economic expectations that increased trade and interdependence between nations would reduce the chances of war.

German interests were in the creation of an economic area incorporating Belgium and the industrial regions of France; to the east the western provinces of Russia and the Baltic would provide foodstuffs. Austria–Hungary, the Balkans, Scandinavia, Switzerland and the Netherlands would remain independent but within a vast confederation and beholden to the German industrial centre.

This was reminiscent of the ideas of *Mitteleuropa* that had been put forward early in the nineteenth century. In many ways, also, it was to be echoed with the territorial ambitions of Nazi Germany in the Second World War. There were inconsistencies, in 1914 as well as in 1939. The landed aristocracy of imperial Germany – the Junkers – had interests that did not always coincide with the industrialists of Germany. They wanted more land to farm or for others to settle, and so divert land hunger at home. But they could not compete with the large estates of Hungary, the Ukraine or the Baltic provinces of Russia. Their interests were in continued protection. Industry, on the other hand, wanted more secure control over raw material resources and freer exports of their industrial produce. Implicitly this meant easier imports. Cheaper food would also reduce pressure on wages. Even if such conflicting aims could be resolved, it was doubtful if *Mitteleuropa* could do it for it would not produce a self contained or complete trading area. It was necessary to import from outside Europe; the naval blockade in the war years seriously weakened the central powers.

Other nations also had economic interests to defend. France wanted to regain the territory of Alsace–Lorraine, lost in the Franco–Prussian war. She also wanted access to (and control over) the coal resources of the Saar. French interests were very much in adjusting the relative strengths of her industry and that of Germany by weakening Germany as well as strengthening France. Britain, the major power in 1914, wanted to maintain that position and defend the status quo which was to her advantage. Britain had much to lose from disruption, and indeed lost much. Italy and Russia, as lesser economic powers, were also cautious. Both had much to lose. Italy had a territorial quarrel with Austria but had close economic links with Germany. Russia's main trading partner was Germany; a continental war would (and did) seriously disrupt the passage of trade with her allies, Britain and France. She had nothing to gain from war. The First World War was fought by nineteenth century generals with twentieth century technology. Whereas earlier wars and battles (perhaps where these generals had learned their skills) had been fought to conquer territory or establish independence, now there were few gains to be made. All nations experienced losses to varying degrees.

The war also brought serious domestic financial disruption to most participants. The costs of war imposed burdens too large to be met from domestic taxation so that governments were obliged to raise revenue by borrowing, in some cases with severe inflationary results. For states that were not directly involved, however, the war presented economic opportunities. Many countries developed import substitute industries or turned to alternative suppliers from European businesses. In particular, the USA and Japan were able to make real commercial advances in the war at the cost of European exporters.

Further reading

General

There are several texts which provide a general coverage of the economic history of the period under review. W.A. Lewis (1948) *Economic Survey, 1919–1939* (London: Allen and Unwin) was published more than 40 years ago but continues to provide a useful economic analysis, from a Keynesian viewpoint, of the inter-war years. A more recent comprehensive survey is to be found in D.H. Aldcroft (1980) *The European Economy, 1914–1980* (London: Croom Helm). F. Tipton and R. Aldrich (1987) *An Economic and Social History of Europe*, in two volumes, 1880 to 1939 and 1939 to the present (London: Macmillan) is very wide ranging in focus, taking in social, cultural and political developments as well as economic affairs. A general study of European industrialisation in the long run is offered by Sidney Pollard (1981) in *Peaceful Conquest – The Industrialisation of Europe 1760–1970* (Oxford: Oxford University Press). More detailed accounts of developments in individual countries can be found in C. Cipolla (ed.) (1976) *The Fontana Economic History of Europe*, volumes 5 and 6 (Glasgow: Collins). Statistical material can be found in B.R. Mitchell (1975) *European Historical Statistics, 1750–1970* (Cambridge: Cambridge University Press).

PART 1

International trends

1

Post-war settlement and reconstruction, 1918–29

The most obvious effect of the war was the loss of life and property and the destruction of capital. Even if the large losses of life in Russia are not included, the war claimed some 12 million fatalities, with a further 12 million demographic loss. Added to this were the many millions of wounded and disabled. These losses were uneven, the greatest being in Serbia and Montenegro, France and Russia.

Physical destruction was much more restricted to those areas where fighting had been prolonged – the eastern front, part of the Balkans and northern France and Belgium. The real effects on industry were much more ones of dislocation than destruction. The loss of markets, sources of raw materials, fuels and transport were more pressing and widespread. Before the days of aerial bombardment, physical damage to factories and even dwellings was very narrowly confined.

The peace settlement was dictated by the victors in their own interests. In the short run, however, the most urgent need was for famine relief. Shortfalls in agricultural production, and especially transport, were urgent. Much of Europe was faced with starvation as food imports could not be supplied or paid for. In Austria in 1918 the daily bread ration fell to 100 to 150 grams; milk consumption was down to 7 per cent of the pre-war level. Malnutrition contributed to post-war mortality. Austrian nationalists claimed that enemies deliberately kept supplies from Austria: Poland and Czechoslovakia refused to supply coal, for example. Previous supplies of food, fuel and raw materials had come from within the empire; now they had to be imported. This break up of former trading areas was to have longer term consequences as well. Similarly, Saxony, cut off from former supplying areas, faced great shortages. In the Ruhr, mines were faced with absenteeism as men went

3

looking for food. Dutch proposals in 1920 for loans to aid food supply and thereby coal production were resisted by the French for fear that increased coal would aid German industry too much. The atmosphere of post-war animosity and distrust did little to alleviate immediate hardship. The United States provided most famine relief, to the tune of $1250 million, but virtually none was as a gift. All but 10 per cent had to be paid for, though private charitable donations contributed a further $500 million relief.

Separate peace treaties were signed with the major belligerents, at Versailles with Germany, St. Germain with Austria and Trianon with Hungary. A crucial clause held Germany responsible for the war and therefore responsible for paying for the losses inflicted. The problems following from the imposition of reparations were to be of great political significance within Germany and are explored more fully below. A further principle enshrined in the peace process was that of national self-determination.

The great multinational empire of the Habsburgs was broken up and new states created or recreated. A number of independent republics, Latvia, Lithuania, Estonia and Finland, broke away from the Russian Empire. (Although on the allied side in the war, the empire was destroyed by the revolution of 1917 and the new Soviet state signed a separate treaty with Germany in April 1918 at Brest–Litovsk. This involved substantial territorial losses to Germany. Soviet Russia took no part in the peace settlement after Germany was defeated, but took the opportunity to renounce the earlier treaty.) Poland was re-established from former Russian, Austrian and German territory. Austria, Hungary and Russia lost substantial territory; Germany was also reduced in size in Europe (by some 15 per cent) and lost all her overseas possessions.

Czechoslovakia and Yugoslavia were established, with national independence for the first time. Romania made huge territorial gains, almost tripling in size. Italy made some modest gains from Austria; France gained the substantial industrial region of Alsace Lorraine from Germany and access to the resources of the Saar (this remained under League of Nations sovereignty until 1935, when it was returned to Germany after a referendum).

Redrawing the map of Europe also exacerbated some economic problems. There were now 38 independent states compared with 26 before 1914. The principle of self-determination was imperfectly applied. Substantial foreign minorities remained, such as Hungarians in Romania, Germans in Poland and Czechoslovakia and Poles in Lithuania.

Insular political attitudes are understandable in this context. For the newly created nations, one great task was to cement national unity. Czechs and Slovaks had little in common; Yugoslavia was a mixture of various nationalities, languages and religious denominations. Even Poland, so long a nation without a country, had to constitute its national consciousness into political reality. So often, one means of doing so was to point to the common enemy – Germans, Austrians, Russians, Hungarians. Political attitudes thus hindered economic activity.

The intense nationalism was manifest in economic hostility to former imperial rulers. Alien property was taken over and landed estates broken up and redistributed, in a general process known as 'nostrification', without prime concern being given to economic considerations. Land reforms often resulted in the formation of family smallholdings with insufficient capital to create a viable farm. At a more general level, also, nationalism had negative consequences. Instead of engaging in cross-border trade, bringing together established resources separated by frontiers, nations deliberately and specifically set out to minimise such trade in attempting to develop import substitutes. Thus an industrial economy like Czechoslovakia imported food from North America rather than neighbouring Hungary. Hungary sought to develop its industrial base and resist imports from Czechoslovakia.

1.1 Recovery

The return to peace faced European nations, victor and vanquished alike, with major economic difficulties. The short post-war boom disguised profound economic problems, many of which were to persist until the next great conflict less than a generation later. The war had brought inevitable changes in the world economy, with a relative weakening of Europe as a whole. Added to these were political measures, internationally and nationally, undertaken as part of, or consequential to, the peace-making process, which were to aggravate the expected process of stabilisation, recovery and growth. Governments were drawn more into the direct management (or mismanagement) of national economies, despite a reluctance to become so involved. Thus, even Britain, the bastion of free trade, extended protective tariffs in peacetime. In 1919, she formally suspended the Gold Standard, which had efectively been in abeyance during the war. In some European nations, especially among the new and successor states, intervention was more extensive and more welcome.

But national governmental measures could do little to correct and counterbalance changes in relative economic strength arising from the war. The first and most obvious was the relative decline of Europe as a whole in the world economy. In part this was accounted for by the virtual withdrawal from the international economy of Soviet Russia, but

Table 1.1 An index of production and trade in 1925

	Production (1913 prices)	Trade
Europe*	103	91
USA and Canada	127	139
Rest of world	130	126

1913 = 100

* Europe excluding the USSR

From League of Nations (1931) *Course and Phases of the World Economic Depression* (Geneva), p. 15

was more the result of decline of European exports during the war years. Before 1914, world industry had been dominated by Britain, France, Germany and the USA, which produced three quarters of world manufacturing output. In 1913 European nations were responsible for 43 per cent of world production; by 1923 this had fallen to 34 per cent (Table 1.1).

The major growth areas were outside Europe. In 1925, manufacturing was 122 per cent higher than in 1913 in Japan, 41 per cent higher in Australia; in much of Europe it was lower.

There were similar moves in shares of world trade; the main beneficiaries were the USA and Japan, which had been able to secure markets from manufacturers cut off from wartime belligerents. Latin America and the British Dominions made gains in the supply of primary products. The pre-war food exports from Russia or the Balkans had been all but cut off in the war and their place taken by producers in the New World. It was thus into an already well stocked market that European producers, especially of commodities like grain and sugar, sought and fought to re-establish their position in the 1920s.

In the short run, as we have seen, the immediate problems were with shortages and hunger. As output increased and agriculture was generally able to recover faster than manufacturing, there was resultant over supply on world markets, a phenomenon which contributed to international recession at the end of the decade.

The deterioration in the terms of trade experienced by primary producers weakened their earning power and capacity to purchase manufactured imports. Within Europe, this relative weakness was more evident in the central and eastern regions, especially the new and successor states. Nation states where agriculture was the major source of income were relatively poor. Further, agricultural incomes tended to be higher in the north and west than the south and east of Europe. One of the most striking characteristics of the inter-war years was that agriculture was richer and more productive in industrial than agricultural

Table 1.2 Agricultural production in Europe

	1909–13		1925–29	
	production	import/ export	production	import/ export
All continental Europe*	1017.3	+137.1	1101.3	+171.1
Including eastern Europe†	340.0	– 26.7	479.0	– 6.1
Net exports from North America[a]		– 63.9		–151.1
From Southern Hemisphere§		– 75.1		–136.1

Cereal production in million quintals and exports (–) or imports (+)

From League of Nations (1943) *Agricultural Production in Continental Europe* (Geneva), pp. 59–65

Cereals = wheat, barley, rye, oats and maize
* Europe excluding the USSR and Turkey
† Eastern Europe, east of Sweden, Germany, Switzerland, Italy
[a] North America = USA and Canada
§ Southern Hemisphere = Argentina, Uruguay, South Africa, Australia and New Zealand

economies. The values of net output per worker in agriculture in 1938, expressed in $US, were: for Romania $80, Poland $130, Hungary $150, Bulgaria $180; in industrial Czechoslovakia the figure was $200 and in Germany and France $290 and $280 respectively.

The weakness of demand among primary producers was one reason why foreign trade was much slower to recover than total production. Another factor, however, was the real barriers placed by governments to international trade. Here was an area where political action contributed to economic difficulties, for it was within the power of government to reduce barriers to trade. Such action, however, depended on international agreement, and this was lacking. The Genoa Conference in 1922 agreed to re-establish fixed exchange rates, based on gold, as far as possible at the pre-war rates of exchange. Such an emphasis was mistaken in attributing so much value to the old Gold Standard.

There were attempts to revive it on the basis of a re-introduced Gold Exchange Standard. Before 1914, the Gold Standard had provided a security of fixed values and ready exchange of currencies for international trade. Incomes earned in one market could readily be spent in another. More particularly, the open British market had been crucial in helping to balance international trade. After the First World War, the mantle of major international creditor fell on the USA. But the USA was a much less open economy than Britain had been before 1914.

Protectionism was not peculiar to the USA, but was evident in almost every European economy as well. To a point this was unavoidable, for all European countries were faced with pressures on trade balances as

Table 1.3   Tariff levels 1927, 1931

	1927	1931
Germany	122	244
France	97.5	160
Italy	112	195
Belgium	77.5	122
Switzerland	160	252
Romania	140	207
Hungary*	131	197
Czechoslovakia*	137	220
Austria*	77	158
Spain	132	185
Bulgaria	296	420
Sweden	72.5	97
Finland	91	134
Poland	74	93
Yugoslavia†	144	207

1913 = 100

* based on pre-war Austria–Hungary
† based on Serbia, 1913

From H. Liepmann (1938) *Tariff Levels and the Economic Unity of Europe* (London: Allen and Unwin), p. 415

short-term import demands tended to exceed or run ahead of their export capacity. But governments were also bound to put their domestic interests first. Despite a general acknowledgement of the need to reduce import barriers made in international arenas by governments, in reality a good many behaved differently. Table 1.3 indicates the way tariffs were increased in the 1920s.

These figures are, however, a simplification, as they aggregate tariffs on different commodities in different markets. They are at best a guide to trends. More specific examples of increases in protectionist duties make the same point, however. In Germany, duties on agricultural products were 55 to 65 per cent higher in 1927 than in 1913. French duties on farm products were actually lower in 1927 than in 1913 but were increased substantially thereafter to become 40 to 50 per cent above pre-war levels.

A further point also relates to foreign trade. Every new state imposed tariffs both for the protectionist reasons referred to above and for the more immediate need for revenue. Financial instability affected the whole of Europe. Tariffs were used for the most common historical purpose of providing income for the state. Financial problems were of pressing concern throughout Europe, and the rest of the world, in the post-war years. These were manifest as inflation and the persistent problem of international debt.

Inflation was a universal phenomenon. The most extreme case of all was in Germany, culminating in the hyper-inflation of 1923, when nominal prices went up to one million million times their pre-war level. Soviet Russia (4000 million increase), Poland (2.5 million), Austria (14000) and Hungary (23000) also experienced hyper-inflation; but every country went through the experience to some extent. For a generation the industrial world had known general stability or secular deflation. The ten years after the outbreak of war brought a new and unsettling experience.

The root cause of inflation is easy to determine. Every nation borrowed to finance war expenditure; taxation was only a partial answer. Taxation was politically unpopular, especially where direct taxes had a short history. In France, for instance, income tax was introduced only during the war years, in 1916. It was politically easier to increase an established tax than to introduce one. It was anyway impossible to finance war expenditures out of taxation. Total war expenditure was reckoned at $210 billion; only borrowing and inflationary printing of money could meet such fiscal demands. The inflationary pressures which built up in the war continued thereafter as governments continued to borrow to finance reconstruction and resettlement. The only real alternative to continued inflationary action by governments was a stringent policy of price reduction, risking social instability, unemployment and reduced social expenditure. At a time of social fragility, with demobilised soldiers returning from the front, no government could take the risk. Even victorious and mildly affected Britain and the USA allowed a short-term inflationary boom. When restrictions were introduced it was at the cost of unemployment and social protest. The fragile new republic of Weimar Germany could afford no such social risks, nor could the new states of the east. There was also an element of deliberate demonstration to the victorious powers that the German financial structure was being ruined by reparations, whether or not in reality this was the case.

Stabilisation was not easily achieved and in some cases needed outside assistance. Austria and Hungary were refinanced, with the League of Nations acting as an agent for government and banking consortia, to create new currencies, the schilling and the pengo. British and American banking loans provided gold backing for the new Reichsmark in Germany in 1924, after domestic stabilisation had been achieved in 1923. By this time the consequences of a balanced budget had become less undesirable than the effects of inflation.

The establishment of international currency stability was equally problematical. Despite the agreed intention to seek the return to pre-war rates of exchange, many nations were unable to achieve this. Where wholly new currencies were established, any return to the values of 'imperial' days was out of the question and barely relevant. In much of western Europe it was easier to achieve pre-war parities but at the cost of adverse economic consequences. Sweden stabilised in 1922, Switzerland and the Netherlands in 1924, Britain in 1925, Denmark in 1926 and Norway in 1928. All these returned to the pre-war rate of exchange. Elsewhere (for instance in France, Belgium, Czechoslovakia and Finland) governments and national banks were unable to achieve this and allowed currencies to float to find a market level which was significantly below pre-war parity, expressed in US dollars. France stabilised in 1926, at 20 per cent of 1913 levels, rejoining gold formally in 1928. This proved to be a temporary cost advantage for French exports. Before stabilisation was achieved, the visible export surplus earned by France resulted in capital exports, as deposits held abroad. After 1926 these returned to France and in 1928 were converted to gold by the Bank of France. This resulted in a substantial increase in France's gold holdings, and comparable drains on international liquidity. It remains a matter of dispute to what extent, if at all, such a low valuation was contrived by the national bank. It should more reasonably be regarded as advantageous *ex post* than a policy objective *ex ante*. The relative contribution of a cheap franc to the fortunes of the French economy in the 1920s is also a matter of uncertainty (see Chap. 6). Belgium stabilised in 1926 at the even lower rate of 14 per cent. The Italian currency reached a rate of 20 per cent in 1926 (3.89 cents per lira). Unusually, Mussolini revalued the lira (to over 5 cents per lira) in 1927. Spain and Portugal showed modest devaluations. Albania, a small country which had achieved national independence only in 1912, introduced its own currency in 1926. Before that date other nations' notes and coin had been used as currency.

The Gold Exchange Standard was in itself fragile. Backing for currency issue could be held in the form of foreign exchange rather than gold proper – as deposits in sterling or dollars. This was a major difference from the pre-war Gold Standard when money issues had been backed, nominally, by gold holdings. Under the new system London became vulnerable to currency movements, as many of the foreign currency holdings were held in the form of sterling on deposit in London. Further, much of the currency backing was acquired through borrowing, sometimes short-term, rather than in earnings from exports. In the longer term both these factors were to prove weaknesses in the international financial system.

International debts were to prove a political problem of great consequence. The foremost and special case of this general phenomenon was Germany. The demand for reparations was a running sore for Germany through the 1920s, though the real economic burden was much less than was claimed (see Chap. 7).

The Dawes Plan of 1924 provided loans as backing for the new German currency and established an ordered system of payment, without reducing the total bill. Annual payments were set at one billion marks initially, to rise to 2.5 billion per annum by 1928–29. More significantly the Dawes Plan opened the way for loans which were greatly to exceed the value of reparations paid by Germany. The Young Plan of 1929 reduced the sum demanded and reparations were finally written off in 1932.

1.2   Inter-allied debts

Inter-allied debts were separate from reparations. The major creditor was the USA but there were substantial sums owed also to Britain and France, principally arising from wartime provisions to imperial Russia. The new Soviet regime refused to acknowledge these obligations. Altogether some 20 countries (not all in Europe) owed $13.2 billion to the USA after the war. These debts were to have been paid at 5 per cent interest over 25 years. For long it was assumed that it was necessary for western powers like Britain and France to impose reparation demands on Germany in order to obtain the means to pay the USA their debts. In turn Germany borrowed money from US banks and so obtained the foreign exchange to pay reparations. There was thus a supposed absurd cycle of debt and repayment which, if once broken, could cause financial chaos. It has further been argued that such a fracture led to international crisis after 1929. There is in reality little to support this view. Inter-allied war debts, like reparations, were of great political importance but less of a long-term economic burden than has often been supposed, largely because they were not paid in full. Had they been paid, such a large inflow of funds would have disturbed world balances of payments. It was nevertheless necessary for the USA to collect some repayment both to help cover the interest on Liberty Bonds, which had been sold to raise the money for the loans, and to appease American public opinion. But the USA extended the repayment period and reduced the rate of interest. In effect, Britain was able to forgo 35.1 per cent of debts, France 64.8 per cent, Italy 81.5 per cent, and Belgium 63.3 per cent. France began to repay her debts only in 1926 and paid $32 million per annum until 1932. Against this American tourists spent $137 million in France before 1929. In a similar period France repaid more to the Netherlands, Norway, Spain and Switzerland for wartime supplies than she paid to the USA. Other loans and expenditures flowed into European countries in the 1920s, and these exceeded the volume of governmental debts to the USA. It is difficult to maintain, therefore, that the repayments of debts to the USA depended upon the receipt of reparations from Germany. The allied debts did not constitute a great burden on the balance of payments of European countries. They were a cost to national exchequers, however. Whereas most of the new cash flows into Europe were private, outstanding debts were an obligation on governments and thus remained of real political concern.

The international debts arose from wartime credits and deliveries in kind, expenditure by forces and so on. There was also vitally necessary famine relief in the immediate aftermath of war; relief for former enemies had to be paid for immediately, that for former allies added to the overall debt burden. In 1931, in the middle of the Great Depression, a moratorium on all inter-governmental debts was declared. By this time the USA had received only a small proportion of the total sums owed to her.

The second half of the 1920s was a period of general economic growth which for some nations amounted to a boom, though more obviously one of investment than consumption. Stock market prices, especially in the USA, increased faster than profits. There was also a considerable volume of overseas investment, especially from the USA, as we have seen, but also from Britain and France. Such international investment went some way to counteracting the limiting effects of tariffs. Tariffs were imposed primarily for raising revenue; they affected prices more than volumes of trade. The quantum of world trade increased by 4 per cent per annum between 1925 and 1929. On the other hand tariffs could also be used for specifically protective purposes, for infant industries in eastern Europe or agricultural protection, such as the swingeing agricultural tariffs which heralded the 'battle for grain' in Italy in 1925. Such protection helped to produce generally faster growth in east than in west European economies, though from lower levels. Of the industrial economies France, Belgium and Luxembourg, Germany, Czechoslovakia, Sweden and the Netherlands grew relatively fast, Britain, Denmark, Norway, Italy and Austria less so. France in particular experienced an export-led boom in the 1920s, helped by an undervalued currency, the development of new industries and a vibrant tourist sector. The major growth in exports was before the stabilisation of the franc in 1926. Industrial production in France increased by over 39 per cent between 1913 and 1929, in Belgium by 52 per cent! British industrial output was about 9 per cent higher in 1929 than in 1913. Most of the growth was in the earlier years; Britain experienced relative stagnation between 1925 and 1929 largely because of structural problems, though she was marginally disadvantaged by an overvalued pound. Germany had a similar overall growth rate, with industrial output 10 per cent higher in 1929 than 1913, but in Germany the boom years were very much in the later 1920s.

In nearly all industrial economies (France, with a labour deficit, was a notable exception) unemployment became an increasing problem before the coming of economic depression, even during the boom years. In Britain the lowest recorded figure was 9.7 per cent (insured persons); in Germany the figure never fell below one million after 1925. In Scandinavia the position was even worse: 10.1 per cent in Sweden in 1924, 10.7 per cent in 1929; in Denmark the average for 1925–9 was 18.5 per cent, in Norway 19.5 per cent. The low overall demand for labour tended to discourage mobility, and trade unions sought to minimise differentials between industries. The growth in the recovery years was thus accompanied by characteristics which hindered some new developments, whether in obstacles to labour mobility or state protective measures inhibiting the growth of international trade.

The persistence or growth of unemployment in the later years of the 1920s suggests, in terms of conventional economic theory, that aggregate demand was failing to grow sufficiently to absorb all potential labour. Further, a serious fall in demand was to lead to recession after 1929. On the other hand an alternative explanation might be found, in more 'classical' terms, in an undue rise in real wages, leading to disequilibrium in wages and prices. Such matters remain unresolved. There were certainly claims in contemporary Weimar Germany that (money) wages were too high; in Britain also, repeated attempts to reduce wages resulted in bitter industrial disputes. Such neo-classical emphasis has re-emerged in the historiography of the German and British economies of the 1920s, and the Depression. It is noteworthy that unemployment was a common phenomenon in Europe, a point which makes the emphasis on a deficiency in aggregate demand more plausible than one suggesting that real wages were too high.

1.3   Further reading

A good international coverage of the First World War is G. Hardach (1977) *The First World War 1914–1918* (London: Allen Lane); an unusual examination of the experience of the war in Germany is presented by A. Offer (1989) *The First World War. An Agrarian Interpretation* (Oxford: Oxford University Press). D.H. Aldcroft (1977) *From Versailles to Wall Street, 1919–1929* (London: Allen Lane) is a good general survey of the international economy in these years. Post-war adjustment and reconstruction is dealt with in different ways: a contemporary critical assessment is in J.M. Keynes (1919) *The Economic Consequences of the Peace* (London: Macmillan). A more recent economic assessment can be found in S.A. Schuker (1976) *The End of French Predominance in Europe* (Chapel Hill: University of Carolina Press). An attitude less critical to the French after the war than Keynes's is taken by D.P. Silverman (1982) *Reconstructing Europe after the Great War* (Cambridge, Mass.: Harvard University Press) and M. Trachtenberg (1980) *Reparations in World Politics. France and European Economic Diplomacy, 1916–1923* (New York: Columbia University Press). Broad social changes are well covered by C.S. Maier (1975) *Recasting Bourgeois Europe* (Princeton: Princeton University Press) and (1981) 'The two post-war eras and the condition for stability in Twentieth Century Western Europe', *American Historical Review*, **86**. A number of articles on the general problem of inflation is collected in N. Schmukler and E. Marcus (1983) *Inflation Through the Ages* (New York: Columbia University Press). For an analysis of US loans to Weimar Germany, see W. McNeill (1986) *American Money and the Weimar Republic* (New York: Columbia University Press). S.A. Schuker (1988) *American 'Reparations' to Germany, 1919–1933. Princeton Studies in International Finance*, **61**, July (Princeton: Princeton University Press) unconventionally questions the real economic cost of reparations to Germany.

2

Recession

At the centre of any history of the twentieth century lies the great
economic Depression that affected virtually the whole world after 1929.
Cyclical slumps, recessions in production and declining profits had all
been known before, but the events after 1929 were of an unprecedented
scale and severity. Falling levels of industrial production from peaks in
or near 1929 were accompanied by rising unemployment and falling
prices for all goods, but particularly for primary produce. The decline in
production was not only more severe but more prolonged than in previous recessions. In many parts of Europe industrial production had not
recovered 1929 levels by 1935 (see Table 2.1). Agricultural production
tended to fall much less, though the price fall was steeper than for
manufactures. As incomes fell, so demand contracted and unemployment increased. Unemployment reached levels never before recorded
and constituted the most serious social and economic problem. In turn
government policies often added to the deflationary spiral, exacerbating
the effects of depression. The depression in prices and production was
followed by a financial crisis which swept through Europe in 1931. Thus
the Depression embraced various aspects of the economy, each of which
requires examination and explanation.

Various factors contributed to recession – cyclical contractions in demand in much of Europe, a general tendency for primary product prices
to fall, financial crises in Europe and the USA. These factors were both
long- and short-term. Causes of an initial downturn in prices or production were not the same as those which led recession into a deep and
prolonged depression. Most historical explanation rests on the Keynesian argument of a reduction in aggregate demand leading to a fall in
production and rising unemployment. However, more recently, some

Table 2.1 Index of industrial production, 1927–35

	1927	1930	1931	1932	1933	1934	1935
Austria	90	81	69	60	62	68	77
Belgium	93	89	81	69	71	72	83
France	79	100	89	69	77	71	67
Germany	102	86	68	53	61	80	94
Hungary	96	94	87	77	84	98	111
Italy	(92)*	92	78	67	74	81	92
Norway	81	101	78	93	94	98	108
Netherlands	86	91	79	62	69	70	66
Poland	87	82	70	54	56	63	66
Sweden	84	99	95	90	96	116	127
UK	96	92	84	84	88	99	106

1929 = 100

* Italy – 1928

From League of Nations Statistical Yearbook 1935/7 (Geneva)
P. Fearon (1979) *The Origins and Nature of the Great Slump 1929–1932* (London: Macmillan) p. 11

neo-classical views have come to place more emphasis on an inappropriate real wage rate as contributing to unemployment. This has been put forward as an explanation for rising unemployment in Germany and Britain. There may be much to support this view: real wages in Germany showed a considerable increase, 1925–30 (at 4.6 per cent per annum), unit labour costs rose and German export competitiveness deteriorated. It is less clear that such factors were of general significance, even if they can explain growing unemployment in Germany. And this remains a matter of controversy. The weight of scholarly opinion rests with the 'Keynesians' and a fall in aggregate demand.

One contributory factor was the fall in prices of foodstuffs and other primary products which resulted in declining incomes and purchasing power for agricultural producers and exporters. However, such price falls contributed to rising real incomes elsewhere. Even where protective measures were adopted by governments to counteract falling prices, the net effect might be expected to have been a redistribution of demand (away from the producer to the consumer or from the exporting economy to the protected home producer) rather than a net fall in aggregate demand. Thus it is necessary to explain what prevented a redistribution of income maintaining total demand and thereby inducing recovery.

There are various reasons why this might have been so. Government deflationary policies were widespread in Europe and they contributed to a reduction in demand by reducing total domestic purchasing power. In some cases there were peculiar or distinctive national factors which inhibited demand: these include the highly cartelised industry in Germany (see Chap. 7) and the unrealistic exchange rates which a number of countries maintained. Price falls should in theory have contributed to rising real incomes for consumers, but in reality this did not happen immediately; there were lags and the positive effects of market movements were sometimes partially offset by government intervention. At a more general level an explanation lies with the failure of the financial system to redistribute purchasing power in the recession, through loans or credits to those producers whose incomes were falling, so inducing a more severe depression and slump. For this reason, there appeared to be a direct link with the Wall Street Crash of November 1929 and the worldwide recession which followed. The balance of modern research would suggest, however, that recession in Europe was not simply imported from the USA but that the trade cycle was already beginning to fall before 1929. This was especially evident in Germany, but also in Britain, which can be said to have imported recession through a collapse in export demand. In both countries unemployment was rising before 1929. Production peaked before November 1929 in Germany, Britain, Belgium, almost everywhere except France. Even in France, a boom economy in the 1920s, visible exports began to contract from 1926. It is evident also that European financial crises in 1931 originated with a decline in confidence in Europe rather than outside. The Wall Street Crash did not cause the Depression in Europe, but the loss of financial confidence resulting from it and the poor monetary policies which followed, together with the collapse of American demand, made the recession more severe in Europe and throughout the world. Thus, although European recession did not originate in the USA, the American Depression undoubtedly adversely affected the rest of the world.

2.1 Primary product prices and recession

Following the early post-war years of readjustment when inflation and real food shortages were evident in Europe, there were almost bound to be price falls as European food production recovered. The major west European countries (Britain in particular) had constituted the largest market for food exports before 1914. In the ten years that followed, the gap in supplies from Russia and eastern Europe had been filled by supplies from the New World. European producers were faced with an over-supplied market from the middle of the 1920s. Thus in many particulars the world was over supplied with basic foodstuffs. World stocks of wheat in 1923 stood at 9.3 million tons; by 1929 they had reached 21.3 million tons. Added to this productivity gains in North America and elsewhere meant increased production and falling unit costs. Average European grain yields increased by 28 per cent in the 1920s. All contributed to a fall in prices. Yet demand was relatively inelastic so that falling prices were not matched by a comparable growth in consumption.

The upshot was downward pressure on agricultural incomes before the onset of severe recession. Within Europe the response, although predictable and understandable, merely served to aggravate the general problem. Most European governments sought to protect their own agricultural producers. Despite the march of industry, agriculture continued to be a major employer in the economies of Europe. This was true in Germany and France as well as in the more obviously agricultural economies further east. Industrial economies in Europe protected their own agricultural sectors through various means, including tariffs and physical barriers. The latter often took the form of import quotas, which could be assigned discriminately to different producers, or minimum domestic milling ratios, which were non-discriminatory. In this way, bread flour, by law, was forced to use a minimum proportion of home produced grain. This minimum could reach staggeringly high proportions – over 90 per cent in France and Italy. Such measures invited retaliation, and this was easier to exercise with discriminatory quotas than *ad valorem* duties. French quotas on agricultural imports were answered by Italian countermeasures, for example.

Even Britain, the major food importer and traditional free trade nation, imposed restrictions and granted favour to imperial producers, from 1932, while remaining a major market for dairy exports from Holland, Denmark and Ireland. The main ones to suffer were the agricultural exporters from eastern Europe who were highly dependent on grain products. It became increasingly difficult for them to find markets. It was not simply a question of Goliath threatening David, however. Czechoslovakia, a small but significant industrial economy, limited agricultural imports from immediate neighbours and industrial imports from the more powerful nations of the west.

The biggest price falls, however, came after the beginning of recession. Although a decline in agricultural incomes contributed to depression, it was more of an effect than a cause. Before 1929 falling incomes for primary producers had been matched by loans and credits, which helped to prevent the deflationary effects spreading. After that date such credits were no longer forthcoming. Protective measures and a general growth of 'beggar my neighbour' policies inhibited international demand and the position was made worse by the high levels of debt. Further credits were cut off just as price falls were at their most severe for primary producers (Table 2.2). Between 1923 and 1933 agricultural incomes fell by 59 per cent in Poland, 36 per cent in Hungary, 58 per

Table 2.2 Agricultural price indices, 1929–36

	Germany (1924 = 100)	France (1926 = 100)	Denmark (1924 = 100)	Hungary (1929 = 100)	European wheat* (1913 = 100)
1929	98	100	65	100	124
1930	83	91	66	76	97
1932	60	83	40	69	73
1934	73	68	47	54	66
1936	79	73	57	65	101

Wholesale prices for agricultural products

* Liverpool wheat prices

From I. Svennilson (1954) *Growth and Stagnation in the European Economy* (Geneva: United Nations), pp. 244, 346

cent in Romania and 52 per cent in Bulgaria. Even in France protection could not resist the decline in agricultural incomes, which fell by 32 per cent between 1932 and 1935. Falling agricultural incomes were not fully transferred to importing nations as increases in purchasing power because so much of the income was absorbed in debt repayment. In 1931, for instance, 48 per cent of Hungary's exports were needed to pay interest on existing debts; for Poland the figure was 34 per cent.

2.2   The Depression in Europe

In examining the European Depression it is appropriate to begin with Germany, for the German economy was the first and most seriously affected. Much of the explanation hinges on the evident tendency towards relative overproduction in Germany well before 1929. The subject remains one of controversy over matters of detail, but there is general agreement that recession began in Germany before the Wall Street Crash. Some writers put emphasis on the downturn in inventory investment in Germany from 1928; others put more emphasis on levels of fixed investment; a decline in public authority investment in 1927–28, resulting from a growing problem of public finance; domestic monetary policy became tighter; growing wage pressure reduced internal liquidity. For many years economic historians in Germany have also stressed the over-production of capital goods arising out of the process of concentration and rationalisation of industry in the 1920s. Others, such as Harold James, attribute problems more to the maldistribution of investment, which created over capacity in some areas, particularly steel, textiles and coal. The output of textiles, leather and building began to fall in 1928. The steel industry regularly exceeded its export quota in the International Steel Cartel. The industry became increasingly export-dependent, so successful was it in increasing production; this in turn made it extremely vulnerable when export markets contracted from 1930.

Such domestic industrial factors helped produce a trade recession but it was international market functions, compounded by insular national policies, which pushed the cyclical downturn into depression and slump. These points can explain why German industry was particularly seriously affected. The price and cost rigidities built into the cartels which traditionally characterised German industry (there were 2500 cartels in 1925, 3000 in 1930) were compounded by agrarian protectionism and, after 1931, a relatively over-valued currency. This helped to prevent a stimulus to demand to aid recovery. In the rival industrial economy of Britain the recession was less severe in impact, partly because industrial growth had been so much weaker and more sluggish in the years before 1929. Further, Britain retained a more open market (though imperfect) for imported food and allowed devaluation rather than the imposition of exchange controls. However, it seems that the Depression was initially imported into Britain because of the collapse of export markets. France too suffered from falling export demand but she was able to resist the worst effects of depression for some time because unemployment did not become the great social problem it was elsewhere. France also had the largest gold reserves in Europe and was therefore able to fend off financial collapse when most of the continent was affected in 1931. The agricultural economies of eastern Europe suffered the worst price falls of all. But all European economies were affected by the collapse of international demand and the break up of the international financial system which followed.

2.3   Finance

A series of financial crises swept through Europe in 1931. Although clearly connected with the depression in prices and production, financial problems followed rather than initiated this decline. However, the ruin of a number of major banks, pressure on national currencies and the defensive measures adopted by governments in response undermined confidence, prolonging and worsening the Depression. Because of the dependence of European economies, especially Germany, on the US capital market, it has been tempting to see a direct connection with the Wall Street Crash. There is little to support this in reality. Rather, European financial crises had their own internal causes. The linkage with Wall Street was nonetheless important: first there was a psychological effect, contributing to a crisis in confidence worldwide; second, the contraction of credit in the USA after 1930 contributed to worldwide deflationary pressures which aggravated the effects of the Depression.

For various reasons European nations, particularly in central and eastern Europe, displayed financial fragility. As we have seen, agricultural exporters found it increasingly difficult to meet debt obligations in the face of falling export prices. Germany had become heavily dependent on American lending in the 1920s. US loans to Germany far exceeded the amount she was required to pay in reparations. Between 1924 and 1929 capital imports reached 17.5 billion RM, compared with reparations payments of 8.6 billion RM. Virtually none of these loans was raised by the central (Reich) government, which was responsible for paying reparations, but the loans nevertheless outweighed any burden reparations imposed on the balance of payments. In fact capital imports funded a balance of trade deficit up to 1930 and thereby helped to finance German economic revival. However, there were points of fragility. Some of the loans were raised by a few large industrial concerns, and many by municipal or state (*länder*) governments. The latter often used the sums so raised for prestigious social overhead expenditures or welfare measures (increasingly unemployment relief). Reichsbank president Hjalmar Schacht was particularly critical of what he saw as irresponsible municipal borrowing. Further, there was a tendency, from 1928, for more of this to be short term – selling short-dated interest-bearing bonds – yet to use the money for long-term expenditures.

The move towards short-term borrowing was in part encouraged by Schacht for political reasons. By increasing short-term debts he hoped that creditors (most of whom were western banks) would put pressure on western governments to reduce reparation demands, for fear that there would be a conflict between short- and long-term obligations. The attractions of speculation in New York also made capital a little more expensive in 1928 and so German borrowers were pushed to more short-term issues. There was no sign that the availability of US funds declined *immediately* after the crash in Wall Street, rather demand for further capital fell as recession began to affect German industry in 1929. (US lending to Canada and Latin America continued into 1930, though there was a reduction in US capital loans thereafter.) Germany ceased to be a major new borrower because of growing recession, and because the electoral successes of the Nazi and Communist parties in 1930 induced political uncertainty among potential investors.

Traditionally German banks had close links with industry – far more so than in Britain for example – providing long-term capital loans as well as short-term credits. In some cases they had become too closely linked to particular industries. The Darmstadter and Dresdner banks, for instance, had invested heavily in textiles and the public sector, both of which showed low returns. In any event all banks had been seriously weakened by the inflation earlier in the decade. Municipal governments which had borrowed heavily in the 1920s were, at the end of the decade, in serious financial difficulty as their social welfare payments made up an increasing share of the budget. As early as 1928, unemployment relief constituted the major outgoing for major cities and it was to become crippling later.

A similar, indeed more extreme, interdependence between banks and industry was evident in Austria, dating from the days of the Habsburg Empire. Viennese banks had large holdings of industrial equity. In fact, industrial share capital made up the largest part of their assets. The same was true for a number of German banks. As recession began to take a hold of industry, before the great crash and financial crisis, the value of these assets diminished. However, some Austrian banks also behaved with what appears to be extreme irresponsibility by supporting their industrial debtors – even sometimes to the point of paying dividends on shares to other stock holders. In order to do so the banks borrowed, again often on short term. In effect they borrowed short to lend long to debtors who were going broke. Thus the banks were weakened by declining industrial profits as much as the other way around. Industrial recession and financial crisis each contributed to the other.

The action of the banks can be explained by the expectation that industrial recession would be short lived and minor. There was a perceived need to keep their main debtors afloat simply because of the extreme dependence on them. It is worth noting that no British bank crashed in the crisis, for in Britain there were no similar links with industrial equity. In Austria the position was the more extreme because the largest bank, the Creditanstalt, had taken over other banks and their liabilities in the 1920s and was thus peculiarly vulnerable (see p. 23). In Germany, Austria and elsewhere the contraction of bank liquidity led to further contractions in domestic credit with increased deflationary effects. Share prices fell and commodity prices, already tending to fall, fell more steeply. The only upward movements were in bankruptcies and unemployment.

In 1931 banking crises arose in a number of major European capitals. They were generated independently in Austria, Germany and later Britain, largely as a result of loss of confidence and eventually panic. In May 1931 the Austrian Creditanstalt collapsed, closing its doors before being rescued by government. For many years the collapse of this major Viennese bank was seen as initiating a general European banking crisis. There is some truth in this, for European banks held large deposits in foreign banks and were thus vulnerable to failure elsewhere (British banks lost deposits in Germany, for example). On the other hand it is important to note that there were also independent causes of bank failure or loss of financial confidence within various European countries. Thus it is perhaps more appropriate to see the collapse of the Creditanstalt as one of a number of parallel developments with similar causes rather than direct links, a symptom of serious and widespread financial instability.

As has been pointed out above, the Creditanstalt had behaved with apparent irresponsibility in the 1920s, lending readily to industrial companies to the point where liabilities exceeded assets as early as 1929. By this time the bank controlled as much as two thirds of Austrian industry. (In the 1920s the number of major banks had been reduced, through amalgamation. In 1929 one of the largest, the Bodenkreditanstalt, had collapsed and been taken over by the Creditanstalt, though in so doing the latter also took on the liabilities of the Boden bank.) Clearly the fortunes of the bank and industry were closely intertwined. The fall of the Creditanstalt also had a political dimension. It followed negotiations between governments of Austria and Germany to establish a customs union. As a small economy Austria was particularly vulnerable in a depressed Europe. However, such plans were in breach of the peace treaty of St. Germain (applying to Austria at the end of the war). These proposals clearly had some economic rationale. It was widely noted that intra-European trade barriers were injurious to European economies. The proposed customs union was designed to deal with this danger. In communicating with the British foreign secretary in 1931 the Austrian foreign minister noted: 'If the countries of Europe were to remove all barriers out of the way of their trade with one another, most duties would become superfluous and Free Trade on a vast scale would be realised.'

Most historical opinion suggests that political motives were stronger than economic in the plans for union and opposition to it was similarly politically motivated. France, fearful of German resurgence, was most hostile. Indeed, it has been suggested that the Bank of France connived at a 'run' on the Austrian bank to cause its failure. This seems unlikely. What certainly did happen was that France, the greatest holder of gold in Europe, refused to ease the difficulties for the German and Austrian banks by providing new loans, thus contributing to failure and effectively scuttling plans for union.

In Germany, financial problems arose in 1930. As depression deepened the real cost of paying current debts increased because of domestic deflation. There were also doubts that Germany would honour even the revised reparations payments (these were reduced in money terms by the Young Plan but still represented an increasing real burden on the state budget because central government income was falling). However, even in 1930 there was little foreign panic to withdraw funds from Germany; much of the early flight of capital which began at this time was domestic rather than foreign. Harold James has shown that at most 50 to 60 per cent of bank withdrawals were 'foreign' and that in reality much of this was German capital in flight. Many German companies had foreign subsidiaries and used these to withdraw capital deposits. There was certainly a banking crisis in 1931 but, James argues, it was essentially caused domestically. The withdrawal of American funds was a result rather than a cause.

A run on the German banks became a panic in June and July 1931 (it followed the bankruptcy of the Danat bank). Crowds besieged banks to withdraw deposits. A 'bank holiday' was declared from 15 July to 5 August after which the banks re-opened with a swingeing Reichsbank discount rate of 15 per cent, deliberately to reduce credit. Domestic liquidity was thus further tightened. Banks were reconstituted; there were several mergers. Rigid exchange controls were introduced together with a 'standstill' agreement on repayment of loans in advance of the Hoover moratorium.

Uncertainty and anxiety did not stop there. The coldly rational men of the banking community moved to convert deposits in London into gold. British banks had lost a lot of cash with the collapse of the German system and Britain was forced to seek loans abroad. These loans could be raised only by a Labour government agreeing to reductions in domestic expenditure, involving cutting unemployment benefit and, among other things, service pay. There followed a cabinet split and the formation of a national government.

International confidence was not restored by this move. In September the withdrawal of funds reached such proportions that Britain was forced to abandon gold and allow sterling to devalue.

This was a major turning point, for in effect the Gold Standard as an international system was destroyed. Scandinavian countries, the British Empire and Japan quickly followed Britain in leaving gold. The USA followed in 1933. France, Switzerland, Holland, Belgium, Italy and Poland formed a 'gold bloc' for a few years. Germany, nominally linked to gold, introduced exchange controls which rendered the exchange standard meaningless.

2.4   Government action

The contribution to economic malaise made by government policies can be interpreted in various ways. Contemporary liberal economic orthodoxy dictated that costs needed to be reduced in order to match world deflationary trends, so that national exports could compete in a declining world market. Devaluation was one means of achieving such an end, though this was rarely resorted to as a matter of policy. Spain, for example, avoided the worst of deflation by allowing her currency to float and considerably depreciate. The British devaluation in 1931 was forced by the market. Devaluation could also easily be matched by competitors and was generally regarded as being dangerously inflationary. More usually, governments resorted to reducing domestic costs through deflationary policies, though their major concern was always with their own financial position, their budgets. Brüning's deflation in Germany was sufficient to produce a balance of payments surplus but at the cost of increased unemployment. Thus reductions in government expenditures, by cutting civil service salaries for instance, were resorted to in order to save government expenditure. However, falling tax revenue, simply because there were fewer people in work and less was being produced, made it an ever more elusive goal for many governments to match expenditure with revenue. Added to this was the simple immediate need to make some provision for the unemployed as well as provide a degree of protection for the agricultural producer.

Such protection, as we have seen, disturbed the weak notions of liberal economics further, for the measures constituted a barrier to trade that cost reductions were designed to enhance. The protectionism that was designed to favour the home market more often worsened the lot of competitors more than it benefited the home economy. Further, it invited retaliation so that everyone became worse off in a downward spiral. In theory reduced import expenditure should have been transferred to home producers of import substitutes but aggregate purchasing power was reduced by government deflationary action as well as by the income effects of the Depression.

It would be misleading and inaccurate to suggest that these difficulties were not apparent to the political leaders and economic advisers of the day. There were several attempts at international resolution of the problems of recession, which foundered on national interests. A world economic conference in Geneva in 1927 favoured reductions in tariffs, subsidies and dumping and an end to trade discrimination, but no action resulted. A further conference, in London in 1933, failed because the USA wanted to take advantage of floating the dollar, though the premise of the conference was that all nations should act in concert and simultaneously reduce trade discrimination of all kinds (see p. 31).

In 1931, however, President Hoover proposed a moratorium on international government debts. In the following year an agreement in Lausanne brought an end to outstanding debts. This applied only to government debts; private commercial debts to banks remained. Such action was rather late and followed the threat of Germany refusing to meet reparation demands. Otherwise the USA behaved with a degree of economic insularity. The Hawley–Smoot tariff of 1930 was the highest in the world. From the US point of view, it is difficult to see Congress not favouring their own farmers at a time of ruin. The contraction in American demand (caused by income fall as well as such protective measures) aggravated European and world illiquidity. Arthur Lewis has calculated that in 1929 the USA, through purchases and loans, injected $7400 million into the world economy; by 1932 the figure had fallen to $2400 million.

The drying up of US capital was arguably the greatest problem, for it reduced sources of credit to the world when the world most needed them. There was thus a crisis of illiquidity with no alternative source of funds. In Kindleberger's terms there was no lender of last resort, a function that had unofficially been performed by the City of London before 1914. Before 1914, British overseas investments had tended to follow an inverse pattern with domestic. Thus when domestic demand for capital contracted, capital outflows increased, thereby helping to stimulate demand, indirectly, abroad. After 1930 the opposite was the case. Domestic contraction in the USA was accompanied by a restrictive monetary policy and reduction in overseas investment, thus causing further destabilisation in the economic system which had come to depend so much on American capital.

Within European states similarly restrictive policies were adopted; conventional deflation and reductions in expenditure helped to drive down the level of economic activity. Policies for national protection sought to export unemployment in a series of 'beggar my neighbour' measures. This is hardly surprising, for all governments were beholden to their electorates, their own nation before the international common good. And the Depression brought the more extreme manifestations of economic nationalism to the forefront. At the time no government in Europe was able to resist the collapse of international demand, though in some respects France was in an unusually strong position.

France continued to earn a trade surplus to 1931. The advantages of her undervalued currency had been beneficial for France but not for the rest of the world. France accumulated vast gold reserves as the rest of Europe was growing short of credit. French gold stocks came to be second only to the USA. In 1925 they stood at 25 billion francs, in 1929 67.5 billion francs and in 1931 88.5 billion francs. These stocks enabled France to resist the international financial pressures which affected most of the rest of Europe in and after 1931 (she was eventually forced to devalue in 1936), though they added to the deflation that affected the rest of Europe. They could not shield her from the collapse in world demand.

The Depression had a variety of causes, as we have seen. Falling demand and price fall were succeeded by widespread financial crisis. But political actions at a national and international level served to make some aspects of depression worse. With the advantages of hindsight and the tools of economic analysis which were not readily to hand at the time we can deduce areas where government measures, or their absence, contributed to economic malaise. Most obvious were the pursuit of a balanced budget, elaborate protection and general deflation. The significance of such policies can be explained in the light of Keynesian theory, and an emphasis on the level of aggregate demand. In essence this postulates that the recession was a function of a contraction in the total volume of demand, nationally and internationally. Almost universally, governments reduced demand further by reducing their own expenditure and cutting domestic costs. Protectionism served to reduce international demand. It was not until the social democratic governments in Sweden and Nazis in Germany used some limited 'pump priming' public investment that there was any significant departure from these policies. Even so it is doubtful if Nazi policies, for instance, can properly be interpreted as Keynesian.

Political actions can therefore be seen to contribute to the cause and continuation of depression. Internationally the USA as the major creditor was arguably in the best position to take remedial action. Within Europe the major gold holder was France. International action was weak and ineffectual. Single events like the Wall Street Crash cannot explain the unprecedented collapse of world trade. There had been substantial stock market losses before, as in 1921, without such widespread effects. In 1929 world demand was already beginning to fall. A trade recession became a slump because of a succession of economic problems, a loss of confidence which political action, at national or international levels, failed to alleviate.

2.5   Further reading

The principles and workings of the Gold Standard are most concisely explained in I. Drummond (1987) *The Gold Standard and the International Monetary System, 1900–1939* (London: Macmillan). A similarly brief and clear survey of the Depression is in P. Fearon (1979) *The Origins and Nature of the Great Slump, 1929–1932* (London: Macmillan). This subject is dealt with in much detail by H. van der Wee (1972) *The Great Depression Revisited* (The Hague: Nijhoff) and C.P. Kindleberger (1973) *The World in Depression, 1929–1939* (London: Allen Lane) which has particular emphasis on financial affairs. The experience of banking in the inter-war years, including links with industry and economic crisis, is examined in a special number (1984) of *The Journal of European Economic History*, **13**. This contains useful articles on France, Spain, Italy, Germany, Austria and Hungary, by various authors, as well as a survey article by C.P. Kindleberger. This latter article casts doubt on the international 'interdependence' of financial crises. A special number (1969) of the *Journal of Contemporary History*, **4**, contains articles on each of the main countries of Europe. The recent survey by B. Eichengreen and T.J. Hatton (1988) *Inter-war Unemployment in International Perspective* (Dordrecht: Kluwer) applies contemporary economic theories to this difficult problem.

3

International efforts at recovery

There was real and effective recovery in the 1930s but it had little association with a revival of international economic exchange. Nation states looked to themselves and protected their own markets and populations rather than risk a more open environment. The trade cycle showed a general upturn from 1932 to 1937 but the developments were uneven. France, Belgium and Czechoslovakia, among industrial countries, showed the weakest recovery; Germany and Sweden the strongest. The particular details are recorded in the chapters dealing with national experiences, but some general observations are appropriate here. Recovery was incomplete in many respects. In most parts of Europe, unemployment persisted, particularly in Britain, Scandinavia, Italy and Czechoslovakia; it was largely removed in Germany and never a great problem in France.

A further, and historically unusual, phenomenon was the failure of international economic exchange to recover. International trade in total declined over the decade. Thus, although intra–European trade was fairly constant as a proportion of world trade (at approximately 29 per cent), it did not change from 1928 to 1938. Foreign trade turnover did not regain its pre-depression levels. Recovery was much more associated with home markets than international. Further, there was some 'trade diversion' to closed trading areas, which are discussed in detail below. Even more striking than the slow growth of trade, there was no recovery of the international investments and capital flows that had characterised the 1920s. Currency instability affected the whole world. The United States devaluation, in 1933, disturbed the international financial market further after world currencies had been disturbed in 1931. However, from 1934 stabilisation was more or less achieved once again. Britain and the USA linked their exchanges. After 1936 and devaluation, France joined in a tripartite agreement. However, this did not influence national recoveries to any great extent, nor reverse the economic nationalism that had firmly taken root in much of Europe. Recovery was determined by government action in large measure; it was national rather than international.

This is not to say that there were no efforts to improve the international climate, for they were many, but they met with little success. The League of Nations was the principal umbrella organisation to bring nations together, but international debate and discussion went beyond the confines of the League; the United States, for instance, was never a member of the League. As early as 1927 there were international attempts to deal with undue protectionism. A diplomatic conference of 29 states in that year initially agreed to abolish all trade restrictions within six months, but each claimed exceptions or exemptions so as to limit severely the effect of the measure even had it been ratified. In the following year a further conference agreed to implement a convention to this effect by September 1929. However, few nations ratified the convention and even these had withdrawn by 1934. In 1929 the Young Committee, in considering the problems of German reparations, proposed the establishment of a Bank for International Settlements. Given the great problems of international debt at the time such a body might have been warmly welcomed; but the bank was restricted in its scope and activities by national banks before it came into operation in 1930.

Obviously the limited international measures of this time did not take the coming crisis into account. They were more modestly designed to deal with the relatively recently introduced protective measures which were seen to hinder free economic exchange, in contrast to the commercially free international environment before 1914. But national interests limited what could be achieved. From now on international action, such as it was, sought to tackle the deepening recession but again national interests often intervened. The League paid most attention to tariffs and other obstacles to trade rather than the recession itself and the collapse of the monetary system. But often tariffs were a political response to the effects of recession. In 1930, for instance, the USA had introduced the Hawley–Smoot tariff, primarily to protect its own farmers. The financial crisis of 1931 had led Britain to introduce emergency duties, and a general tariff in 1932.

Many of the initiatives trying to deal with high levels of protection came from the smaller states, for they had most to lose from the closure of export markets. This was especially the case for the agrarian economies of central and eastern Europe. In 1930 an International Agricultural Conference met in Warsaw to consider the special trade problems of agricultural exporters. Bulgaria, Czechoslovakia, Hungary, Poland, Yugoslavia, Romania, Estonia and Latvia attended but made little progress in their collective attempts to gain preferential access to European markets. There were some limited regional agreements: Denmark, Norway, Sweden, the Netherlands, Belgium and Luxembourg signed a convention for economic rapprochement in 1930, and were later joined by Finland. This achieved little in itself but did establish a basis for inter-governmental consultation and advanced warning of tariff adjustments, which in turn fostered the closer economic identity of the Nordic countries from 1934. Similarly the Low Countries had common interests which brought them closer together. Luxembourg, hardly a national economy, had joined Belgium in economic union in 1922, while retaining full sovereignty. In 1932 these countries joined the Netherlands in the Ouchy Convention, which agreed an immediate 10 per cent tariff reduction with further cuts to follow annually. However, as other states failed to co-operate, this idea foundered also.

Great hopes rested on the World Economic Conference of 1933, held in London. The presence of so many prime ministers, finance ministers and presidents of national banks gave the conference enormous prestige and moment. But nothing could be achieved unless all acted together, and nothing was achieved. The USA was to take advantage of floating, and devaluing, the dollar. For the major economic power to steal a march on others in this way was inconsistent with the supposed atmosphere of cooperation. At the same time the countries remaining on gold (France, Belgium, Poland, the Netherlands, Switzerland, Italy) were anxious to retain tariffs and liberty to employ exchange controls in order to avoid devaluation. Nations were competing with each other and employing a variety of measures to do so. Unless the political environment of distrust and competitiveness could be replaced by one of genuine cooperation there was little hope of progress.

After the failure of the conference of 1933 the world in general and Europe in particular (which accounted for the greater part of world trade) moved closer to autarky and trade restriction. Subsequent attempts to alleviate these restrictions were modest. The USA passed the Reciprocal Tariff Agreement Act in 1934, to negotiate mutual tariff reduction, but on a bilateral basis. This she did with Belgium, Sweden, Finland and the Netherlands in Europe as well as Latin America, but the measure had little effect on world trade as a whole. Attempts to regulate the wheat trade in 1933 failed; the 1937 International Sugar Conference was more successful in regulating this trade.

The Tripartite Declaration in September 1936 promised much but ultimately delivered little. France, Britain and the USA were the three partners declaring their desire to foster international economic relations.

In particular it was agreed that the French devaluation, which immediately preceded the declaration, would not be followed by others, thus avoiding a renewed competitive spiral. Switzerland, Belgium and the Netherlands shared in this agreement – significantly, for these countries had formerly been partners of France in the 'gold bloc'. Tariff or quota reductions were announced in France, Switzerland, the Netherlands, Czechoslovakia and Latvia, which briefly helped international business. But the 'success' was short lived. Germany and Italy were notable in not acceding to the agreement. In 1937 commodity prices fell again and there was a renewed recession.

International measures to alleviate depression had been limited. Although they had been almost entirely concentrated on encouraging international trade this recovered only slowly and under restrictions. Pollard makes the interesting observation that in this environment the most favoured nation clause, which had made such a valued contribution to the growth of international trade before 1914, was a hindrance. Few nations were prepared to extend trade concessions to another for fear of having to make similar concessions to all.

3.1   International trade and trade blocs

The inter-war years as a whole were characterised by a contraction in international trade and this was especially true of the 1930s. The Depression finally destroyed the multilateral trading system that had been imperfectly resurrected since the Great War. Although the recovery years did bring a limited revival in foreign trade it was restricted, in large measure, by treaties, tariffs, quotas and other such political intervention.

This was especially the case for the major industrial producers of Europe, Britain, France and Germany. Competition from the USA and the Far East (in particular Japanese textiles, but Britain was also affected by the Indian cotton industry) adversely affected extra-European trade. Britain and Germany lost manufacturing markets in the 1920s; France, which had boomed in that decade, suffered greater losses after 1931. Similarly these three major economies experienced a contraction of their intra-European trade and this influenced the continent as a whole, for these nations constituted the major markets.

Historically, and it remained true through the inter-war years, most international trade was conducted between industrial nations. An expansion of trade and growing trade dependence was an apparent function of industrial development. If we take the League of Nations definitions of industrial and agricultural economies (agricultural: Denmark, Spain, Norway, Poland, Ireland, Hungary, Finland, Romania,

Yugoslavia, Portugal, Bulgaria, Greece, Turkey, Albania, Iceland, Latvia, Lithuania and Estonia; industrial: Britain, Germany, France, Austria, Belgium, the Netherlands, Italy, Sweden, Switzerland and Czechoslovakia), we find that within Europe most trade was between the 10 industrial economies: even in 1935, 44 per cent of their exports were to each other, only 16 per cent to the agricultural economies of Europe. At the same time agricultural economies were dependent on industrial countries for markets. This put the smaller agricultural countries of Europe into a weak bargaining position when that became crucial in the years of depression. Europe as a whole imported raw materials and some foodstuffs from outside Europe. Again the industrial countries were the main importers. Other continents sent 45 per cent of their exports to industrial Europe, only 5 per cent to agricultural Europe. These aggregate figures were inflated somewhat by Britain, which was the largest market for food exports and a major one for manufactures. Germany was the largest export market for the Netherlands (24 per cent of exports in 1928), Austria, Czechoslovakia (over 20 per cent) and Poland (40 per cent) as well as the agrarian countries of south eastern Europe. France was the largest market for exports from Belgium and Spain.

As the three largest industrial powers were such important markets, any contraction in their demand would be bound to have widespread effects. This is part of the story of the 1930s. On the other hand the smaller industrial economies of Europe (i.e. Italy, Belgium, the Netherlands, Sweden and Switzerland) were able to increase their mutual trade during the decade. But these developments could not counteract the generally negative picture of the 1930s. International trade was increasingly characterised by protectionist measures, bilateral treaties and the establishment of restricted trading 'blocs'. France, Britain and other European powers with overseas colonial or imperial dependencies increased their trade in this direction. Germany, without such an overseas empire, was to extend her influence within Europe. Germany, above all, perfected the manipulation of clearing agreements to her advantage, though she was far from being the only nation to resort to clearing. (A clearing system enabled the value of exports and imports to be balanced in international clearing accounts without the necessary transfer of cash payments between one state and another. Details of their operation varied from place to place.) By 1937, 12 per cent of the world's trade was conducted through clearing arrangements. For some European countries the proportion was much higher; over 50 per cent for Bulgaria, Germany, Greece, Hungary, Romania and Yugoslavia.

Clearing agreements were one way around trading obstacles and the difficulties of funding international payments. The variety of trade barriers

Table 3.1 Value of imports subject to quota and licence, 1937

France	58%	Ireland	17%
Switzerland	52%	Norway	12%
Netherlands	26%	Britain	8%
Belgium	24%	Sweden	3%

From League of Nations (1942) *Commercial Policy in the Interwar Period*, p. 70

was itself in part the result of the breakdown of the Gold Standard. Few national currencies remained linked to gold after Britain and the USA abandoned the system. A small 'gold bloc' of France, Switzerland, the Netherlands, Italy (to 1934), Poland and Belgium (to 1935) remained. These currencies were consequently overvalued, with the result that imports needed to be highly restricted and exports often bounty-fed. Other nations retained artificially high currency values but prohibited free exchange with rigid controls. These included most notably Germany and, after 1934, Italy. A third group had depreciated currencies after the great readjustment which began in 1931, yet also exchange controls: in Europe they included Denmark, Czechoslovakia and Greece. The most numerous (on a world scale) were those countries which devalued their currencies and continued to allow free exchange throughout the 1930s. They included Britain, the USA, Norway, Sweden and the British Dominions.

As well as tariff barriers to imports there were physical obstacles, and these were more likely to apply where there was free exchange of currencies. In 1937 the proportion of imports (by value) subject to quota or licence is shown in Table 3.1.

3.2   British foreign trade

As a major trading nation, any contraction in Britain's demand was likely to have widespread effects. Further, as a major market, Britain was in a strong bargaining position when negotiating trade treaties and other arrangements. Given that British exports fell by 26 per cent in volume between 1929 and 1938 there was a major incentive to save imports or relate imports to agreed exports. Such policies were followed, though British participation in bilateral trading arrangements by no means initiated the process, which became widespread within and beyond Europe.

After 1932 Britain made bilateral trading agreements with Denmark, Sweden, Iceland, Finland, Lithuania, Latvia, Estonia, Poland, France, Germany and the USSR. There was also a similar treaty with Argentina, a special trading relation with the Irish Free State and, most significantly, the system of imperial preference following the Ottawa Agreement, also in 1932. When negotiating with those countries in a weak trading position, in particular the smaller primary exporters (Denmark, Iceland, Finland, the Baltic States) and, to a lesser extent, Sweden, Britain was in a position to drive a hard bargain, just as Germany was in relation to south east European economies. Denmark was particularly dependent on the British market; in the 1920s over 50 per cent of exports had gone to Britain. By 1932–3 the proportion was as high as 67 per cent.

The treaty between Britain and Denmark of 1933 allowed Denmark to provide 62 per cent of non-empire British imports of bacon together with a minimum quota of butter, eggs and fish. In return, however, Denmark was required to make significant concessions by reducing tariffs on imports from Britain and above all agreeing to take 80 per cent of her coal imports from Britain. Previously she had been able to import cheaper coal from Poland. Thus the terms of trade were turned against her. (Denmark was less adversely affected by international price movements than other agricultural economies because she was a net importer of grains, which showed the greatest price fall.) As a result exports to Britain contracted (to 53 per cent in 1937, 56 per cent in 1938) and imports increased (28 per cent in 1933, 38 per cent in 1937, 35 per cent in 1938). Significantly, in 1934 a Danish trade treaty with Germany was less disadvantageous to Denmark because Germany was much less significant as an export market.

On the other hand Denmark continued to enjoy a huge trade surplus with Britain. While British exports to Denmark increased in value between 1932 and 1938 from £10 million to £16 million her imports declined from £41 to £38 million, still more than double the export figure. Similar trends were evident for smaller northern economies highly dependent on a small range of primary product exports: Iceland (fish), Latvia, Lithuania and Estonia (foodstuffs and timber), Finland (timber and pulp). They were more or less forced to take British coal and manufactures in return for a secure export market. Yet all benefited from the market access in a highly protective world market, and usually they maintained an export surplus which helped to finance imports from elsewhere. For instance, in 1921–5 Britain took 38 per cent of Finnish exports and provided only 19 per cent of imports; in 1936–8 the figures were 40 per cent for exports, 18 per cent for imports.

Norway, with growing exports of ores, metals, and especially shipping services, was less dependent on a single market but even so maintained about 25 per cent of exports to Britain. Similarly Sweden had the same proportion of exports to Britain and a continued surplus. For the other countries with which Britain made bilateral treaties there was nearer to

Table 3.2 British trade with Empire

	1928	1931	1937	1938
UK imports from Empire	30.4	28.7	39.4	40.4
UK exports to Empire	41.5	41.1	44.4	46.3
Empire imports from UK	35.0	33.9	30.9	32.1
Empire exports to UK	33.9	36.3	37.8	40.7

Figures are percentages

From Political and Economic Planning, (1947) *Britain and World Trade* (London), pp. 22–4

a proportionate change in the trade volume. The level of dependence on the British market can be seen from the following figures, showing the proportion of total commodity production exported to that market: Ireland 35 per cent, Denmark 29 per cent, Finland 20 per cent, Norway 14 per cent, the Netherlands 11 per cent and Sweden 9 per cent.

The best known British trade deals were with Empire partners. The Ottawa Agreement of 1932 established a series of bilateral agreements, within the sterling area, together with Canada. The effect was a marginal diversion of trade to imperial markets but very little in the way of trade stimulus. Again, the overseas markets gained more than Britain. In effect Britain's imperial partners gained at the expense of other producers, many of which were within Europe. All such restrictive trade treaties did little to boost trade as a whole. On the other hand, Britain constituted a major market for primary, especially food, exporters who might otherwise have been in a far more serious plight (Table 3.2).

3.3   German trade and bilateral treaties

1930s

Germany took bilateral treaties further than Britain or any other nation. Unlike Britain, Germany had introduced exchange controls in 1931 and she used clearing accounts to settle imports and exports, as far as possible on a bilateral basis. In some cases she was able to manipulate trade to her advantage and accumulate trade deficits with primary product exporters. Although she established bilateral trading and clearing arrangements with many countries, within and outside Europe, her main sphere of influence was in south-eastern Europe (Yugoslavia, Romania, Hungary and Bulgaria).

The pattern of trade for Weimar Germany, before the economic crisis, was comparable with that of Wilhelmine Germany before 1914.

German exports had been directed to relatively high per capita income economies. Consequently Germany had earned a surplus on trade within Europe and a deficit outside Europe, especially the USA. Germany gained particularly from her trade with Britain. Put simply, German industrial exports funded imports of raw materials and a margin of foodstuffs. In the international economic environment of the 1930s, securing the supply of imported foodstuffs and raw materials became a major political priority.

Whereas Britain set out to maximise exports through trading deals, Germany appeared to exploit bilateral treaties to maximise imports with minimal exports. This was certainly the case under the Nazi regime though, as with much Nazi policy, the methods were developed before their advent to power. A feature which greatly influenced German foreign trade was the strict control of currency exchange, introduced in 1931. In a sense this was a substitute for devaluation but it enabled government, through the state bank, to ration currency for imports. Such a means of control was taken up and extended by the Nazis to determine (though imperfectly) not only the type and volume of imports but also whence they came. From 1931, before the Nazi advent to power, Germany made preferential trade treaties with Romania and Hungary which allowed these agricultural exporters access to a major market at a time of severe price depression. Under the Nazis such bilateral treaties were extended and elaborated, initially for political reasons though eventually as a vital means of securing food imports (see Chap. 7).

The significant aspect of German trade treaties was the clearing arrangement made necessary by the imposition of exchange controls. Again this was not peculiar to Germany but was elaborated into a system in the Nazi period. Under the clearing system exports to Germany were paid for by a deposit into a special clearing account, exclusive to that trading partner. German exports to that partner were paid from the same account. There was no recourse to free currency exchange. Over time, especially after 1936, war preparations and increasing domestic demand for foodstuffs in Germany increased import demand but reduced potential export supply. Thus Germany's trading partners accumulated substantial balances in the clearing accounts, but these could only be reduced by importing more from Germany. In this way Germany was able to increase imports without immediately funding them with exports. What began as a relatively favourable move for agricultural exporters soon turned to their disadvantage. For instance, Hungary signed a new treaty in 1934 which guaranteed a quota of food exports to the German market. Later treaties (technically they were renewals of the original treaty of 1931) in 1936 and 1937 insisted on wheat exports to Germany and minimum deliveries at a time when

Table 3.3 German trade with eastern Europe, 1928–39

		1928	1933	1936	1938	1939
Austria	I	1.6	1.4	1.8	0.3	–*
	E	3.5	2.5	2.3	0.5	–*
Czechoslovakia	I	3.8	2.9	2.6	3.1	1.9
	E	5.4	3.3	2.9	2.9	1.7
Hungary	I	0.05	0.8	2.2	3.1	4.6
	E	1.3	0.8	1.7	2.6	4.4
Romania	I	1.3	1.1	2.2	2.9	4.4
	E	1.4	0.9	2.2	3.0	4.1
Yugoslavia	I	0.5	0.8	1.8	2.8	2.7
	E	1.0	0.7	1.6	2.6	3.5
Poland†	I	2.7	1.8	1.75	2.3	2.0
	E	4.1	1.7	1.6	2.8	1.9

Figures are percentages of German total

I = German imports
E = German exports

* included in Germany
† includes Danzig

From D.E. Kaiser (1980) *Economic Diplomacy and the Origins of the Second World War* (Princeton: Princeton University Press) p. 319

improving international terms of trade made exports elsewhere more attractive to Hungary.

Using this system Germany was able to make a marginal transfer of trade to the economies of south-east Europe, but this was trade diversion rather than creation. By 1936 the successor states (Czechoslovakia, Hungary, Yugoslavia, Bulgaria, Austria, Romania, Poland) and the Baltic together provided nearly 13.8 per cent of German imports against 5.9 per cent in 1928. Over the same period total German imports had fallen to 41 per cent of their 1928 level. What these figures also illustrate is that the German sphere of influence in east and south-east Europe was far from being a self-contained trading area (Table 3.3). Germany continued to rely on trade with other partners over which she could not exercise such control. In 1934, for instance, she made an agreement with Britain, which included clearing arrangements. In this case the trade was kept roughly in balance.

From 1937 German domestic demand generated more imports, especially of foodstuffs. At the same time the economies of south-east Europe were finding it a little easier to export elsewhere, which gave them a little more bargaining power. Germany was forced to make minor concessions. The shift in relative bargaining power can be illustrated by the fact that, after 1937, although continuing to exercise considerable influence over the terms of trade with her small neighbours,

Table 3.4 German share of trade in eastern Europe, 1928–38

		1928	1933	1936	1938*
Austria	E	18.5	15.1	16.1	–
	I	19.9	18.7	16.9	–
Czechoslovakia	E	22.1	17.7	14.5	20.1
	I	24.9	19.8	17.5	19.1
Hungary	E	11.8	11.2	22.8	45.9
	I	19.5	19.7	26.0	40.8
Romania	E	18.4	10.6	17.8	26.5
	I	23.7	18.6	36.1	36.8
Yugoslavia	E	12.1	13.9	23.7	42.0
	I	13.6	13.2	26.7	39.4
Poland†	E	34.2	17.5	14.2	24.1
	I	26.9	17.6	14.3	23.0

Figures are percentages

E = Exports
I = Imports

* 1938 figures include Austria in Germany
† includes Danzig

From D.E. Kaiser (1980) *Economic Diplomacy and the Origins of the Second World War* (Princeton: Princeton University Press), pp. 325–6

Germany was required to exchange goods on a more equitable basis rather than continue to accumulate endless deficits. As a result Germany exported arms in exchange for food, despite the priority given to domestic war preparation. Czechoslovakia and Poland remained outside the German orbit of *Grossraumwirtschaft* and were always economically more independent. Poland could drive a hard bargain and insist on hard currency payments for exports to Germany or for carriage dues across the Polish corridor (as it happens this was quantitively unimportant as most trade was sea-borne). But Poland remained in a generally weak trading position through the 1930s and her trade dependence was reduced. Czechoslovakia was the most industrialised country in eastern Europe and was able to relax trade restrictions in the 1930s (Table 3.4).

For the south-east of Europe there is no doubt that Nazi Germany exploited her position as a major market. On the other hand she did provide a market at a crucial time, often at above world market prices. The multiplier effect of the increased income generated internally thereby stimulated domestic economic activity and recovery. The difficulty was that there was no escape. Even as the terms of trade for agricultural producers improved in the later 1930s, the clearing system restricted freedom of imports. Clearing certificates could be and were traded in Romania, for example, to allow holders to trade elsewhere. That such certificates were traded at a discount after 1937 indicates how the commercial terms of trade had moved to Germany's disadvantage, though effectively they remained in her favour.

Such trading arrangements allowed Germany extraordinary political influence over smaller nations. In all cases Germany was a far larger market for these states, especially the Danubian economies, than they were a market for German exports. Unlike France and Britain, Germany had no overseas empire. The economies of south-eastern Europe came closer to quasi-colonial status in the 1930s. In important respects Germany was paying a high economic price for the trading arrangements that have been referred to: the main benefits from the German viewpoint were political. The determining motive was probably political also. Germany's trading partners, in central and south-eastern Europe, were rewarded economically for political acquiescence. By 1938 Germany had clearing arrangements with 25 countries, accounting for 50 per cent of her trade, but it was only in central and south-eastern Europe that she was able to take political advantage of this.

3.4   International trade

France

The collapse of international demand was particularly serious for the French economy because France, unlike Britain and Germany, had experienced an export-led boom in the 1920s. While the British industrial economy stagnated relatively and Germany laboured, as a trading nation, with a visible trade deficit, France prospered in the markets of the world. This success was based, at least in part, on the low valuation of the franc which made French goods cheap internationally, especially before stabilisation was achieved in 1926. French exports flourished, before this date, in relatively high income markets – luxury goods, like high quality textiles, perfumes, motor cars. Most exports were to European neighbours, though North America was important also. Like Germany she had a trade deficit with non-European markets but an overall surplus, with resultant accumulations of gold, until 1931. Visible trade was boosted by earnings from tourism (25 per cent of export earnings; in 1929, 10 billion francs) and receipts from reparations deliveries (in 1929, 7 billion francs).

The recession all but destroyed this favourable picture (though visible exports ceased to grow after 1926, France maintained a trade surplus until 1931). Tourist receipts fell to 3 billion francs in 1932; reparations payments to nothing at all. World demand for luxury items fell more steeply than average and in the face of devaluation of other major

Table 3.5 French trade turnover

	Algeria		Belgium		Britain	
	I	E	I	E	I	E
1931	3428	3976	3633	3582	3851	5088
1935	2330	2578	1406	1816	1583	1639
1939	4760	3702	3046	3921	2978	4153

Figures are million francs

I = Imports
E = Exports

From A. Sauvy (1965) *Histoire économique* (Paris: Fayard) vol. 2, pp. 565–70

currencies the franc was left relatively over-valued in the 1930s. Thus French exports declined, though she continued to maintain a small surplus with industrial nations in Europe, at a much lower level of turnover than in the previous decade. Belgium, Germany, Switzerland and Britain, her major European markets, took 24.7 billion francs in exports in 1928; in 1932 this fell to 7.4 billion. Foreign trade turnover was at its lowest in 1935, in the most severe period of domestic deflation. Devaluation (1936) and a modest expansion of domestic demand contributed to a minor, but incomplete, recovery of trade. In 1938 exports to major markets were well below the 1929 level: Belgium at 58 per cent of 1929; Britain at 46.6 per cent; and Switzerland at 57 per cent. Only the Netherlands showed a small increase (107 per cent). Imports from the three major suppliers in 1938 were: the USA, 73 per cent of the 1929 level; Britain, 55 per cent; and Belgium, 81 per cent. Germany took only 39 per cent of the French exports she had in 1929 and supplied 54 per cent of the imports.

In a manner similar to Britain, France increased trade with her overseas territories, though as in other instances this represented a trade diversion rather than generation. In most cases the trading partners became more important as sources of supply than as markets proper. In other words French imports from colonies grew faster than exports to them; the real gains were greater for the colonial markets than for metropolitan France. This was a similar pattern to Britain and other imperial powers. Imports from French Equatorial Africa increased from 511 million francs in 1931 to 1896 million francs in 1939, exports from 334 to 1025 million francs. For French Indo-China the figures were: 1931, imports 404 million francs, exports 537 million francs; 1939, imports 1495 million francs, exports 1197 million francs. Algeria was by far the major 'colonial' market with trade turnover comparable in scale to that of Britain or Belgium (see Table 3.5). French imperial trade was similar to the British case, and for that matter the German sphere of influence in south-east Europe, in that the trading area was not self-contained. Marginal shifts to colonial trading partners could not substitute for losses elsewhere.

Italy, Spain and Portugal

Italy was less trade dependent than France, though her population was comparable in size. Total trade turnover for Italy was lower indeed than for Belgium or Holland. However, the economy was much affected by the recession, with the loss of tourist receipts (similar to but of a lower order than France) and particularly the reduction in remittances from emigrants. These difficulties reinforced the aspirations towards self-sufficiency already evident in the fascist economy. Campaigns to reduce imports, especially of foodstuffs, were increased; on leaving the Gold Standard in 1934 exchange controls were introduced and, in the following year, rigid control of imports. Over the decade there was a marginal shift in trade to Germany and the east – a trade treaty with Hungary in 1934 for instance – and away from western Europe.

Attempts to incorporate overseas territories in a trading orbit met with limited success. However, overseas possessions were more important as markets than as sources of supply, largely because they preferred to export to free exchange markets where possible rather than be restricted by clearing arrangements. Altogether Italy made a minor impact on European trade. She moved modestly towards self-sufficiency but in a manner far less systematic than Germany.

Spain and Portugal had an even smaller impact. In the 1920s Spain's major trading partner had been France so she was adversely affected by French contraction and protection in the 1930s and, to a lesser extent, by the fall in Italian demand. There was some marginal shift towards Germany but overwhelmingly Spanish trade was disturbed by the Civil War from 1936.

Portugal, as a residual imperial power, continued to trade outside Europe. This enabled her, at best, to reduce the rate of decline of foreign trade in the 1930s.

Others

As we have seen the trading position of the smaller economies of Europe was determined to a large extent by the behaviour of the larger markets of the continent. Many smaller industrial economies were affected by the growing restrictions of the German market especially. The

Baltic States and Scandinavia came to depend more closely on Britain, though Germany continued to provide a major market for Sweden. In the 1930s smaller, highly trade-dependent economies (such as Belgium, the Netherlands, Czechoslovakia, Sweden, Switzerland) increased trade with each other as an imperfect substitute for the decline in staple markets.

No such adjustments could overcome the general contraction of demand and the political determination of trade in the 1930s. This, in nearly all cases, meant greater self-sufficiency. The industrial economies, largely for political reasons, moved towards agricultural autarky, producing a higher proportion of basic temperate foodstuffs at home at the cost of high domestic prices, restrained living standards, and market losses to agricultural exporters. (Imports of non-temperate foodstuffs increased as there was no direct competition with home producers.) In response there was little alternative for the agricultural economies of Europe but to reach for greater self-sufficiency in industry – a function more of relative prices than political determinism. Where markets could be secured they were welcomed. The results were general constraints on international trade, shifts to bilateralism and various clearing arrangements and overall political interference in buying and selling. Markets, in the strict sense, had less and less to do with trade in the 1930s and international exchange of goods and services had very little to do with the halting process of recovery.

3.5 Further reading

A good background to the patterns of economic interdependence is to be found in J. Pinder (1976) 'Europe in the world economy, 1920–1970', in C. Cipolla (ed.) *Fontana Economic History of Europe*, volume 5 (Glasgow: Collins). A thorough, but dated, account of the 1930s is H.W. Arndt (1944) *The Economic Lessons of the 1930s* (Oxford: Oxford University Press). International economic relations, particularly as affecting Germany, are examined in L. Neal (1979) 'Economics and finance of clearing agreements in Germany 1934–1938', *Economic History Review*, **32**, pp. 399–404 and D. Kaiser (1980) *Economic Diplomacy and the Origins of the Second World War, Germany, Britain and Eastern Europe, 1930–39* (Princeton: Princeton University Press).

PART 2

Sectors

4

Agriculture

4.1 Introduction

The importance of agriculture in twentieth-century Europe is easy to demonstrate. In the 1930s primary production often contributed between one-quarter and one-third to gross domestic product; only in Great Britain, the Netherlands and Belgium was the share of agriculture and forestry at or below 10 per cent in 1938. But only in Britain was agriculture essentially marginal to the total economy, even though 5 per cent of manpower delivered about 5 per cent of domestic product, a ratio much more favourable than in the continent. Continental states cherished their rural population and measures to support agriculture loomed large in their economic policies, especially after the First World War. Peasants were seen as the bulwark of society because of their persistent political influence; but the peasantry was also often enlisted in the battle against industrial discontent and radical insurgency. Peasants were not necessarily anti-revolutionary and the arts of government were widely deployed to make the rural population well disposed towards their rulers or towards the maintenance of bourgeois authority. This rural population was typically composed of peasant-like family farms. Nevertheless, not all agricultural regimes were dominated by peasants, nor was peasant husbandry always autarkic and self-absorbed. Many of the most successful agrarian regimes of Europe in 1900–50 were founded upon peasant holdings, while many of the least were managed in large, extensive, exhaustive estates. In terms of physical output mini-culture was invariably productive. For all its domination by peasants, European agriculture in 1913 and 1938 would have produced sufficient output to provide the requisite energy for the population of the continent and for most of its livestock if the distortions

Table 4.1 Employment in agriculture

Percentage of employed population *circa* 1930

Over 55% in agriculture
Albania, Bulgaria, Lithuania, Poland, Romania, Spain, Yugoslavia
40–54%
Eire, Estonia, Finland, Greece, Hungary, Italy, Latvia, Portugal
25–39%
Czechoslovakia, Denmark, Norway, Sweden
15–24%
Austria, Belgium, France, Germany, Netherlands, Switzerland
Under 15%
United Kingdom

Numbers employed in agriculture in Europe (excluding the Soviet Union)

1920–21	73 793 000
1945–50	67 884 000

Source: F. Dovring (1960) *Land and Labor in Europe, 1900–1950* (The Hague: Nijhoff)

caused by differential transport costs, tariffs and regional preferences in consumption had been discounted.

Europe, excluding the post-war territory of the USSR, contained almost 250 million hectares of agriculturally serviceable land, which in 1930 employed about 43 million active workers (Table 4.1). Despite the counter-attractions of emigration, urbanisation and industrial and commercial development, this number had probably increased modestly between 1900 and 1930, except in north-western Europe; and then declined no less modestly to 1950. Agriculture comprehended production schedules influenced by differences in climate, altitude, rainfall, slope and surface geology, with an emphasis upon livestock production in mountainous and/or cold, temperate regions, and upon arable production that depended traditionally upon cereals as the mainstay in the lowland zone. But most peasant holdings, so far as possible, were mixed enterprises because peasant households were faced with the need for self-sufficiency on the one hand and for maximum land use on the other. But however inefficient, peasant agriculture was not as a rule merely subsistent; most households had the will or the compulsion to produce commodities for the market, if only to pay rent, taxes and dowries. The degree of market penetration differed from one region or one country to another. In intensive regions of production, such as Flanders or Valencia, the supply of urban markets at home or abroad had been paramount for centuries. In Yugoslavia or Poland, by contrast, the quantity of traded farm produce was still negligible as a proportion of total peasant output in the 1930s. Yet even in so-called backward regions, farmers

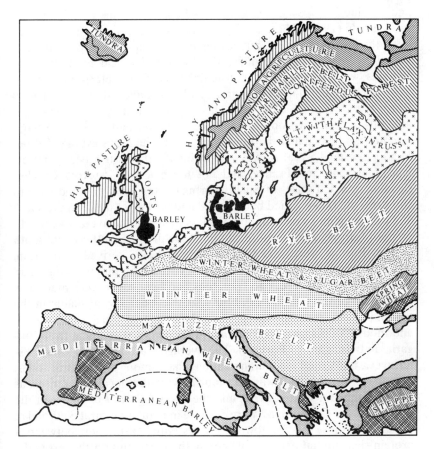

Figure 4.1 Map of European crop belts
Source: *Geographical Journal*, 1937

were open to commercial opportunities when communications were sufficiently improved to provide the incentive.

4.2 Output

The zones of production in Europe are well illustrated in L.D. Stamp's famous map (Fig. 4.1), which indicates the prevailing systems of agriculture in the 1930s. As a rule these conditions had not changed for a long time, perhaps even for centuries, because production schedules, despite the peasant's own needs, inevitably reflected conditions of vegetable growth. The differences between north and south and between highland

and lowland Europe are brought out by Paul Lamartine Yates's study of food supply (1960). The quantity of food available obviously depended upon the means of supply, but customary working-class or peasant diets varied by reason of the foodstuffs available in local markets. Thus Iberians, when they were not consuming much fish, preferred a diet that was much higher in cereals, fruit and vegetables than in northern Europe, and in which butter and cheese played little part beside vegetable oils in the provision of fats. Whereas butter and cheese consumption in Scandinavia and the Low Countries in the 1930s averaged about 11.5 kg per head a year (it was equally high in the British Isles, Switzerland, Germany and France, and not much less in Austria, Czechoslovakia and Estonia), in Spain, Portugal, Italy and in some eastern countries the range varied between 1.3 and 6.5 kg per head. In the south and east even milk consumption was less than half the average of northwestern Europe. Furthermore, although the diets of southern and south eastern Europe were very high in carbohydrates derived from grain, wheat, maize and some buckwheat were virtually all that was consumed by humans. Barley, rye, oats, potatoes and beet sugar were much less used south of the Garonne and the Danube. Beer was available in the towns, but was generally less popular than wine, of which there was an enormous production of *vins ordinaires* throughout the south, from Bulgaria and Hungary to Portugal. The average European diet varied extensively, but varied less among nations than among agricultural zones. Lamartine Yates (1960) was very much aware that local differences, as between the Bordeaux district and the *Massif Central* or between the *Alföld* and the Carpathians, were decisive in regulating rural diets and in influencing those of the towns. The essential distinction between a protein-rich, animal-derived regimen in the north and north-west and a starch-rich, vegetable-based regimen in the south and south-east was confirmed by his analysis of the statistics. One result of this difference was that southern diets were less calorific than northern. Energy values for each adult were less by 500–800 calories per day in the Mediterranean than around the North Sea.

If agriculture determined the character of regional food supplies, dietary preferences went far to sustain inherited agricultural practices. Unless an important inter-regional trade in primary products were to develop, the prospects for improving or altering the prevailing system of husbandry were restricted by the settled habits of local markets. Observable changes in consumption, and therefore perhaps in production, were frequently the result of unlooked-for shortages in supply. No new farm crop of significance was introduced into Europe after 1914. Wartime expedients sometimes resulted in the permanent adoption of new production plans, by changing the mix of grains or by introducing potatoes

Table 4.2 Percentage of GDP supplied by agriculture

1938–50
Over 30% Albania, Bulgaria, Eire, Estonia, Finland, Greece, Hungary, Italy, Latvia, Lithuania, Poland, Portugal, Romania, Spain, Yugoslavia
10–29% Austria, Belgium, Czechoslovakia, Denmark, France, Germany, Netherlands, Norway, Sweden, Switzerland
Under 10% United Kingdom

Source: F. Dovring (1960) *Land and Labor in Europe, 1900–1950* (The Hague: Nijhoff)

or sugar-beet into new areas, for example. In general, however, the process of diffusion in European agriculture had almost reached low water between 1900 and 1940.

This does not imply that European agriculture was stagnant or failed to raise the levels of production in the period. Each of the three main classes of farm crops whose output was systematically recorded – cereals, potatoes, sugar-beet – increased in volume of production. Grains – wheat, rye, maize, barley, oats and mixed corn – expanded in total output by more than one-third across the continent, from an average of 97 million tonnes in 1920–24 to 124 millions in 1935–39. Potatoes increased in output from 108 to 148 million tonnes and sugar-beet from 34 to 48 million tonnes between the same quinquennia. The other principal product about which complete data are available is wine, which, thanks to a significant decrease in France, Italy and Spain, actually fell in output from 156.7 million hectolitres (1920–24) to 151.7 million hectolitres (1935–39). Comparison with the period before 1919 is virtually impossible because of frontier changes, but it is a reasonable assumption that the output of most field crops was marginally lower in the early 1920s than it had been on the eve of the war. The quinquennium 1940–44 is in many ways the most interesting of all, but the data available are seriously distorted by war measures and by under-reporting; for several states no returns were collected. What is apparent is that the continent did not succeed in raising output substantially, if at all, even though in many countries the exigencies of war threw men back on to the land and/or increased the proportion of GDP contributed by agriculture (Table 4.2). In the Netherlands, for example, the sectoral share of agriculture in national income approximately doubled between 1938 (7 per cent) and 1946 (15.5 per cent), although its value in real terms fell by at least one-third. In Italy also agriculture/GDP rose from 28 per cent in 1934 to 37 per cent in 1946.

Table 4.3 European agricultural production in the inter-war years

	Grain ('0000 tonnes)	Potatoes ('0000 tonnes)	Sugar-beet ('0000 tonnes)	Wine (000 hl.)
1920–24	96 934	108 470	34 055	156 721
1935–39	124 356	148 398	48 072	151 727

	Livestock
1920	*Cattle* 93.7 m. *Sheep and goats* 141 m. *Swine* 54.6 m. *L'US* 930 m.
1939	*Cattle* 106.7 m. *Sheep and goats* 170 m. *Swine* 80.8 m. *L'US* 1285 m.

Percentage increase of livestock: 38%

Five-year averages; percentage increase of arable production: 34%

L'US = Livestock Units

From B.R. Mitchell (1975) *European Historical Statistics* (Cambridge: Cambridge University Press), Section C

Livestock production is less easy to gauge (Table 4.3). The population of goats, poultry and small mammals used for food was seldom estimated. For horses, cattle, sheep and pigs numbers were taken fairly regularly after 1920. Horses were essentially to be classed as intermediate goods, even though they were sometimes consumed as food. Oxen too were still widely used as draught animals. All animals provided some materials for manufacture – hoof, horn, bones, hides, wool, feathers, even grease. Livestock husbandry was essentially dedicated to food production, whether of dairy goods or of meat. There appear to be no statistics either of milk production or of carcase meat brought to market for the whole of Europe.

4.3 Farming types

A comparatively small part of Europe is dedicated to highly intensive agriculture of the kind associated with market gardening. The best practice in the south was of this type. In Spain, whereas the high plateaux were notorious for their backwardness and inefficiency before the 1960s, the coastal plains of Valencia and Murcia possessed a husbandry, a Moslem legacy, practised on smallholdings in which five crops could be taken every two years, with fruit trees, producing citrus, apricots, peaches, almonds and olives, undersown with potatoes, maize and alfalfa. Part of the Po Valley was similarly given up to market gardening, but horticulture there has always existed side by side with grain production, dairying and pig-keeping. Italy had a long tradition of careful, intensive husbandry, but it was not celebrated for such minute specialisation in the 1920s. Part of the agricultural plan of the Fascists was to encourage double cropping on irrigated land in the central regions. Outside the areas in which wheat could be grown effectively, labour-intensive small farms producing fruit, vines and olives, interspersed with ground crops, were successfully established in the period. The most diversified system of garden-like farming in the south was concentrated in western Provence and the lower Rhone valley, where the holdings tended to be larger than in Valencia or the Romagna, at about 5 ha., but the pattern of production was similar – fruit, vegetables, sunflowers, maize, vines, early potatoes, which were destined for markets in Marseilles, Lyons or the north.

It was only in temperate Europe that cultivation on such an intensive model was widespread, although in the cooler latitudes it was seldom possible to obtain more than two crops a year. Flanders had a reputation for 'spade' husbandry on minuscule holdings as long-established as Valencia, where the production of cash crops for the towns or for exports, interspersed with forage plants for the livestock kept to supply milk, meat and dung, provided the key to all modern rotations in Europe. Cultivation had been modified in the nineteenth century to provide for the growing industrial towns of the region and was amended yet again after 1900 in response to overseas competition, but a sixteenth-century peasant would still have recognised his descendant's husbandry in the 1920s. A more recent development in horticulture and specialised agriculture had transformed similarly fertile districts in the Netherlands, eastern England, Strathmore in Scotland and the Mittelrhein plain in Germany. On some of the thinnest of sandy soils, as in the Belgian Campine, two or three generations of effort to build up soil structure and fertility had begun to pay handsome dividends by the 1930s. With the same result reclamation from the sea or on estuarine alluvium encouraged cash cropping on an unprecedented scale. Near all the large towns there grew up similar market gardens to supply local markets with perishable produce. Not all intensive arable farming was dedicated to these short-range internal markets, however, since some were already devoted to particular commodities and had attained a national or international celebrity for asparagus, celery, figs, soft fruit, Salerno lemons, pot plants, herbs and cut flowers, etc.

One major aspect of intensive farming was specialised livestock-keeping. Many dairy herds, for example, were very small: the cows produced high yields of rich milk because, as in Switzerland or the Netherlands, they were closely tended and expertly fed. 'High feeding', which in Victorian Britain had been associated with large mixed enterprises, was more characteristic on the continent of peasant smallholdings, sometimes as in west Flanders so tiny as to defy the lore of the agronome about cow-keeping. Most of the renowned market-garden districts of the north produced milk or pigmeat as part of a balanced pattern of land-use. Dairies making butter, cheese or processed milk goods were as numerous in Belgium as in Denmark or Holland, though in Flanders and Hainaut they were usually very small. In Switzerland and Norway, where arable farming was of little account, the efficiency of agriculture was chiefly measured by the contribution of the dairy sector. Even in Lombardy commercial agriculture, particularly on the larger holdings, was founded upon dairying. The *cascine* were substantial enterprises producing quantities of milk, part of which went into cheesemaking and part into feed for pigs and calves, kept to produce Parma ham and veal. Since *cascine* sometimes exceeded 100 ha. in extent, the order of magnitude differed from Swiss or Dutch dairying although the system was essentially similar.

Peasant agriculture in a less specialised sense was often better able to produce high-yielding commercial crops than the large *latifundia*, or great estate farms, of continental Europe. In Hungary the great estates not significantly disturbed in the cataclysm of 1918 delivered most of the substantial surplus of grain which fed the country's great flour mills, but purely in terms of yield per hectare they were less productive than peasant holdings in similar conditions of climate, rainfall and altitude. Peasant farming was enormously variable. Its success often depended upon a tradition of secure tenure, stable political conditions or prevailing social values. Bulgaria, for instance, had not only a more prosperous but also a more efficient agriculture than Yugoslavia between the wars for all of these reasons, although in geographical terms the situation of the two economies was broadly similar. With a few exceptions, however, the real problems of European agriculture resided in the *latifundia*.

These *latifundia*, in Spain, southern Portugal and the Italian *Mezzogiorno*, were situated on dry, infertile soils which even after substantial investment in improved techniques would have remained marginal. Large farms in any event were characteristic of thin-soiled plateaux, scarp-and-vale landscapes, windswept heaths of sand, gravel or chalk. In the Beauce or Picardy, as in the Dunantal or in Mecklenberg, these large holdings were efficient in the sense that they produced fair crops, with yields per hectare varying from 15 per cent below to 10 per cent above the national average, and also because they made good use of the relatively scarce resources of labour available in barren districts. In Picardy, for example, the labour productivity of 100 ha.+ farms was up to 20 per cent greater in the 1920s than the productivity of neighbouring smallholdings. It is difficult to find comparable figures for Sicily or Andalucia but the inference is that there was no effective competition in the districts dominated by *latifundistas* for geographical as much as social reasons. In the Spanish *secano*, overrun with sheep or rangy cattle, peasant holdings apart from homestead crofts were almost non-existent. In such conditions the very few livestock per hectare managed on the surviving magnate estates had only rabbits to contend with in their search for food. What could be done to remedy this situation defied the ingenuity of agricultural experts before the war, except in those parts accessible to running water or on the previously no less unproductive marshes still in the hands of traditional institutions or aristocratic families which could be improved by drainage.

Productivity

The variety of farming types in early twentieth-century Europe testifies to the adaptability and versatility of peasant economies. The question of productivity already mentioned, however, raises more complex issues than the farmer's often inherited response to the constraining influence of geography. How productive was European agriculture before 1940? If productivity means yield per hectare or per unit of livestock, or alternatively gross output per holding in relation to effective demand, the evidence is quite favourable. The higher output of peasant holdings by comparison with large farms was obtained generally from a combination of greater assiduity in cultivation and greater labour participation by peasant families. But productivity is about the comparative costs of supplying a non-agrarian population with primary produce, and representative peasant systems of husbandry responded weakly to external market opportunities before the Treaty of Rome. It must also be measured against relative labour and capital costs. The fact that almost all European states before 1940 deployed an active labour force in primary production, which was proportionally greater than the agricultural contribution to domestic product, is telling. In terms of labour efficiency, primary production was less successful than manufacturing; hence the gains in aggregate productivity earned by industrialisation. Peasant family farms almost invariably were afflicted by under-employment that could not always be relieved by work outside their holdings. Moreover, mechanisation and new fixed investment (in buildings, under-drainage, irrigation and improved farm layouts), although not neglected on peasant holdings, tended to proceed most thoroughly on large holdings in which economies of production were easiest to achieve. There were undeniably more backward *latifundia* than progressive large farms in pre-war Europe, but the best of the latter were already organised as capitalist enterprises turning out quantities of marketable produce upon which inter-regional commerce generally depended.

Geological and climatic problems were not the only defects of *latifundial* organisation, but the greatest impediment to their progress was natural rather than man-made. Before 1914 there had been some convergence of production plans and technology on large, quintessentially estate farms, in Norfolk and the Beauce, in Hungary and Pomerania, depending essentially on British ideals of agricultural efficiency translated into continental usage. Where appropriate this 'improved' standard was maintained, although since many traditional districts of large-scale agricultural production suffered the consequences of post-war expropriation and redistribution the old landmarks were moved. The peasants who replaced the *latifundistas* were not necessarily less efficient; the assumptions upon which the calculations of productivity are made, however, must be changed in these circumstances.

One test of the productivity of the large farms is to compare their yields per ha. with those obtained in the New World. More wheat or barley per ha. were customarily obtained in Europe than on the American prairies. On the other hand, costs were greater than in the New World, not least because of expensive cultivation in old soils which required repeated fertilisation and intricate ploughing. European land was never treated as an exhaustible resource as were the virgin soils of the Americas, since it bore burdens of political and social obligation and opportunity that were keenly expressed in the support by the cereal magnates for state intervention to protect their markets.

British farmers, not being favoured by protection before the 1930s, gave up cereal growing on a scale not matched on the continent. Yields in Britain had always been high by world standards: a Norfolk farmer, for example, often grew twice as much wheat or barley per hectare as his contemporaries in Picardy, Mecklenberg or Nebraska, but his profits, in the 1880s or the 1920s, were lower because his inputs and capital costs were expensive and he enjoyed no price protection.

Wheat production, shielded by tariffs, expanded on the continent after 1919, but changes in productivity were much less predictable. Wheat, like several other desirable crops, maize, sugar-beet, olives, citrus fruits and vines, was carried into areas or on to soils that were less suitable to its production. The conversion of rye land to wheat, for example, was only sustainable if new techniques, rotations, seed varieties and top dressing were adopted. But much of the impetus towards improvement of this kind, visible in the nineteenth century, lost momentum early in the twentieth in such districts, not as a result of land reform, but because price differentials favoured wheat when urban taste increasingly found traditional breadstuffs repugnant. The commercial decisions of farmers, even of peasants well placed to exploit wider markets, therefore often over-rode agricultural preferences. Although the world trade in primary produce became more uniform after 1870, the rules of comparative advantage were not permitted to determine *national* programmes of production, and tariffs also tended to distort the course of agrarian development in a continent rapidly becoming urban and industrial.

Yields mattered to agricultural planners, since their improvement formed one stile in the ladder of enlarging effective output. Making agriculture more intensive was an object less often pursued, because it was more difficult than the encouragement of extensive land use. Mussolini's 'battle for grain' was intended to make Italian land more *productive*; in effect it succeeded in obtaining more grain, chiefly wheat, at the expense of other crops and even, in several areas, of livestock. Italy could not sustain a monoculture but the prestige attached to corn in the 1920s pushed the nation's agriculture hazardously near a public obsession with bread and pasta.

If we admit that many elements in the discussion of agricultural productivity even in the twentieth century are incongruous and may even miss the point that in most states agriculture was a way of life in which the majority of the people actively or passively participated, and for them output was first of all a matter of direct consumption, it remains necessary to compare regional variations in husbandry as a guide to the *potential* for agriculture as an 'industrial' enterprise. The yardstick of excellence often used by agronomes was Great Britain. British seeds, British progeny, British fertilisers, British machinery, less often British social ideas of the countryside, were in great demand on the continent among the liberal, progressive landowners who regarded themselves as the vanguard of agricultural change. British livestock were the beau ideal of the world around 1900 after two centuries of methodical breeding; they produced more meat to bone, more milk in each lactation, more wool per fleece than their foreign counterparts. Cross-breeding seemed the answer to most continental problems of pastoral agriculture. The effects, however, as with a considerable portion of all the transplanted 'improvements', were equivocal. Yields of animal produce in Europe improved modestly between 1900 and 1940 and more spectacularly between 1945 and 1960, but the contribution of selective breeding was marginal. On certain intensively-managed capitalist enterprises British-bred dairy or beef cattle did enrich their owners and improve local markets. For most farmers, however, British breed types were unattainable or inappropriate exotics, which by changing the character of the carcase, of milk quality or of resistance to disease actually interfered with sound local practices. The cattle of Denmark, the Netherlands, Lower Saxony, Switzerland and Lombardy were already superior in several respects to imported kinds. Similar problems resulted from the transfer of British improvements that offered the promise of higher yields in arable farming. In essence British agricultural progress was founded upon a rural social order that scarcely existed on the continent and the high yields of corn, milk and carcase meat were specific to the country which had set little store by growing industrial crops, hemp, flax, coleseed, or fruit and vegetables or other delicacies such as veal and high-grade poultry meat. The vulnerability of British agriculture after 1878 did not deter experts from envying the nation's technological proficiency but the disjunction of high farming and high exposure was not ignored by continental improvers in the protective envelope of twentieth century agricultural policy-making.

British excellence was always rather chimerical, being an issue of learned sentiment rather than practical achievement. Yields per hectare for most temperate crops or per head of most livestock commodities were as high, or higher, in Flanders, Holland, Zeeland, Denmark and many parts of Germany. Comparable data from southern or eastern parts of Europe are less easy to find. Switzerland certainly produced milk of very high quality in quantities equal to northern Europe, but the Swiss were hampered by geography from producing such large arable yields as the Dutch. Yield standards, in other words, were often a matter of relative specialisation. Although peasant farms achieved the highest levels of physical productivity, there was less uniformity across the continent on the smaller family farms that dominated the landscape from Ireland to Greece than on the commercialised, capitalist farms. Arable and livestock yields were very high everywhere, as much as or even more than twice the continent's average, in regimes of intensive mixed husbandry, marrying cattle and pigs with cereals, sugar-beet, vegetables and other cash crops. Such holdings, peasant enterprises in Belgium or Holland, moderate family farms in Denmark or large undertakings in Britain, East Germany, Picardy, etc., accounted for no more than one-fifth of holdings in Europe, which delivered less than one-third of aggregate output. It is important to stress that these improved farms were situated on virtually all soils and cut sharply across the conventional, anthropological division between farmers and peasants.

The measurement of physical productivity has been attempted with much trepidation (Table 4.4) since interpretation of the statistics, themselves often untrustworthy, will mislead anyone who does not allow for regional, social or climatic variations within countries and between states. Useful data for several important commodities are not available. The five for which reasonably consistent information is forthcoming count as the most significant products in European agriculture and may be taken as representative of the whole sector. Table 4.4 divides the data for gross yields more or less at each end of the period, based on average yields aggregated into a single standard. Barley was chosen for northern countries and maize for southern, and for no country except France is

Table 4.4 Comparative productivity in European agriculture

Physical productivity: mean yields of selected produce (five-yearly averages)

	1920–24 tonnes per hectare				1935–39			
	wheat	barley/maize	milk*	potatoes	wheat	barley/maize	milk*	potatoes
Britain	2.2	B 1.9	2360	15.6	2.3	B 2.1	2480	17.25
Belgium	2.4	B 2.1	2300	17.6	2.6	B 2.7	2400	22.3
Netherlands	2.8	B 3.0	2460	16.0	3.2	B 3.4	2600	31.0
Denmark	2.4	B 2.9	2600	14.6	1.9	B 2.8	2750	16.9
		B 1.3				B 1.5		
France	1.4	M 1.1	1560	8.0	1.5	M 1.6	1600	11.0
Germany	1.8	B 1.75	1350	12.6	2.4	B 2.4	1500	18.8
Italy	1.0	M 1.5	(1000)	6.9	1.5	M 1.9	(1200)	6.6
Hungary	1.1	M 1.2	n.a.	5.6	1.4	M 1.9	n.a.	7.6
Poland (rye)	0.9	B 1.1	n.a.	10.0	(rye) 1.2	B 1.2	950	10.8
Europe average								

Labour productivity (index of aggregate net output/agricultural employment)

	early 1920s	year	late 1930s	year
Britain	100	1924	100	1937
B/NL/DK	78	1923/4	83	1937/8
France	46	1923	43	1936
Germany	53	1922	50	1938
Italy	17	1924	15	1938
Czechoslovakia	44	1924	53	1937

* litres per annum for all cows in milk

Note: The index of agricultural employment was struck as the balance between *total* employment in the sector (66%) and an estimated full-time equivalent (34%), which is imputed from the known statistics of part-time work on the farm. The years cited relate specifically to returns of agricultural output/income.

From B.R. Mitchell, (1975) *European Historical Statistics* (Cambridge: Cambridge University Press), plus Statistical Yearbooks of the various countries listed in Mitchell, p. xv-xix *Trade Yearbooks* (Rome: FAO)

the mean of both spring-sown grains included in Table 4.4. We have taken the evidence from certain *national* statistics – hence the deficiency in returns for 1909–13, which for many territories are not comparable with the post-war political geography of Europe.

Well above average in grain production were Denmark, 'Benelux', Great Britain, Germany, Switzerland, Ireland and Sweden. In the middle rank stood Austria, Bulgaria, Czechoslovakia, Hungary, France and Norway. The Baltic States, Finland, Greece, Italy, Poland, Portugal, Romania, Spain and Yugoslavia all produced average yields well below the mean. Nevertheless many highly productive countries grew cereals on a small portion of the agricultural land available (Ireland, Switzerland, Sweden) and among the most backward regions much arid or otherwise marginal land was sown with wheat or maize intermittently or without much thought to increasing productivity. A similar if not exact pattern applied to the cultivation of potatoes, although some of the apparently least productive countries, e.g. Italy and Greece, tended to cultivate a higher proportion of 'early' varieties that naturally produced less than the 'main crop' sorts dominant in northern Europe. Dairying in general has already been discussed. In particular, in the least productive countries, milk was either not highly valued or was taken from goats and sheep as often as from cows. Significantly the Italian statistics suggest that the national average yield – at or just above the mean – was inflated by the contributions of Piedmont and Lombardy where commercial dairying was widespread. For meat the problem is to relate *both* the value and the weight of the carcase to the annual slaughter, which is virtually impossible. There is no doubt, however, that Denmark once again carried off the laurels in both pigmeat and beef productivity. Altogether north-western Europe was the most highly productive agricultural region in all livestock commodities throughout the period.

There was some improvement of yields between 1918 and 1938. In most territories this change varied between 15 and 25 per cent, but in the very productive regions, above all in Denmark, Britain and Belgium, the possibilities of further progress in the inter-war years, without the application of new scientific techniques, were restricted. German experience in cereal productivity is significant but not easy wholly to explain. The difference between the best and the worst scarcely narrowed, but there was a modest upward displacement in the levels of productivity across Europe which most affected those countries just below the mean point in both 1913 and 1922, e.g. France and Czechoslovakia.

Labour supply

In 1930 agriculture in Europe outside the USSR employed about 43 million males, which made it easily the largest sector by employment in the economy of the second most industrialised continent on earth. In France and Spain there were at least 4.5 million workers in agriculture: Italy still possessed 6.6 millions and Germany 3.5 millions. By contrast, Great Britain, about equal in size to Italy, counted fewer than 1.2 million in 1931. There was much overcrowding of cultivable land in the most populous, fertile or climatically select districts, although in Europe as a whole the average ratio of workers to land was quite favourable at 5.8 ha. per active worker. Expressed in terms of national statistics, the variations, though wide, were not excessive. Significantly below the mean, with densities of 3 to 5 ha. per worker, were Italy and Belgium, both of which were very crowded (*c.* 3.3 ha./worker), Norway, the Netherlands, Portugal and Czechoslovakia, which suggests an interesting geographical dispersion. Great Britain already achieved a ratio of 15.5 ha. or more per worker, and several other states exceeded 8.0 – Denmark, Estonia, Latvia and Greece, while substantial parts of other countries had an equally generous ratio – eastern Germany, Poland, Hungary and Spain. The erratic progress of land reform chiefly accounts for these exceptions, since there is clear evidence of an increase in the rural *population* between 1891–1911 and 1921–47. Spectacular changes may often have been owing to variations in the methods of enumeration, although the recorded decline of manpower numbers in France from 5.9 to 4.5 million, 1895–1930, and the rise in the Danube/Balkan region from 8.4 to 10.7 million, traced genuine shifts in the rural population of some magnitude.

In general there occurred a decline in agricultural *employment* in western Europe (but not in Scandinavia) between 1900 and 1940 of about one-fifth (less if one assumes the French figures to be untrustworthy). Elsewhere the situation was more ambiguous. No fall in numbers took place but the increase is difficult to assess. Regional analysis, however, suggests that the agricultural population and with it the manpower available to agriculture was as much affected by industrialisation as in north-western Europe. Thus in the central belt of Sweden (Gothenburg to Stockholm), the farm population showed a marked downward trend when elsewhere in the country the agricultural population actually expanded. In Bohemia also, male employment in farming fell by 50–60 per cent, 1910–47, and the total agricultural population by almost 50 per cent. Even in the Mediterranean much the same trend is apparent in Piedmont, Lombardy and Catalonia. In the industrialising zones of Europe, male employment in agriculture declined by a percentage variously between 25 and 67 between 1895–1910 and 1931–47, which even allowing for distortion caused by depression and war is significant.

A mean swing against agriculture of 35 per cent in these regions disguises some other developments – the proliferation of part-time holdings, the increase of female labour on farms and the extension of market gardening which preserved the elements of peasant agriculture better than could have been predicted from the crude equation of industrialisation with rural depopulation.

The greatest structural problem in twentieth-century Europe has not been overmanning in itself, but the frequently recurring mismatch between rural population and the *quality* of land available. The ratio of workers to land is not of much value in assessing either the market opportunities or the potential for subsistence of peasant families in districts as different as the Landes or the Beauce in France (superficially not too dissimilar) or Emilia-Romagna and the Basilicata in Italy. Furthermore, there was often diversity within a district or a particular commune. Nature tended to regulate the density of agrarian populations, but the equilibrium between land and people was easily thrown off-beam by social pressures.

Social policy

The peasant problem was a complex amalgam of social traditions, fused with economic disequilibria and political calculation. The purpose of policy on the continent for upwards of a century had been to institute a free-standing rural community no longer reliant upon feudal *seigneurie*, in which self-help, reciprocal interdependence and economic opportunity were freely mixed. The idea filtered down that peasants with rights in property and a stake in the social order would sooner or later emulate the bourgeoisie and participate in the conduct of public affairs, in the expectation that their legitimate interests would be advanced in the process. In north-western Europe, excluding Great Britain, this convenant between the state and the farmer was in action by 1900. Where rural society was essentially egalitarian, based on the dominance of the peasant community, law, social tradition and political propriety combined to form a skein of common interest which was readily integrated into the framework of the constitution. In few states were peasants or their agrarian parties able to control the political establishment, at least in north-western Europe, but in all, the peasant voice was profoundly important. The attempt at political involvement had been less successful in the south and more erratic in the east of Europe before 1920. Laws affecting land tenure and property rights had been amended by liberal or modernising governments in Italy, Spain and Greece before the Great War, but with few positive results. Parliamentary parties in fragile reformed constitutions could ill afford to enrage the landed elites, however inefficient or domineering the stewardship of their estates, at least until the *fuerzas vividas* of commerce and industry could assert themselves against reactionary traditions. Even in France and Germany this was an incomplete social phenomenon before the 1930s.

Conditions that favoured extensive land reform in the inter-war years were not improved by the ascendancy of dictators in Portugal, Spain, Italy, Greece and Hungary, since the despots sooner or later became hostile to radical change. In the Habsburg successor states, in Romania, Poland and the Baltic countries, circumstances were rather different. Many governments, whatever their complexion, were able to initiate further land reform, if only because much land became free for redistribution through sequestration. By the mid-1920s all these states were poised, doubtless precariously, upon the edge of becoming peasant polities in the fashion of Bulgaria or Yugoslavia. In the former, the importance of the peasantry had been recognised since the founding of the state. Pre-war Romania had moved in the same direction after 1907 and the new kingdom of the South Slavs after 1919. Alexander Stamboliiski in Bulgaria is an important figure in the formulation of agrarian polities of this kind. His plan for a coherent peasant state under the Crown were overturned in a *coup d'état* in 1923, but his idea of a 'green' revolution to match the Red Revolution in Russia, with the peasants as the stabilising force against rampant bolshevism, reverberated around continental Europe for at least a decade. Every east European state produced one or more agrarian leader of force and influence – Wincenty Witoś in Poland, Stjepan Radic in Yugoslavia, Antonin Švehla in Czechoslovakia are merely the best known examples. The pattern was repeated in Scandinavia, especially in Finland and Sweden.

These men found that the chief obstacle in the way of fostering the peasantry was not the commercial class in their nations but entrenched magnates in the countryside, whose attitude to peasant ascendancy, even in the teeth of bolshevism, was hostile or ambiguous. Needless to say states that adopted wide-ranging policies of agricultural protection enriched the landlord class as much as the peasantry, as in Hungary, Latvia and Poland. By the end of the 1920s the majority of eastern states had fallen under the control of dictators or aristocratic juntas which resembled the masterful inertia of Salazar in Portugal or Primo in Spain more than the busy interventionism of Mussolini. Social reform benefiting the farming population in these circumstances was extremely limited. Witoś in Poland was able to promote the interests of his agrarian constituency when he was Prime Minister but the political instability of the country reduced his effective contribution to their long-term wellbeing. More successful, for reasons which tell us much about the political morass of the east, was Antonin Švehla in Czechoslovakia, who served a long term as Minister of Agriculture under Masaryk and laid the foundations of Czech agrarian modernisation.

Co-operation, including the spread of Raiffeisen banks, was extensive but not densely distributed in the east. Most ventures were based on western models, but were seldom actively promoted by governments, which tended to leave the establishment of co-operatives to agrarian initiative. Admiral Horthy in Hungary, no special friend to his peasant subjects, nevertheless encouraged the development of agrarian banks because of the immense importance to the national economy of a commercially effective agriculture. Bulgaria had an interlocking set of economic institutions to support the numerous peasantry of the country.

Indeed, Bulgaria also developed a complex network of processing and distribution installations to underpin the national market in primary produce.

Serfdom, except in the informal guise of peonage, may have been dead in Europe by 1900–20 but landlordism was still a widespread phenomenon. In eastern Germany, for instance, the great estates, intact in 1914, were still competing successfully with peasant holdings in terms of land use. The ground lost before 1930 was not vital to the survival of junkerdom, even though the *Gutsherren* had come to depend not upon serfs but upon immigrant labour or dispossessed migrants from the east. The *latifundia* of Hungary, unlike many of the great estates of the east that had been expropriated, flourished more or less intact under Horthy. The persistence of a land-owning aristocracy also held together the great estates of the south through liberal or autocratic regimes. When the *latifundistas* of Sicily or Andalucia required labour to cultivate their rundown estates, they could still draw upon a virtually dependent body of manpower entrapped by customary ties of duty or the nexus of credit into the web of subordination. It was often the bailiffs, whose exactions and indifference exacerbated social relations, that prompted the frequent outbursts of discontent in the south. But even when estate-based agriculture was more efficient, in the Po Valley for example, peasant disaffection was rampant. Red Emilia obtained its name from peasant communism as much as from radical Bologna. After 1922 little was done to disturb the capitalist structure of agriculture in the region. The Fascists broke the power of radical opposition in the early 1920s and were then content to leave the grateful beneficiaries of *squadrismo* largess in charge of their property. The Italian dictatorship, however, was often ambiguous about the inherited power of rural land-ownership. Much depended upon local affiliations and the standing of each *ras* with the national government or with the party. Several of the autocracies of pre-war Europe mistook the shadow for the substance of order in rural and provincial affairs. Dictators, in general, like most of the liberal democracies, earned the support of the agrarian majority by restoring or maintaining social cohesion as much as by economic and financial assistance. Nevertheless, the great issues of rural reform that had excited the European mind for a century after 1780 offered less potential for further improvement in the twentieth-century than the microscopic adjustments that alone could provide a more rational basis of peasant agriculture. As a rule, policies of land reform engaged peasants more closely as well as more directly in husbandry, since the statesmen who enfeoffed villagers with land of their own caused the people to make the best of what was provided in order to support families freed of all customary obligations other than public taxes and, perhaps, residual rents. Peasants with land were rather more likely to stay in their villages than those whose ties were feudal or wage-dependent. Nevertheless, a process of slow displacement of surplus free peasant populations did take place, although it may have required two or three generations of adjustment. Those parts of Europe in which emancipation was late or where redistribution trailed behind the abolition of serfdom were characteristically those regions in which both labour participation and population pressure were greatest after 1900. But as one might expect, the creation or proliferation of modest peasant holdings, in all but the most advanced territories, had the result of reducing *effective* employment. Under-employment was widespread throughout the continent. It was contained as a problem in the proximity of industrial towns where the men and/or women were able to obtain alternative or additional work. In central and southern Italy, in the Danube/Balkan region and in Andalucia, the situation was difficult to remedy. It was a chronic malaise wherever low productivity, amounting often to mere subsistence, reduced the peasants' ability to save and diversify. One spectre of rural over-population, however, had retreated into the deep shadows. Starvation hunger was a much rarer affliction of peasant communities in 1920–40 than it had been before the 1850s. Dearth was kept at bay by a resolute attention to household self-sufficiency. At its worst it could be relieved by inter-regional or inter-continental trade in foodstuffs. But for peasants who knew not the name of Malthus, keeping the balance between the land's production and the family's needs was not only perennial: it was also instinctive and over-rode all other preferences. That in essence is the meaning of the low productivity of agriculture.

Technological innovation

Problems of farm structure certainly limited productivity in many parts of Europe. Mere smallness of size was less of an obstacle than fragmentation. With more or less severity, the dispersion of plots increased the effort required for cultivation and reduced the benefits of mechanisation and even of co-operation. The problem did not exist in Denmark where enclosure and legislation to prevent the break-up of family farms had created a remarkably uniform pattern of homesteads, and for similar, if less carefully planned, reasons, holdings in Britain and Ireland were not subject to fission: the trend of two or three centuries had been towards consolidation. Land law elsewhere encouraged the division of holdings upon inheritance. Partible transmission not only led to fragmentation but also caused farmers endless difficulties in reconciling tenurial claims, in repurchasing alienated plots or in forging amicable co-operation among relatives. Since peasant families customarily intermarried, the distribution of plots in any village changed from one generation to the next in an unstable kaleidoscope, which had the effect of distracting agricultural minds from husbandry to property. Resources which could have been invested in the fields and buildings of the holding were allocated to dowries, portions, provision for dependants with reversionary interests in the estate or in buying out legatees. Whether partible inheritance slowed the process of urban migration is unclear, but in the twentieth as in the seventeenth century the overmanning and morcellation of agricultural land led in some instances, in Baden and Württemberg or the Swiss Jura for example, to occupational involution as part-time work proliferated.

The defect of fragmentation was ubiquitous in all but the three countries mentioned, although its effects varied considerably from one district to another. But even in areas of intense fragmentation, the will to change the system which sustained it was muted by acknowledgement in political circles that the peasants would resist interference in their way of life. Even after the Treaty of Rome of 1956, structural reform of the peasant landscape, thought to be imperative, was held up by failure to repeal the relevant sections of Roman land law until the Mansholt Plan was adopted.

Most states did what they could to rationalise the rural landscape before 1940 by attempting both to reduce the number of very small holdings and also to promote amicable exchange of plots, sometimes with cash incentives. The German *Flurbereinigung* policy of the 1950s reflected policies of long standing. In the inter-war years, as in the nineteenth century, the best success occurred when expropriation and redistribution or successful reclamation allowed new initiatives. New holdings on Dutch polders were laid out more generously than was generally the case in Holland, and it was customary to redefine the rights of inheritance so as to impede *morcellement*. Danish land law was applied to the expropriated estates of the German landlords who abandoned north Schleswig after 1918. In the east and south-east of Europe the resettlement of estates with peasant farmers was less coherently organised, but in parts of east Germany, Poland, Hungary and the land appropriated from the Turks some standardised family holdings were created, and an attempt was made in law to maintain them. The general impression is that peasant customs were little disturbed in post-liberal Europe and the problem of miniaturisation was not successfully addressed.

The difficulty was compounded by the remoteness of work from home in many peasant and *latifundial* regimes. Residential villages designed to serve the fields round about existed everywhere, but a majority of European land-workers in the 1930s apparently lived at more than a comfortable walking distance from their employment. At the extreme were found villagers who expended half or more of their available time – and a similar proportion of their energy – in transit. Draught animals too consumed much effort in the daily grind of moving between plots. The overmanning of agriculture and the apparent over-supply of beasts of burden, above all in the south, were the result of excessive unproductive labour. Even on the big estates of Sicily or Extremadura labour was extensive, inefficient and wastefully deployed. The explanation of this displacement of resources is rooted in tradition. The preference for occupying houses in defensible townships, in mountain *pueblas* or *borghetti* or in the rural *shtetl* of east European Jewry, and the equally deep-seated attachment to villages or market towns because of their social variety and vivacity, were difficult to change by officials however convinced they were that farms and fields should coincide. In some districts, of course, the countryside was hazardous because of infestation by mosquitoes, flooding or frequent droughts. Policies of reclamation increased the land open to rural settlement. New farming communities were created upon Italian marshes, in the valleys of the Ebro and Guadalquivir and in Polish Mazuria, where before husbandry had been a matter of seasonal opportunism. It is not known how much relocation of farmsteads into the fields occurred nor how many new *rural* villages were created between 1920 and 1940 but, if we mean to use the process as a yardstick of successful structural reform, the results were negligible.

The chief problems of agrarian Europe before the Second World were thus as much social as technical. Given that few governments were prepared to disrupt the pattern of rural life too severely for fear of peasant reaction, or to protect the pillars of agrarian society, measures to modify land law and settled customs were not to be expected. In any event the contemporary benefits of modernisation so as to promote mechanisation were far from obvious to governments whose object was to preserve the rudiments of agrarian society.

Technical innovation relates to mechanisation, to the application of chemical, biochemical or genetic discoveries to agriculture, and to the adoption and widespread dissemination of cultural practices that were understood to improve productivity. The use of machinery was transformed by the development of the internal combustion engine. Most of the evidence collected in this century has related to tractors, which may be misleading. Peasants who possessed horses, and even more those who kept oxen, were not easily persuaded to change to mechanical traction, because draught beasts represented such a large portion of their capital and replacement was relatively inexpensive. On smallholdings, horses or mules were more versatile than tractors. Moreover, nineteenth-century agricultural engineering left a legacy of machines or implements apt for horse-, ox- or hand-power that was normally better suited to mini-culture than innovations designed for American, British or East German capitalist enterprises. On the other hand oil-powered machines were more adaptable to small-scale cultivation than steam-power, a fact reflected in the ownership of steam equipment by machinery contractors rather than by farmers themselves, even in comparatively advanced parts of Europe. Mechanisation is at the head of a process of technological development that by 1920 was incomplete and disjointed. Peasant preferences for hand tools, for example, had changed little since Courbet had depicted the unnecessary back-breaking effort required in field labour in the 1860s. New ideas in design or performance percolated slowly through Europe before the Second World War, not least because engineering companies, in Germany, Belgium, Britain, Switzerland and north-eastern France, contrived to make innovations and to create demand for them, but the variety of sickles, shovels or ploughs marketed by leading suppliers in the 1930s, such as Cockerill or Spear and Jackson, underlines the continuing diversity. It is therefore not surprising that adoption of new horse- or ox-drawn implements should have been so patchy between 1890 and 1940. No-one attempted to count the total of horse-hoes, hay-rakes, rollers, seed-drills, mowing or reaping machines there were on European farms in the period. What statistics there are are unusually unreliable. More certain is the number of horses available to farmers, although the increase recorded before 1940 disguises a decline in draught oxen and of mules or donkeys (not counted in all relevant countries). Whereas manpower, expressed as *equivalent* to full-time adult male labour (counting casual labourers, women and children *pro rata* with fully employed males), went up by about 5 per cent, 1900–1940, horsepower increased by 12 per cent. In the same period mechanical traction increased by perhaps 2 million h.p. Just before the war there were 30 000 tractors in Germany, over 5000 in Hungary, about the same number in Italy, 3500 in Denmark and 1400 in Belgium. Most of the 200 000 in the later OEEC area of Europe did not exceed 20 h.p. and none was provided with hydraulic transmission to its implements. The pre-war tractor was of two kinds, the heavy, cumbersome field machine appropriate to large-scale ploughing, often imported from or imitative of the United States; and the light, manoeuvrable vehicle characteristic of horticulture. There was little in between to replace horse-teams in seeding, hay-making or harvest. Ford dominated the market, closely followed by International Harvester. There were no comparable manufacturers of European origin, although most automative engineers and several of the old heavy engineering firms in Belgium, Britain, Germany and France produced some tractors. Ransomes of Ipswich, for example, devised a successful light tractor for market gardeners and the German *Volkspflug* tractor of the late 1930s found a niche not occupied by the large American manufacturers in the peasant sector of domestic agriculture.

The tractor was symbolic of the new order in agriculture but its effectiveness before the invention of hydraulic transmission was less striking than the dissemination of chemical fertilisers, which probably doubled in application in the 40 years before 1939 and doubled again in the following 20 years. Most chemical products were lower in price in most European countries in the 1930s than similar products had been in the 1890s. Although governments were less prepared to subsidise fertilisers in the 1930s than in the 1950s, various schemes to extend their use, as well as new seed and improved breeds of livestock, were in operation, often by way of co-operative enterprises in both fascist and liberal states. The most complete programme of technical improvement in agriculture was initiated in Social-Democratic Sweden in the 1930s, but even in the most backward countries, in Greece or Portugal for instance, the ministries in charge of agriculture were eager to spread the word before the 1950s.

In the use of fertilisers there was no wholesale replacement of organic materials by industrially processed chemicals. Nevertheless a considerable proportion of the output of the great chemical works of Europe, IG Farben, ICI and Solvay as well as of more specialist producers such as Fisons and Hoechst, was intended for agriculture. Ammonia and super-phosphates together with balanced inorganic fertilisers were characteristic of this important trade, but there was also profit in the supply of industrial waste products like the basic slag that was taken from blast furnaces of the Gilchrist-Thomas type. There was also a considerable traffic in processed urban sewage, especially for market gardening around the larger towns. Chemical producers in general were well aware of the potential of agriculture for business since, in addition to the rising demand for fertilisers, there was an expansion of output, at least in north-western Europe, of veterinary products and cleansing agents.

Willingness to exploit technical innovation was not determined by farm size. Flemish and Dutch peasants had been as open to scientific discoveries as British farmers, often with even more gratifying results, in the nineteenth century. What mattered was opportunity: the concentration of both engineering and chemical industries in north-western Europe was instrumental in promoting agriculture in the region. But there was also inventiveness in relation to this opportunity: the Hungarian invention of roller-grinding of flour was specific to the commercial system of farming in the country and the contribution of Swedes, Danes, Dutch and Swiss to the technology of dairying equally related to their agricultural preoccupations. No less important, however, were education and professional training. By 1913 peasants in north-western Europe and in substantial parts of the Habsburg Empire had general access to elementary schooling, although a considerable proportion of the agrarian population was still functionally illiterate. Governments, however, varied in the degree of their commitment to support rural education and in several states quite a high level of technical proficiency had been achieved in schools. Bourgeois writers were divided in their expectation of the peasant's ability to absorb propaganda between optimism and scorn. But the tenet of official policy was to raise the standards of rural instruction sufficiently to influence agricultural practice and preferences. It was a complex problem since part of the exercise stirred up ancient resentments against the tax-hungry authorities. But the offspring of the free-standing peasantry of northern Europe were introduced to the mysteries of public and private hygiene, sound animal husbandry, dairy technique, elementary book-keeping, etc., in addition to basic literacy and other civil accomplishments, at least from the end of the nineteenth century. No-one seriously doubted the benefits of professional education, in Lithuania and Bulgaria as much as in Denmark or France during the 1920s and 1930s. The results perhaps disappointed the sanguine hopes of the technocrats of the age, especially in countries such as Italy hastening too fast to join the modern world. Even in the east the desire for an informed peasantry affected nearly all governments. In the case of Czechoslovakia, the farmers' leader and long-serving minister of agriculture, Švehla, took it upon himself to introduce the best western practices he could transplant into central Europe and created a Slavic version of Belgium or the Netherlands.

This requires a wider perspective. In subsistence agriculture the portion of gross receipts (including consumption) expended on such purchased items as feeding-stuffs, seeds, new livestock, fertilisers, fuel, electricity, etc. perhaps averaged 5 per cent and in very few agricultural systems in southern or eastern Europe before 1940 did such purchased inputs exceed 10 per cent, whereas in Britain the average before the war was already about 40 per cent and on the commercialised peasant enterprises of western Europe the proportion probably fell between 20 and 35 per cent. Even in France the *national* average before the war was almost 15 per cent. Another measure is the density of manpower employed in agricultural advisory work relative to the number of farms. Data from the early 1950s suggest that advisors were seven times more numerous in Britain, the Netherlands and Denmark than in France, while in the south the difference was very much greater. The proportions are unlikely to have been much different before the Second World War, even though the total strength on the advisory side had been increased in the interval, probably by a factor of three.

4.4   Agriculture and industry

The relationship of agriculture to industry had many facets, but there were two direct connections. First, farmers, and to an extent also isolated peasants, purchased industrial goods both as householders with a modest appetite for consumption and as entrepreneurs who made use of metal goods, fertilisers, hydrocarbon fuels and veterinary products. However we characterise pre-war agriculture in Europe as subsistent or self-sufficient, peasants in and after the railway age were not immune to the attractions of the market. Industrialists and merchants could ill afford to neglect the rural population of potential consumers, even though countrymen were generally regarded in the towns, in the 1930s perhaps even more grimly than in the 1880s, as infertile ground for merchants to till. The increased output of agricultural implements, tractors and chemical fertilisers was not inconsiderable between 1920 and 1940 but agricultural demands upon heavy industry, even in Britain and Germany, added little to total industrial production, altogether in Europe below 10 per cent in the later 1930s. Certain firms of course depended upon the agricultural trade in engineering and heavy chemicals. The United Kingdom, Germany and Belgium possessed substantial export industries that relied upon the prosperity of agriculture around the world. Several had owned subsidiaries or assembly plants elsewhere in Europe before 1914, some of which were retained, others were resumed after an interval in the 1920s and the majority lost forever to become nuclei of new industries in Austria, Hungary or Romania. These new national industries were matched by the outgrowth of manufacturing in western states, especially Italy and the Netherlands, originally to supply their own farmers but during the middle years of the 1920s destined to break into export markets in competition with Britain, Germany and the United States. The manufacture of goods consumed by farmers was a bread-and-butter activity in most European states, but the trade was still too significant to be left to others in a protectionist age, even though exporting was an object of most industrialists' ambitions from the Danube to the Meuse.

The second aspect of this relationship touches the processing of primary produce. Most of this activity was small in scale, ubiquitous and disjointed, on a par with the structure of farming itself. Nevertheless there were industries founded upon agriculture. The importance of flour-milling in Hungary was still central to the national economy of the Magyar Republic, where the attempt of government to diversify industrial production in the 1920s merely disguised the dominance of milling. In Britain and in Germany flour-milling was also an industry with a higher degree of concentration than was common in agrarian states. In Britain especially its development owed much to the adaptation of imported technology in an essentially import-led pattern of primary processing. Flour-milling centred upon the sea-ports was complemented by an equally concentrated organisation of oil-milling, feeding-stuff manufacture, malting, brewing and distilling. Even on the continent large creameries, margarine factories, preserving and canning establishments were set up in several countries. The general pattern of regional exploitation of primary products by manufacturers was scarcely disturbed by the limited influence of industrialisation before the 1930s, although Danish, Dutch and Swiss dairy products already had international *réclame*. Where raw material was in local surplus, however, a craft-based or factory-organised manufacture grew up processing hemp, flour, mohair, wool, leather, horn, grain, sugar and fruits. Some of these crafts were ancient, but underwent partial transformation in the twentieth century and then fell into decay. That is what happened in the Belgian flax industry around Kortrijk, 1870–1940.

The successful adaptation of peasant modes of production to the market, as in Bulgaria, stimulated small-scale processing across a wide front. In Hungary, conversely, peasant surpluses were drawn increasingly into industrial production that was geared to the large agricultural enterprises. But even in Switzerland, where the processing of agricultural commodities added substantially to the value added by manufacturing in the total economy, village millers, cheese-makers, *chocolatiers* and wine-pressers easily outnumbered the small but influential group of commercial companies such as Nestlé.

Urban expansion from Athens to Dublin, from Barcelona to Riga should have modified the pattern of disaggregated food manufacturing, but because in many regions peasants adapted well to the demands of urban consumers, the industrialisation of their products was a good deal slower than in Britain or the United States.

4.5   Tariffs and protectionism

Fiscal policies for agriculture after 1920 had their roots in the preference for tariff protection displayed by numerous European states after grain prices had embarked upon their downward course in the early 1870s. Tariffs seemed to offer a painless solution to falling agricultural incomes within economies not dependent upon a large export trade in primary produce. The protection of agriculture was an object of policy everywhere except in the United Kingdom, where for all its formidable reputation for productive efficiency the sector had become marginalised by rural depopulation and the more insistent claims of industry and the urban working class upon cheap food. The fields and livestock ranges of the New World had become an extension of Victorian Britain. Britain's openness to imports was not accepted by everyone with an easy conscience before 1914, not least because the promises of free trade were not maintained with equal enthusiasm within the international economy. But the fact that Britain was not self-sufficient in agricultural production by 1870, and was therefore a prize worth contestation among suppliers the world over, influenced some European states to sustain the essentials of free trade in farm commodities, because their access to British and other deficient markets remained vital to their economic wellbeing. The Danes and the Dutch were reluctant and half-hearted converts to fiscal protectionism, while the Belgians and the Swiss devised limited and particular tariffs for their agriculture so as not to endanger their export markets. Not all countries with a predominant agriculture in the composition of their foreign trade retained a wholly liberal policy before 1914, but the more exports outweighed imports in government calculations the less the appeal of grain duties. The classic territory of agricultural tariff protection before the war was in France and Germany, where the motives implicated in their taxing of imports were mixed and not necessarily coherent. The instinct was to keep out New World produce, but, if that proved impossible, to equalise the price of foreign and domestic supplies on internal markets. The *raison d'être* was wider than the mere support of peasant incomes in an epoch of falling prices. The role of government in preserving agrarian society acquired sentimental, even mystical, force, especially in France. This perception, merged with the *dirigiste* tradition in French politics, was held with renewed vigour, but emitting an odour of desperation, throughout the inter-war period. Tariffs were preferred as a means of support chiefly because they were easy to administer and incurred few public costs. As the first line of defence they were insufficient, but more and more states were converted to the device in the twentieth century and logic proposed that the tariff wall should steadily be elevated to counter the effects of each succeeding crisis. Where autarky strongly influenced policy-making the range of dutiable commodities was extended to provide effective cover for all branches of agriculture not invulnerable to import penetration by the perishable nature of produce. One problem which appeared after the 1870s was the invention of bulk refrigeration which made meat and cheese supplies from the American west or Australia as palatable as those on offer in local markets, and therefore added to the difficulties of European farmers, hitherto largely protected from long-range competition in pastoral products. Nevertheless different states had different priorities in setting their tariff levels. Although the trend between 1900 and 1940 was upward, national variations make a general comparison rather difficult. Michael Tracy (1989) made use of Liepman's estimate of 'potential' tariffs for foodstuffs, which he expressed as a percentage of the export prices in European countries. His figures suggest that between 1925–27 and 1931–32 these potential tariffs at least doubled in weight, although in Germany the rise, even before the coming of the Nazis, exceeded 200 per cent, while in several eastern states the increase, usually in the aftermath of good harvests in 1929 and 1931, was 250 per cent or more. Except where tariffs were superseded by measures of direct control over imports, the levels continued to rise in the 1930s, when even the UK had a tariff of sorts on cereal imports.

The economic benefits of tariffs were equivocal. Duties upon imports did not themselves force up prices. It is even uncertain whether the tariff effectively preserved the price differences that existed between Europe and the chief exporting zone, North America. Before 1913 wheat prices, for example, declined on virtually the same trend in France and Germany as in the United States and Britain. Both the former started from a higher point in 1870 than the latter but fell by broadly the same percentage to a nadir in 1893–95. Thereafter all four countries showed the same upward tendency until the Great War. Yet the price gap between France and the United States was narrower in 1910 than in 1870. A similar, though less clearly indicated, pattern of fluctuations around parallel trends occurred in the inter-war years. Indeed, where differences were apparent, especially in the 1930s, the cause seems to have been the operation of physical rather than fiscal controls over supply. States which still relied upon the tariff for their protection were exposed to international price trends at least indirectly, whereas fascist or bolshevik command economies could avoid some of the consequences of world price movement. But neither Germany nor Italy was immune from external influences in its agricultural policy, not least because both were still engaged in foreign trade in primary produce. The supplementation of tariffs with secondary controls, production quotas, milling ratios, the insertion of 'floor' prices to stabilise farm incomes, etc. improved the management of agricultural markets, but at an increasing public cost, and in some sense the subsidisation of agriculture in relation to prevailing market prices was a transfer payment from industry or the service sector to the farmers, even though industry itself was in receipt of a similar kind of subvention. One striking difference between Britain, America and Australia and France, Belgium, Germany and northern Italy was the greater cost of urban working-class budgets, especially of food, on the continent, certainly in relation to average earnings but even, in some countries, in absolute terms. There is irony in the 'margarine standard' enjoyed by the Ruhr working-class in the 1890s or 1920s when German peasants were encouraged by the state's apparatus of subvention to produce great quantities of both butter and cheese.

Cheap food, even in the industrialising economies of the continent, was not an object of policy, although the corporatism of fascist governments in the 1930s allowed them an option of regulating consumer prices as an act of will.

As tariffs became more general and their value increased the question of their effectiveness assumed more importance. The hope in the 1920s that duties would achieve a 'floor' price for agricultural products was severely tested when glut coincided with depression in 1929–31. The inadequacy of tariffs led to a rather desperate search for alternatives. Imports still threatened, because producers of agricultural commodities in the New World were forced by circumstance to dispose of their surpluses at whatever price they could command, tariff or no tariff. The rise of tariff levels was designed to choke off this effort to break open continental markets, but the cumulative effect of these defensive measures distorted the superstructure of internal markets, not least because it was often necessary to admit exceptions. Moreover, tariff policy after 1925–27 conveyed the wrong message, by encouraging farmers to deliver yet more produce on a glutted market. The gap between protected and open prices for commodities such as wheat became unmanageable. In these circumstances a second line of defence had to be constructed. One scheme was to link imports to a predetermined proportion of domestic produce. In flour and meal for instance a ratio between foreign and domestic grain in milling was adopted by most continental states after the idea was enacted in Norway in 1927. This milling ratio was amended from time to time, almost invariably to the disadvantage of imports. By 1934–36 the proportion of domestic produce required in flour-milling varied between 35 per cent in the Netherlands and 100 per cent in Sweden, and even in large countries such as Germany, France and Italy the ratio exceeded 90 per cent. Similar measures were devised for other commodities: margarine had to contain a proportion of domestically produced butter in Sweden, the Netherlands and Switzerland and of lard in Denmark; states which had considerable surpluses of low-grade carbohydrates encouraged or required refiners of petrol products to mix alcohol derived from sugar-beet, wine, fruit or grain with the mineral oil. Substitution was very common in the 1930s in command economies deprived of adequate supplies of crucial imported commodities, but the process seems to have begun as an *agricultural* measure. The connection between import purchases and domestic supplies, like the later Swiss *prise en charge* system, was first made in 1931 in Latvia for sugar. It was soon followed by rye, wheat and oats and then adopted in several east European countries where 'linked purchasing' regulations were often tied to bilateral trading arrangements. The nationalists in Spain made the scheme a cornerstone of their agricultural and overseas commercial policies from the end of the 1930s and the Swiss were making tentative experiments of the same kind before war disrupted their commercial plans.

Quotas of different sorts were employed to supplement tariffs in the attempt to match supplies to demand in order to stabilise prices. Deficiency payments made directly by treasuries to guarantee price levels were not widespread, even though in Britain this kind of subsidy gradually became normative. Elsewhere similar measures were introduced only in a few northern states, and then briefly or for a restricted range of primary products, chiefly because the scheme was so expensive and the commitment potentially so difficult to control. Linked to production quotas deficiency payments were especially effective, as the Dutch discovered. But to manage production and to eradicate fraud were well-nigh impossible in such vast agricultural domains as France. Remedies had therefore to be specific to particular products or regions. The variety of ideas tried in practice during the 1930s attests both the ingenuity and the desperation of agriculture ministers across the continent.

A distinction has to be made between those states seeking autarky and those merely attempting to mitigate agrarian distress. It is not a clear distinction, because most governments, liberal or fascist, kept faith with their peasantry; but the differences of emphasis are crucial. The objective of autarky was to eliminate dependence upon foreign trade in theory if not always in practice, to produce all the agricultural commodities possible within the geographical limits of the country and to substitute domestic for exotic products. No European state in the 1930s was fully self-sufficient, but the denial of classical theories of comparative advantage, especially in fascist states, reinforced the idea of the state as a gigantic corporate enterprise, in which the producers were given a dominant role because the essential feature of inter-war autocracies was to magnify the physical capacity of the economy. Autarky in these conditions was not merely a means of policy but the end to which the state aspired. Theory and practice often fell apart, especially in inefficient totalitarian regimes, but the mystique of production, and therefore of those who delivered it, was ineradicable.

4.6   Further reading

Michael Tracy's (1989) *Agriculture in Western Europe since 1880*, 3rd edn, (London: Granada) is authoritative and comprehensive within its frame of reference. It includes useful studies of France, Germany, the UK and Denmark. For the eastern lands, there is an up-to-date study by I. Berend (1975) in M.E. Kaser and E.A. Radice (eds) *Economic History of Eastern Europe* (Oxford: Oxford University Press).

The East is also covered adequately in O.S. Morgan (ed.) (1933) *Agricultural Systems of Middle Europe* (New York: New York University Press) and by Doreen Warriner (1939) *The Economics of Peasant Farming* (Oxford: Oxford University Press). For the West, P.L. Yates (1940) *Food Production in Western Europe* (London: Macmillan) and E.M. Ojala (1952) *Agriculture and Economic Progress* (Oxford: Oxford University Press) offer useful new insights into the industry both generally and for particular countries.

National histories of agriculture and rural society in English, apart from Tracy and Morgan, are scarce and perfunctory, but F. Skubbeltrang (1953) *Agricultural Development and Rural Reform in Denmark* (Rome: FAO) is an outstanding exception. Much the best of these national histories is H. Gervais *et al.* (eds) (1977) *Histoire de la France Rurale*, vol IV (1914–present) (Paris: Seuil). Also very good are P. Bevilacqua (1990) *Storia dell'Agricoltura Italiana nell'età contemporanea*, vol I (Venice: Marsilio); Z.W. Sneller (1951) *Geschiedenis van de Nederlandse Landbouw, 1795–1940* (Amsterdam: Mouton). M. Augé-Laribé (1950) *La politique agricole de la France de 1880 à 1940* (Paris: Seuil); Ernst Klein (1979) *Geschichte der deutsche Landwirtschaft in Industriezeitalter* (Wiesbaden: Wirtschafliche Paperbacks) and H. Haushofer (1963) *Die deutsche Landwirtschaft in technischen Zeitalter* (Stuttgart: Ulmen) are adequate but not exciting surveys of Germany.

For particular topics the following books are recommended: G. Wright (1964) *Rural Revolution in France. The Peasantry in the Twentieth Century* (Stanford: Stanford University Press); S. Mallet (1962) *Le paysan contre le passé* (Paris: Seuil); H. Tiltman (1935) *Peasant Europe* (London: Benn); F. Dovring (1960) *Land and Labor in Europe, 1900–1950* (The Hague: Nijhoff); P.L. Yates (1960) *Food, Land and Manpower in Western Europe* (London: Macmillan); R. Dumont (1953) *Voyages d'un Agronome* (Paris: Plon).

5
Industry

In 1913 the greater part of world industrial production was in the USA, Britain, Germany and France. In the years following the First World War, as we have seen, the relative share of industrial production in Europe declined as that in Japan and other parts of the New World increased. Within Europe also there was a relative if minor shift. In particular the USSR experienced rapid growth and there was real development in Scandinavia and some smaller states in eastern Europe. The most significant relative decline was shown by Britain. These comparative developments were in part a function of shifts in industrial structure.

The major industrial centres of the nineteenth century had tended to be concentrated on sources of energy and raw materials. Thus the principal industrial regions were on or near to coal fields. In western Europe these were in the north of England, Scotland, Wales, the Ruhr, Belgium and part of the southern Netherlands and the iron fields of Luxembourg. Coal and iron resources extended also to the Saar and Lorraine. Further east there were industrial centres in Silesia and Bohemia, centred on Pilsen. Sweden and Spain produced iron ore, there were engineering and textile centres in northern Italy and Switzerland. Yet the bulk of production was relatively concentrated in regions determined more by resources than markets; industrial strength was associated with iron, steel and engineering. The staple industries of the nineteenth century had been textiles, iron and steel, shipbuilding and engineering. Shipping not only carried goods but also provided a major market for coal just as railways had been a major market for steel and engineering as well as fuel inland. The growth in demand for basic industrial products was reinforced by cost-reducing innovations in steel manufacture and new ore discoveries. Such stimuli were lacking in the inter-war years.

It is important to remember that industry did not simply mean large-scale or factory production. A large proportion of industrial employment was, throughout the period, in relatively small units. These included labour-intensive family-based enterprises and artisans. The relative importance of such small scale industry was most evident in east and south-east Europe. In Bulgaria, for example, rapid industrial development in the inter-war years took place in handicraft or artisan industry. Even in Germany, an industrial leader, the *handwerke* continued to play an important part in many industries. Nearly all leather shoes in Germany (with one major exception, Salamander) were made in small workshops. In Denmark most of the textile industry was on a similar small scale; in France, despite the growth of technologically advanced industries in the 1920s, small scale, specialised industries continued to play a major role in total production.

Distinctions between 'old' and 'new' industries, although commonplace, can be equally misleading. What were old and established industries in one place could be new and dynamic elsewhere: textiles had been staples for centuries in Britain, France, Switzerland, Italy and Germany and in the inter-war years stagnated or declined; in Hungary and the Low Countries, however, they were a fast-growing sector. The manufacture of sugar from beet had been established in early nineteenth century France, Germany and Austria (Bohemia); after the First World War it became among the fastest growing of industries in the Baltic, southern Europe, even Britain.

The variety of structural change and patterns of development between countries and regions is one of the features of continental Europe in the early twentieth century. Yet there were common underlying themes as well. New technologies and changing markets brought the development of new products. It is thus legitimate to refer to new industries based on recent technologies, such as internal combustion, electrical engineering or inorganic chemistry. Nearly all such industries were based on inventions dating from well before the First World War but they grew in scale of production and demand thereafter. Synthetic textiles and motor cars, for example, dated from the 1880s but became major and fast-growing industries in later years.

At the end of this period, despite real structural change, the relative distribution of industrial strength had changed little. On the eve of the Second World War the great powers in industrial terms were very much the same as they had been in 1913. Thus Britain, France and Germany were significantly greater industrial powers than other countries. Germany recovered industrial leadership from the loss of resources in the post-war settlement and the severe downturn of the slump. Italy, too, had seen real industrial growth to become the fourth industrial producer in Europe (discounting the USSR) by 1938, though some way behind the leaders.

In 1938 Germany accounted for 32.1 per cent of the net industrial output of Europe, excluding the USSR. She produced 42.8 per cent of the iron and steel and took 29.2 per cent of energy consumption. This leadership, particularly the primacy in steel, was associated with the rearmament programme. In the same year Britain produced 23.7 per cent of net industrial output (20.7 per cent iron and steel, 27.7 per cent energy consumption) and France 11.2 per cent (12 per cent and 11.7 per cent). This industrial leadership was not merely the product of size though *per capita* comparisons on a broad basis give a more varied picture. Germany, with a little under 17 per cent of the population, and the UK (near to 12 per cent) were still significant in *per capita* terms; France (10.2 per cent population) less so.

France was one of the boom economies in the 1920s, especially because of new industries, but did not maintain that position after 1930. Belgian industry grew quickly but was based more on staples like textiles and steel. Both benefited from under-valued currencies in the 1920s. France became a European leader in motor vehicle production and electrical power generation. The early development of hydroelectric power, coupled with bauxite deposits, led directly to the early establishment of aluminium production in France. She also developed chemicals, artificial fibres and engineering. In *per capita* terms Italy, with a population similar to that in France yet with only 6.4 per cent of new industrial product, was some way behind. Countries like Sweden and Switzerland were major industrial producers *per capita* though modest in aggregate. Belgium (with Luxembourg) and the Netherlands also had a larger share of total product than population, by a small margin. Thus there were small countries or regions (like north Italy or Bohemia) where industrial production and employment had a major impact and was an important source of income, even though in aggregate terms these countries were not major producers.

In the inter-war years industry faced far more than stagnation. The setbacks of the war and post-war readjustment and the recession after 1929 were deep cyclical downturns but there was, nonetheless, secular growth. Real incomes improved overall, though at a rate probably slower than in the generation before 1913, contributing to an extension of the market. Labour productivity also showed secular increases, though averages conceal a host of variations. Nevertheless such developments contributed to cost reductions and market expansion.

There were thus contrasting developments in the inter-war years: on the one hand there were declining or stagnating industries for which demand was growing slowly or not at all; on the other were growing industries which increased their share of total production. In between, as it were, were industries experiencing mixed fortunes, relative stagnation or modest growth. The declining sectors included coal, shipbuilding, railways, cotton textiles; growing industries included motor vehicles, electrical power generation and electrical goods, and some branches of the chemical industry. Those industries which might be included in the third group are steel, chemical dyestuffs, building and related trades and food processing.

5.1 Declining sectors

It is difficult to be precise about which industries were declining and which expanding for fortunes varied in different parts of the world and Europe. Traditional natural textiles constituted a major growth industry in India and other parts of Asia. Yet such expansion was in part the cause of the relative decline of the cotton industry in Britain in particular. Faced with overseas competition for the first time and protective measures in former export markets, the Lancashire cotton industry went into severe decline; the German and Italian industry also declined. In other parts of Europe, though, the cotton industry was a leading sector, particularly in the east and south-east (Hungary, Bulgaria and Romania) where the industry was built up in the 1920s using redundant machines sold off from Lancashire mills. There was some degree of competition also from artificial textiles, principally rayon, though this was less significant than competition from the cotton industry in former markets within and beyond Europe.

The decline was most serious for Britain as the industry had previously been so export-dependent. France just about maintained its level of cotton consumption; Belgium, Switzerland, Sweden and the Netherlands all showed an increase. The initial spur had been to replace imports in the war; growth thereafter was unspectacular but continued as import saving and to serve more specialised, high-cost markets than the British industry (Table 5.1).

Table 5.1   Raw cotton consumption

Percentage change 1925–38			
UK	–22.9	Belgium	+29.7
Germany	–11.2	Netherlands	+96.5
France	0	Sweden	+ 4.7
Switzerland	0		
Italy	–28.6		

Adapted from I. Svennilson (1954) *Growth and Stagnation* (Geneva: United Nations), p. 143

Two further examples of industrial decline in Europe were coal and shipbuilding, though both these cases were disproportionately influenced by the British example. The demand for coal was reduced by the development of alternative fuels, especially oil, and greater efficiency in the use of coal. The biggest setback for the British industry was the decline in bunkering trade. More ships were diesel powered, though this was a slow change; as trade was slow to recover there were fewer ships in use. Britain also faced more competition. For Poland coal was a major export earner. The decline in total was a more serious problem for the traditional exporters. Thus various attempts to improve efficiency and manipulate markets were invoked. In nearly all these, Britain was unsuccessful. Attempts to reduce wage costs led to a prolonged dispute in 1926; productivity increases were modest by international comparison. In the 1930s various bilateral trading treaties depended on agreements to import British coal, though cheaper alternatives were available.

Other producers appeared to be more successful, though the essential problems were similar. In Germany, rationalisation often meant that ownership was concentrated in a few companies and output similarly concentrated in the most productive pits and fields. This, and the increased mechanisation of coal cutting, enabled output per man shift to double between 1924 and 1931. By 1929, 91 per cent of coal in Germany was cut mechanically. In Belgium the figure was 89 per cent, in France 72 per cent, in Poland 31 per cent and in Britain only 28 per cent.

Britain again performed poorly in shipbuilding, in which she had been world leader before 1914. The drying up of trade after the First World War resulted in general overcapacity. The seizure of much of the German merchant marine as part payment for reparations did little to help new demand. The British shipyards later became centres of seriously depressed areas. In the 1930s deliberate government policies of scrap and build were instituted, though with minor effect. There was general malaise in Europe, though Italy, the Netherlands, Sweden and Denmark were able to increase their share of total production.

5.2   Expanding industries

In the chemical industry Germany quickly re-established her leadership in Europe in the 1920s, though chemical production was more widespread than before the war. There was more rapid growth beyond Europe (especially in the USSR and Japan). Although dyestuffs remained an important branch of the industry, there was virtually no growth in this sector in the inter-war years. Germany retained first place, with Britain, France and Switzerland also major producers. Similarly, superphosphates remained fairly stable. The European growth sectors were synthetic nitrogen, plastics and synthetic textiles (especially rayon). In 1913 rayon had been produced in Britain, Germany, France and Belgium. In the 1920s the Netherlands, Czechoslovakia, Hungary, Poland, Spain and Sweden all introduced the industry; in the 1930s Romania, Portugal, Norway and Finland followed.

Nowhere else did the chemical industry have the prominence that it did in Germany. In the late 1920s the chemical industry employed close to a third of a million people; the firms which made up IG Farben alone employed 84 000 in 1924; by 1928 the combine employed 114 000. In the 1930s this dominance increased.

Electrical power and the internal combustion engine were together the leading sectors in power in the twentieth century. These new resources transformed much of industry. Between 1920 and 1939 European electrical power consumption increased by a factor of four. Such an increase was enabled by technological improvements in power generation and distribution, to reduce the cost and increase efficiency of supply.

The early leaders in power supply were Norway, Switzerland, Austria and Sweden, because of the exploitation of hydroelectric power. France too had HEP resources but was slower to exploit them. In the 1920s thermal power stations, burning coal or lignite, increased much faster in volume. Germany and Britain quickly became major producers/consumers (there was little cross-border trade in power). In thermal production improved transmission efficiency, so that power could be transported great distances to the point of use, enabled concentration of production in larger power stations. This in turn made for economies of scale and lower unit costs. Another and equally important improvement was in the efficiency of fuel consumption. The amount of power per ton of coal improved significantly; this was one reason why demand for coal did not increase in accordance with the demand for electrical power. Further, standardisation of voltages, which was slow to come about, reduced complexity. National or virtually national systems enhanced the markets further.

There was steady expansion in the 1930s and a rapid take up in these years in eastern Europe. Generally speaking, demand grew slowly in the 1930s where industry grew slowly, though there are some contrasts here. In Britain and Denmark, for instance, demand came especially from the domestic sector rather than industry. France and Belgium, on the other hand, had a relatively slow uptake in domestic demand but a more rapid one for industrial uses.

The availability of electrical power not only enabled more decentralisation of industry, it also spawned a new consumer market in

Table 5.2   *Per capita* consumption of electricity, 1929–38

	Kilowatt hours	
	1929	1938
Norway	547	747
Switzerland	249	317
Austria	62	71
Britain	58	187
Belgium–Luxembourg	56	69
Denmark	37	79
France	31	57
Czechoslovakia	20	26
Poland	6	12
Greece	4	11
Bulgaria	4	7

From I. Svennilson (1954) *Growth and Stagnation* (Geneva: United Nations), p. 118

Excluding industry and transport

domestic appliances. In the inter-war years such domestic appliances were largely a middle class preserve. But radio and electric lighting were classless. Not surprisingly consumption remained low in the poorer countries of the east and south east of Europe. In western Europe, Scandinavia and Switzerland had high consumption levels, France relatively low (see Table 5.2). Germany was the largest producer of radio sets. The number licensed in January 1924 was 1500, by 1930 it was over 3.5 million, and by 1938 11.5 million.

The motor vehicle industry was the outstanding example of a new, growing industry in the inter-war years. The industry employed new, or almost new, technologies (the internal combustion engine was young, and there was a host of innovations in braking, transmission, tyres etc.). More particularly, there were innovations in production, especially the assembly line and standardisation of parts. Technological developments contributed to a decline in unit costs and an expansion of the market. Further, the industry had multiplier and technical 'spin-off' effects. Thus although manufacture was effectively confined to six European countries (Britain, France, Germany, Italy, Sweden and Czechoslovakia), the derived demand for servicing, petrol sales and above all road building affected all Europe.

The European leader in the 1920s was France. In the following decade Britain overtook France, and production increased quickly in Germany (Table 5.3). All European producers imposed tariffs both to protect producers and to levy a tax on what was still, in the 1920s, a luxury. Thus non-producers imposed duties also. In 1929 Britain levied import duties of 30 per cent, Germany 20 per cent, France 45 per cent, Switzerland 28

Table 5.3 Motor vehicle manufacture

	France		Germany		UK		Italy		Sweden		Czechoslovakia	
	C	P	C	P	C	P	C	P	C	P	C	P
1925	56	121	10	39	35	132	3.6	46	0.3		5	
1929	42	212	32	96	57	182	3.2	52	1.3	0.5	3	12
1932	28	136	8	43	61	171	3.1	27	2.9		3	10
1935	22	143	42	205	114	354	9.5	41	3.0	1.5	1	7
1938	45	182	63	275	104	341	12.0	59	4.8	2.2	2	11

Figures are in 000s

C = commercial vehicles
P = private cars

From B.R. Mitchell (1975) *European Historical Statistics* (Cambridge: Cambridge University Press), p. 488

per cent, Finland 32 per cent, Bulgaria 25 per cent, Italy only 6 per cent, but this was increased to 95 per cent in 1932. Czechoslovakia imposed a 65 per cent luxury sales tax in the 1920s and Germany also had high domestic taxes until 1933.

The industry had begun as a labour-intensive, luxury business; in the inter-war years the character began to change, though small scale specialist manufacturers never disappeared. The greater part of production began to be concentrated in fewer firms. In 1921 there were 150 French manufacturers, 96 in Britain and in 1925 200 in Germany. By 1928 three firms dominated the French market, Citroën, Renault and Peugeot, with 68 per cent of the market in cars. By 1937 three firms took 74 per cent of sales in Germany; in Britain 41 factories in 1929 had been reduced to 32 by 1939.

French producers led the continent in the 1920s. Renault was one of the great innovators, Citroën a great entrepreneur who was in the forefront of Europeans' import of American technology. As well as a large home market the French were leading exporters; only Britain had a higher rate of usage of cars in the 1920s and a good many of these were imported from France. In turn the car was a stimulus to other branches of the economy. In 1932 there were 15 000 French retail dealers in cars, motor cycles and bicycles. Further, although not yet a legal requirement in France, 95 per cent of drivers were insured in France in 1935. A reversal of the economic fortunes of the 1920s for France saw her leadership eclipsed in the following decade. In Britain real incomes increased, while France endured relative stagnation, and the popularity of cars increased – the peak demand for motor cycles had been in the 1920s. The small, affordable family car became commonplace in Britain in the 1930s. At the same time manufacturers in several European economies began to develop cheap cars to serve more of a mass market. In

Table 5.4   Motor vehicle usage

	France	Germany	UK	Italy	Sweden	Czech	Austria	Switzerland
1922	161	900	136	2640	767	260	775	199
1925	84	452	75	1097	369	137	598	102
1929	44	237	45	433	153	72	340	62
1932	34	217	40	229	135	62	290	61
1935	27	171	35	162	85	60	252	57
1938	23	148	24	148	51	54	194	40

Number of inhabitants per car

From T. Barker (ed.) (1988) *The Economic and Social Effects of the Spread of Motor Vehicles* (London: Macmillan), p. 204

the 1930s Citroën and Fiat as well as Morris and Austin looked to a more popular product. The famous Citroën 2CV was designed and developed in the later 1930s, though not yet made commercially. A 500cc. Fiat was also begun, though again production was interrupted by the war.

In Germany popular car ownership was slower to develop; the car remained a luxury item for longer than in France and Britain. High taxation limited the market, fewer German cars were small than in France or Britain. In 1933 the Nazi regime instituted a deliberate policy of motorisation, removing car taxes and increasing expenditure on road building. Before then cheap, extensive, efficient rail travel had been more than an able substitute for travel by road. By 1935, however, expenditure on roads exceeded that on railways for the first time. Plans to develop a 'people's car' were drawn up, though the vehicle was never produced commercially in the Nazi period. The 'strength through joy' vehicles (which became the Volkswagen) and the road network eventually served military purposes. Nonetheless car usage (many for business purposes) increased in the 1930s, but remained behind other parts of Europe (Table 5.4).

The industry in Czechoslovakia followed a pattern similar to other parts of Europe, though it developed slowly in the 1930s with general stagnation in the economy. Ownership was concentrated in Bohemia, especially in and around Prague. In nearly all cases the production of cars exceeded that of commercial vehicles, the sole exception being in Sweden. Lorries were not yet in a position to compete with rail and water for carrying bulk loads. Further, motor cycles made up a major part of the industry, though with lower added value than cars. Demand for motor cycles persisted longer in Germany and Czechoslovakia as the car market was restricted.

The steel industry, so long the indicator of industrial advance, underwent mixed fortunes in the inter-war years. Demand from new sectors such as the motor industry was insufficient to replace demand that was lost in other markets. European production as a proportion of the world's total declined, from 51 per cent in 1913 to 41 per cent in 1936–37 (as a percentage of steel ingots and castings by weight). Within Europe, production stagnated in France and Belgium in the longer term and grew in Britain and Germany. In the 1930s armaments industries became a great source of renewed demand. Overall the European steel industry showed only modest progress in the inter-war years; proportionately steel manufacture declined as a European industry.

Although not a new industry by any means, food processing constituted a growth sector in the least industrialised regions of Europe. Sugar manufacture from beet grew in almost all parts of the continent and Britain. However, food processing as a sector was far more important in the Balkans. From very low beginnings the Balkan countries experienced some of the fastest rates of industrial growth and food processing, such as fruit canning in Bulgaria, was among the leading sectors in those countries. At a technical level, however, they remained relatively backward by international standards, especially compared with the mass production techniques of British and American producers.

There was thus growth and structural change in European industry in the years between the two world wars. The examples given above can be only that; there are numerous other examples of industries to illustrate the case. Old or stagnating industries in one region could be the growth sectors in others. Textiles and clothing were fast-growing in Hungary and Czechoslovakia, for instance, while tending to stagnate in many parts of western Europe. New products were developed to serve consumer markets but in all cases also the state deliberately sponsored or encouraged industry, for purposes of maintaining employment or, very often, from military motives. Thus aeroplanes and air transport developed virtually from nothing, yet were almost entirely dependent on government support, direct or indirect, in one form or another. In turn this stimulated demand for new products like aluminium production, which showed dramatic increase. Leading producers were France, Germany, Norway and Britain. In the 1930s armaments production became more important in the economies of Europe, affecting far more than aircraft.

5.3   Rationalisation and cartelisation

One of the most frequently used words about European industry in the 1920s is 'rationalisation'. This usually refers to a process of organising or reorganising production to reduce or eliminate inefficiencies – by saving labour, standardising production, replacing labour with machinery. Such developments were hardly new – standardisation in Germany had been introduced in the 1890s, for instance. But there was a renewed effort to improve the efficiency of production through technological modernisation in many industries, especially after 1925. It is in this period that there is much emphasis on rationalisation. The process often had negative consequences by rendering labour or plant redundant. On the other hand it was intended to reduce costs. The process could have been confined to a single manufacturer but is also commonly taken to refer to some element of agreement among firms. The smaller or less efficient producers might be bought up and closed. Thus it is important to identify two different meanings of 'rationalisation', the elimination of redundant capacity, including labour, and the modernisation of productive processes. These two senses were not mutually exclusive.

The quest for rationalisation was common in Europe, though British manufacturers were less obviously successful than others in introducing cost-saving measures. Much of the process was associated with the introduction of productive techniques, often called 'Taylorism', after F.W. Taylor (1856–1915). This involved the reduction of processes to their most simple component forms with the elimination, as far as possible, of skills. Taylorism was the subject of much debate in the 1920s, but nowhere took root in undiluted form. The assembly line was much more associated with Henry Ford and the motor car, though the ideas of Taylor became fashionable in many industries. Such ideas of 'scientific management' were taken up with enthusiasm by some European entrepreneurs, learning from American counterparts or through US companies setting up subsidiary plants in Europe. French and Swedish business people were among the leading lights in this movement but the rationalisation process has, in historical literature, become particularly associated with industry in Germany and to a lesser extent Austria and Czechoslovakia.

It was long assumed that the great extent of rationalisation in Germany contributed to the growth of unemployment in the 1920s and eventually to the slump after 1929. The extent of rationalisation in German industry, and especially its role in bringing about depression, has recently been questioned, however. While there is some evidence for the phenomenon it is limited. Harold James can find only two examples, the motor industry and Ruhr coal mining. Direct investment by Ford and General Motors introduced American methods. However, as we have seen, the German motor industry remained rather less developed than elsewhere in Europe, and there is no evidence of structural unemployment in this industry, rather the opposite. This was an example of productive modernisation reducing unit costs and helping to expand the market. Similarly in France Citroën was an enthusiastic proponent of

American technology. His compatriot and rival, Louis Renault, bit by bit transformed the process of production in his Paris plant in the 1920s. Such sophistications of production engineering did not lead to redundancy of labour, however. Taylorism had little real influence; other factors were historically more important.

In the coal industry of the Ruhr, and to a lesser extent Holland and Belgium, there were significant improvements in productivity in the 1920s and a lower demand for labour as a result. Redundant capacity was eliminated through the closure of relatively inefficient pits and may be seen as negative rationalisation. In Germany 76 Ruhr collieries were closed between 1924 and 1928 (see Chap. 7). To these examples must be added others. The textile, steel and mechanical engineering (machine building) industries in Germany undertook investments in the 1920s which contributed later to excess capacity and labour shedding, with the closure of less profitable units. The number of blast furnaces in Rhineland-Westphalia declined from 118 in 1913 to 72 in 1928, though the average weekly production increased from 1491 tons to 3207 tons. In such developments the concentration of ownership was as important an influence as techniques of production.

There were other examples of combinations of productive enterprises, involving vertical and horizontal integration. German examples are again the best known. IG Farben was formed in 1925, soon to be followed by ICI in Britain. In 1926 the giant Vereinigte Stahlwerke (of German steel producers) was formed. In France the Schneider works, based in Le Creusot, was well known as an armaments and metallurgical concern. In the 1920s the company extended ownership into new sectors within and beyond France. These included coke making, steel manufacture, railway engineering, machine making of all kinds, diesel engineering, ship-building, optical instruments, motor cars, electrical power generation. The company had manufacturing and banking interests in Belgium, Austria, Poland, Romania, Hungary and Czechoslovakia (including the Skoda works).

Such a case was extreme but not unique. Far more common, however, and possibly more significant, were controls over markets and sales through cartels. These did not necessarily have any influence on production or ownership; they were marketing agreements. Cartels were long established, from the nineteenth century, in Germany; they increased in number in the inter-war years. In Czechoslovakia the number of cartels doubled in the 1930s under state support. Cartels also operated in the British cotton industry, Swiss watch making and the greater part of European steel manufacture. Cartels thus came to influence much of European industry, internationally as well as domestically. One of the earliest international agreements was an association of glue makers. In

1926 a Franco–German potash agreement was signed; copper and zinc also became subjects of international cartels, as well as most dyestuffs manufacturing in Europe. The best known example was the International Steel Cartel of 1926. The original signatories, Germany, France, Belgium and Luxembourg, agreed to limit total production (25.3 million tons) and to distribute this total on a quota basis. In 1927 Austria, Czechoslovakia and Hungary joined as a unit, with a joint quota of 7.27 per cent to be distributed among themselves as they decided. All such measures were means to share out a limited or declining market, and avoid competition. But even such agreements could rarely survive the pressures to reduce prices and undercut competitors in the industrial depression.

5.4   Further reading

The development of industry and technology is covered in D. Landes (1969) *The Unbound Prometheus. Technological Change and Industrial Development in Western Europe from 1750 to the Present* (Cambridge: Cambridge University Press), though it really deals only with Britain, France and Germany. I. Svennilson (1954) *Growth and Stagnation in the European Economy* (Geneva: United Nations) has extensive data on some major industries. Particular industries are also dealt with by N.J.G. Pounds and W.N. Parker (1957) *Coal and Steel in Western Europe* (London: Faber & Faber); J. Gillingham (1985) *Industry and Politics in the Third Reich. Ruhr Coal, Hitler and Europe* (London: Methuen); L.F. Haber (1971) *The Chemical Industry 1900–1930. International Growth and Technological Change* (Oxford: Oxford University Press); P. Hayes (1987) *Industry and Ideology. I.G. Farben in the Nazi Era* (Cambridge: Cambridge University Press); T.C. Barker (ed.) (1986) *Economic and Social Effects of the Spread of Motor Vehicles* (London: Macmillan). The growth of multinational industry has a large literature, including these useful sources: L.G. Franko (1976) *The European Multinationals* (Stanford: Greylock), J. Foreman-Peck (1982) 'The American challenge of the twenties. Multinationals and the European motor industry', *Journal of Economic History*, **42**, pp. 865–882.

PART 3

National experiences

6

France

Before the First World War France was one of the major economic powers in Europe but one which had begun to fall some way behind her competitors. The principal industrial producers, Britain and above all imperial Germany, had opened a gap in total industrial output in the latter part of the nineteenth century. Even Russia, so long regarded as a backward economy, had come to exceed French output of major industrial commodities such as steel. This apparent retardation of France – which a century before had been probably the richest and briefly the most powerful state in Europe – exercised considerable political concern and no small subsequent academic interest.

Although statistical certainty is always dubious it is undoubtedly true that, in aggregate, French industrial production was eclipsed by the rapid growth elsewhere. In *per capita* terms the picture remained more positive. And herein lies one explanation, for the population of France grew very slowly in the half century before 1913, and stagnated in the inter-war years. This had limiting effects on overall growth both in terms of the elasticity of labour supply and growth of aggregate domestic demand. A number of other factors have been adduced to explain the phenomenon, many of which continued to influence the features of the French economy in the inter-war years.

As well as the major natural resource of population were other major resources: coal, which was abundant and cheap in Britain and Germany, was scarce in France. In particular coal suitable for coking was expensive (unusually, France continued to use charcoal burning for iron smelting well into the nineteenth century). Thus, France produced 40 million tons of coal from her own mines in 1913 but consumed 61 million tons. On the other hand, France had abundant iron ore and had been a pioneer in the development of hydroelectric power; natural resources cannot explain economic performance completely. Cultural factors, particularly associated with the legal and property relation stemming from the Napoleonic code, were also of great influence. The Third Republic was the bourgeois society *par excellence* and the characteristics of bourgeois France were more conservative than adventurous. There was a strong desire to avoid risk and play safe. In particular this was evident in the countryside, where the small scale family unit predominated. The social structure of French agriculture and its weakness in the face of world competition in the last quarter of the nineteenth century are generally seen as having a retarding effect on the economy as a whole. But small scale and family ownership were by no means confined to farming, and this continued to apply through the years before the Second World War.

The story was by no means altogether negative before the Great War, but the economic cost of war was particularly great for France. The seeds of later advance in 'new industries' were sown before the conflict of 1914. France had by far the largest automobile industry in Europe, Renault having become the major manufacturer in the continent by 1907–12. Automobiles made up 3 per cent of total French exports in 1912 (excluding motorcycles).

Similarly France had become a leading producer of aluminium, based on cheap HEP, and even aeroplane engines. Such industries were to be growth areas in international demand in later years. The bulk of industrial exports, however, were in those sectors for which demand was growing slowly or stagnating, especially textiles (silk was the largest single export).

Wartime fighting and the occupation resulted in great economic losses for France because much of the fighting took place in the industrial regions of the country. Large areas of the cotton textile industry, much engineering and many coal mines were in regions occupied by invading forces. The steel industry was perhaps the most seriously affected, with 95 from a total of 123 blast furnaces under occupation. Agriculture in the occupied areas was also damaged with some systematic destruction by occupying forces and confiscation of livestock. But the negative effects did not end there. First were the population losses of 1.3 million dead or missing from an active male population of 13.1 million. Second were the financial losses of overseas assets (liquidated to finance the war or written off in Russia) and the problem of repaying internal and external loans after the war.

Thus the French economy came out of the war in 1918 having endured major losses, though with some real and potential gains. Many years ago the economist Alfred Sauvy estimated the economic costs of the war to be equivalent to 1.25 times the national income for 1913. And this would not take account of the human and psychological effects for, apart from those killed, there were some 388 800 injured. Few families escaped direct or indirect losses from the war. In such an environment hostility to Germany, which coloured the post-war settlement, is understandable. Accounting for the losses remains problematical. As government compensated those who lost their property, there was a natural tendency for costs to be exaggerated. Keynes, a participant in the peace negotiations at Versailles, criticised French claims as being over-estimated. The gains to France were real and large. There was some confiscated German property (as in chemical works or merchant shipping included under reparation payments) but above all the territorial gain of Alsace-Lorraine. This was one of the major industrial regions of Europe and provided France with an additional steel industry (though little metallurgical processing of steel). There were also coal mines (though it did not produce coal suitable for coking), iron ore and potash deposits and a number of textile factories. Most of these assets were handed over to private companies, though potash deposits and the railways remained in government hands. In addition to Alsace-Lorraine France gained access to the coal from the Saar, though the territory was never ceded to France.

In the post-war treaty with Germany, and its implementation, France was the most intractible of the Western allies. The actions of the government have often been judged by historians, especially those of American or British origin, as unreasonable and vindictive towards the defeated power. As has been mentioned, this was even suggested by the contemporary observer J.M. Keynes. More recently historiographical opinion on this point has mellowed.

The major economic problem facing French governments after the end of hostilities was that of inflation. While this was never as severe as in Germany or central Europe it was more extreme than in Britain. As elsewhere, French inflation began in the war with printing money to meet expenses. When the USA entered the war in 1917 she agreed to help support the exchange value of the franc. However, with the ending of hostilities, inflationary pressures persisted but without the external support from Britain and the USA for the franc. Reconstruction of war-torn industries was generously financed by government compensation and grants but in the absence of sufficient revenue, and a political culture hostile to direct taxation, this generosity was in itself bound to be inflationary. Further, it demanded that government expenditures be made good from elsewhere – hence the continued stress on the need for reparation from Germany (see also Chap. 1).

Governments were also faced with debts to the USA and Britain, which increased the French demands on Germany. In the long run neither reparations nor allied debts were paid in full (see Chap. 2) but in the early 1920s they greatly influenced the political options of European governments.

Continued domestic inflation in France after the war led to falling confidence at home and abroad with the result of a 'flight of capital'. When Britain and the USA ceased supporting the franc in 1919 there was a virtual collapse of the exchange rate. France, like Britain and other European powers, had hoped to return to a gold standard at the pre-war rate of the *Franc Germinal* at 25 to £1 sterling. This was an elusive goal. The (paper) franc fell to nearly half pre-war parity in December 1919, a third by 1920. By 1924 the exchange value had reached crisis levels of 122 francs to £1. Neither currency was yet convertible for gold; in dollar terms the effective devaluation of the franc was even greater. At the time the French press blamed this on a British–American plot in retaliation at the French invasion of the Ruhr but it was more likely a result of declining confidence at home. Lack of domestic confidence among banks and the bourgeoisie was more pronounced subsequently when a left-wing government of the *Cartel des Gauches* was temporarily in power. Further printing of money, without foreign currency reserves (the fiduciary issue) induced renewed inflation and depreciation. Although a cheap currency had real economic advantages, as we shall see below, there were social and political problems. Such was the hostility to some foreign tourists who gained from this that one US group was attacked in the streets of Paris. A low point of 243 = £1 was reached in July 1926, but confidence returned with the return of Poincaré to office and he was able to oversee a stable rate of exchange of 124 to £1, or 20 per cent of pre-war value. It was at this rate that gold convertibility was established in 1928.

This new rate was probably a modest undervaluation of the true market rate in 1926 – in contrast to the effective overvaluation of the pound sterling in the previous year. This has led to some suggestions that the Bank of France might have been contriving a low exchange rate to give French exports a competitive advantage. This is uncertain as depreciation was initially greeted with alarm. However, there was some concern at the rate of appreciation of the franc after Poincaré resumed office in 1926, which suggests that the French went for stabilisation at a deliberately low rate. In so doing France avoided the need for deflation, which was happening in Britain, or the excessive inflation and problems of Germany. In effect the franc was strengthened by being allowed to reach a low level. The stable franc attracted foreign currency which the Bank of France was able to convert to gold. France in later years accumulated larger gold holdings than any other west European nation. The experience of inflation and exchange depreciation, however, induced in the cautious bourgeoisie of France, especially those creditors who had seen savings washed away, uncertainty and mistrust of government. In the Depression of the 1930s, government financial remedies were limited by this experience, as devaluation was ruled out as a viable option.

Despite the financial instability and the problems of post-war recovery the 1920s were, on balance, a decade of relative boom for the French economy, especially in the industrial and service sectors.

Growth was particularly marked in new industries and in exports. For the latter, exchange depreciation was a positive factor. This was especially so for tourism, for in this sector the exchange value of the currency had a direct and positive effect. For viable exports a depreciating currency can give the exporter a price advantage, but by the same token import costs rise, thus affecting raw material and component costs. These are less significant for tourism.

France had certainly been a tourist playground in the '*belle époque*' of the 1890s and later years, but it was a playground for the rich. The nightlife and culture of Paris, the casinos of Deauville and Biarritz attracted the princely from all over the continent. In the 1920s the market expanded (though modest by today's levels). This was the golden age of the Riviera. The well-to-do of Europe were added to by many Americans crossing the Atlantic to enjoy the fruits of France and the cheap franc. Cultural changes which made sunbathing and exposure to the sun more acceptable enhanced the process. Tourism and receipts therefrom came to provide up to 25 per cent of export earnings. It was indeed a major industry.

Visible exports were also enhanced by a cheap currency but the stimuli were more broadly based, with the marked expansion of new products. The foreign trade position was markedly affected by the loss of many foreign assets in the First World War. Like Britain, France had been something of a *rentier* economy before 1914 with invisible earnings substantially from foreign investments covering a deficit on visible trade. In the 1920s traditional or staple exports continued to provide the major income, among them textiles, clothing and luxury items. Even within the textile sector there was more emphasis on the high-cost producers like silk, in contrast to Britain mass-produced cottons. In the 1920s iron and steel became a major French export, a development assisted by the acquisition of Alsace-Lorraine. In general French exports grew at a rate faster than total product. World demand for industrial products from France grew quickly in the 1920s, especially in high-income markets like the USA or western Europe. Staple French exports were associated with high quality, such as gloves, luxury clothing, perfumes and cosmetics as well as 'luxury' food products, for which there was a relatively high income elasticity. These traditional sectors were to suffer particularly with the collapse of world trade in the Depression. 'New industries' (such as automobiles, chemicals, alloys) also boomed relatively in export demand in the 1920s but continued to make up only a small part of total values. On the other hand, they were less seriously affected in recession.

It is difficult to judge how important a part was played by the exchange rate. Clearly a cheap franc gave French exports a competitive edge, especially in industrial products, such as iron and steel, where there were many direct competitors. That exchange depreciation was important can be further supported by the fact that exports began to decline with stabilisation after 1926, though France was able to maintain an active trade balance until 1930. On the other hand, the industrial boom of the 1920s cannot be attributed entirely to the cheap franc. Productivity gains were real; industrial production grew more quickly than elsewhere in western Europe and Malinvaud estimates that GDP grew by 4.4 per cent per annum 1922–29. These positive trends were the result of innovations and efficiencies, and the exploitation of new developments made before 1914. This was especially evident in new industries.

6.1 New industries

New industries grew most rapidly in France in the 1920s and were a major factor in her industrial success, though not yet sufficient to produce fundamental restructuring in the economy (see also Chap. 5). These industries were associated with new or recent products, incorporating innovations of the late nineteenth and early twentieth centuries. Also they were associated with new methods of production or marketing. Shortcomings in entrepreneurship or business organisation have often been put forward as a factor in industrial retardation in France before 1914; this was far from the case with the new sectors of the 1920s.

The best known example is the motor industry. In the 1920s this was dominated by three major companies: Renault, founded in Paris in 1898, Peugeot, originally a tool maker and bicycle manufacturer, and Citroën. Citroën bought a small manufacturer, Mors, after the First World War, having made a fortune as an armaments maker during the war. Citroën above all was a great entrepreneur and innovator (he was later to introduce the first front wheel drive model in 1934) and set out to extend the market by reducing prices and eliminating the luxury image of the motor car. In 1919 he launched such a model, using the Model T Ford as an example and Ford production methods. Renault, too, learned from

Ford, having visited the US plant in 1912. The motor industry was in the forefront in introducing 'scientific management' and mass production techniques. The French all but dominated European motor makers in the 1920s (see Chap. 5). Some of the techniques of production had been developed in the war – Citroën, for example, produced ammunition on an assembly line and substitutes had to be developed for German patent magnetos.

For military suppliers also war orders brought great fortunes and sources for investment in the 1920s. Renault produced tanks for allied armies and aeroplane engines. Before 1914 the French were already leaders in the infant aircraft industry. In 1913 French companies produced 2240 aircraft engines and 1148 airframes, nearly half of which were exports to the UK. War demands boosted the industry. Although there was some technical connection with automobiles, particularly with engine construction, few of the same companies were involved. There were further linkages with rubber for tyre manufacture and more particularly oil and petroleum refining. Aluminium was another 'new' industry which was to have an important part in aircraft manufacture. France had become the major producer before 1914, based on bauxite deposits and above all cheap HEP. In this way a substitute for scarce coal before 1914 was to provide major dividends in later years.

Before 1914 Germany had dominated the production of chemicals, pharmaceuticals and dyestuffs. In the 1920s rival producers grew up in France and elsewhere, taking advantage of new markets and the ability to use German patents without payment. The chemical industry was one of the fastest growing, from low beginnings, in France but one where France was much less dominant than in automobiles. Relative 'giants' were formed – Kuhlmann and, in 1929, Rhone Poulenc, comparable to IG Farben in Germany or ICI in Britain.

New industries were associated with various aspects of rationalisation and scientific management, though these processes were by no means confined to strictly 'new' sectors. The coal mines of the north were some of the most 'rationalised', using the generous post-war government compensation schemes to mechanise production. Growth was especially marked in steel production, though this was greatly helped by the acquisition of Alsace-Lorraine. Output grew from 4.6 million tons in 1913 to 9.7 million in 1929. Rationalisation in the sense of amalgamation of productive plants was most marked in chemicals and also in electrical power generation. In the motor industry the dominance of three large companies did not result from amalgamation but the elimination of rivals through competition.

Overall the 1920s was a decade of industrial growth, modernisation and innovation not only in new industries and products but in service sectors, banking and retailing. 'Rationalisation' and innovations in production resulted in general improvements in productivity. They were, however, unevenly applied and some structural problems remained.

An index of industrial production moved from a base of 100 in 1913 to 57 in 1919, 55 in 1921 but had grown to 127 by 1928. This growth was weighted up very much by the capital goods sector and building. Consumer goods, with some notable exceptions like motor cars, which were in any event hardly yet a commodity of mass consumption, grew more slowly. In part this may have been because of the persistence of the small scale, sometimes family, production unit. Relatively small scale production tended to characterise the consumer goods sector, partly because of the limits in the size of the home market. However, the same was also true of the Lyons silk manufacturers – a highly export-oriented industry. It has long been asserted that the dominance of the small scale producer induced a conservatism in attitude which inhibited innovation and enterprise and therefore restrained growth.

In 1931, of 1.6 million registered industrial establishments, 64 per cent had no paid employees at all, depending entirely on family labour, and 34 per cent had fewer than 10 workers. At the other end of the scale a quarter of all industrial workers worked in enterprises employing more than 500. Such large scale works were thus atypical for industrial enterprises. There was something of a dual structure in manufacturing and the labour market.

6.2   Agriculture

Agriculture remained easily the largest industry in France. Its position was changing in the later nineteenth century as industrial and commercial developments become more prominent, but even in 1911 a large part of the population still depended upon the land. Forty-two per cent, or 8.5 millions, of the active population was 'agricultural' on the eve of the war. By 1936 the proportion had fallen to 36 per cent, or 7.14 millions. Rural emigration had begun well before 1890 and was only partly compensated by an influx of foreign workers, chiefly from Italy, Spain and Belgium, who gravitated towards agrarian occupations. The exodus from the countryside increased through time. One estimate is that the rate of loss was twice as great in 1920–40 as in 1892–1912. This outflow caused anxiety at all levels of French society, not simply because it seemed to foreshadow a derelict countryside but also because peasants represented the masonry in the French military edifice. Countrymen, as they knew full well, were the infantry of France; they had contributed most in bloodshed in the Franco–Prussian War and again bore the brunt of the national military effort in 1914–18. The losses of manpower through death or disablement in the Great War reduced the agrarian population by 750 000 or more, so that the chronic complaint of manpower shortage was transformed in 1917–22 into acute crisis. To aggravate the position, thousands of peasants, dispossessed by hostilities or merely seeking the opportunity of improvement, moved into towns and munition factories. The isolation, backwardness and social tedium of village life were still active deterrents for ambitious peasants in the 1920s and eventually prompted governments to propose the modernisation of the countryside by means of electrification and improved local transport. But apart from a brief interlude in the mid-1930s when unemployed industrial workers returned to their roots, the trend of depopulation continued until 1940 and had resumed by 1950.

Since French agriculture had been traditionally bedevilled by low productivity, low yields and poor labour efficiency, the haemorrhage of manpower could have resulted in persistent problems for aggregate production. In fact, although there were several significant changes in the pattern of agricultural output after 1870, aggregate production was maintained or perhaps improved through time. Thus the volume of output was about the same in the 1920s as in the 1870s, with one-fifth less manpower. The 1920s does represent a significant decline by comparison with the decade before the war but, as in the 1870s, production improved as the decade progressed. According to L.A. Vincent the index of agricultural production in 1925–29 was 96 (1909–13 = 100) and in 1935–39 it was 106. If productivity is expressed in terms of labour efficiency, the improvement between 1913 and 1938 was at least 25 per cent.

The landscape of France changed perceptibly after 1870. First the total cultivated areas contracted as much sub-marginal land was converted to woodland or tumbled down into rough grazing. Between 1908–14 and 1934–38, according to J.C. Toutain, the area of France left uncultivated increased from 6.6 million ha. to 9.7 million ha. and the area in woodland increased from 9.9 million ha. to 10.8 million ha. Grassland expanded by 1.6 million ha. while arable fell by about 3 million ha. The principal loss occurred in the area devoted to cereals and especially to wheat and rye, which together had accounted for 7.8 million ha. in 1905–14 but only for 5.6 million ha. in 1934–38. Since the land under vines, potatoes or sugar-beet fell only slightly or remained constant, the chief gainer by the loss of the area under corn was temporary grass and other forage crops. In other words there was a notable shift towards pastoral farming. The livestock statistics do not wholly support this suggestion, chiefly because there was a great fall in the number of sheep (Table 6.1).

Table 6.1 French agricultural production

Output of major crops (5-year average)

	wheat		potatoes		s/beet		wine	
	m.ha.	m.kg	m.ha.	m.ks	m.ha.	m.ks	m.ha.	m.hl.
1909–13	6.35	8.65	1.55	13.32	0.3	7.85	1.6	6.4
1919–23	5.2	6.9	1.4	10.05	0.16	3.1	1.52	59.7
1929–33	5.3	8.3	1.4	18.54	0.3	8.7	1.53	54.1
1935–39	5.0	7.77	1.36	15.4	0.31	9.0	1.52	60.7

Yield (quintals per ha.)

	wheat	potatoes	s/beet	wine
1909–13	13.2	85.6	260.8	29 hect.ha.
1935–39	15.55	113.2	290.0	40 hect.ha.

Livestock numbers (millions)

	horses	cattle	swine	sheep	goats
1910	2.9	14.52	6.79	20.19	1.56
1920	2.2	14.53	8.9	17.11	1.42
1930	2.64	13.22	4.94	9.41	1.34
1934	2.84	15.71	7.04	9.57	1.41
1939	2.12	14.19	6.38	8.95	1.28

Livestock output (metric tonnes)

	milk	butter	meat
1923	12.07	–	–
1929	14.28	0.22	1.31
1935	14.69	–	1.69
1939	14.18	0.196	1.65

Table 6.2 Self-sufficiency in French agriculture

	1865–74	1905–14	1925–34	1935–38
Cereals	98.1	90.3	87.9	93.3
Potatoes	101.2	100.5	99.4	99.5
Wine	104.8	91.4	83.1	82.3
Meat	99.5	100.2	95.9	98.6
Dairy produce	107.5	101.1	98.4	101.2
Wool	24.9	8.2	8.3	–
Oil plants	30.1	15.8	7.6	4.5
Flax, hemp	65.0	24.0	30.7	57.3

Figures are percentages of production

Yields, however, increased significantly. All arable crops produced greater output per hectare in the 1930s than in the 1900s. In some cases the increment was considerable. Thus wine production rose from 29 hectolitres per hectare in 1905–13 to 40 hl. per ha. in 1935–39. The yield of potatoes increased by one-third and sugar-beet by 15 per cent. There were less impressive returns, however: grain yields rose by 5–10 per cent, although there had been an improvement of about 15 per cent between the 1870s and 1950s, and milk yields, carcase weight and fleece size showed only modest increments, probably under 5 per cent in total.

Agricultural change did bring about improvement in some degree. It is interesting to note that, despite the Méline tariff, the relative self-sufficiency of agricultural production actually diminished. The war was devastating. The loss of production in the war-affected departments was grave, not less because of the traditional efficiency of the Nord and Artois, but the decline in 1915–21 was not confined to the war zone. French agricultural production in 1919 at 52 (1909–13 = 100) was not only much below pre-war levels, it was insufficient to feed the population even on the reduced dietary standard made acceptable by the war. Effective self-sufficiency, on the assumption that the volume of demand was constant, fell from 100 in 1865–74 to 94 in 1905–14, fell to about 60 at the nadir in 1919 and then rose to about 90 in the late 1920s and slightly more in the late 1930s. Yet on the eve of the Second World War metropolitan France was less self-sufficient, if only by a little, than she had been in 1914 (Table 6.2). The population had grown slowly; agriculture was more productive; demand therefore must have been rising throughout the period despite the effect of depression on industrial living standards.

Peasants were renowned among the French for their propensity to save. They provided a fund of savings on which the economy often depended. That was only true if the savings were put to use, if peasants could be persuaded to deposit in banks, not to spend their reserves of money. The Crédit Agricole Mutuel increased the countryman's willingness to participate in banking, but it also encouraged him to borrow on his own account.

By the later 1920s the credit bank had advanced at least three times as much to the clients as it held on deposit, although an attempt was made to keep deposits and short-term loans more or less equivalent. The Crédit Agricole was charged to furnish loans for modernisation and development, so that the expansion in business only partly reflects the process of agricultural improvement. However, much was still dedicated to consumption or unproductive investment. Total deposits in 1926 amounted to 269 million francs; total loans in the same year equalled 906 million francs. The equivalent data for 1938 were 1.639 billion francs and 6.292 billion francs. Long-term loans increased from 476 million francs to 1.892 billion francs. A considerable proportion of these loans was laid out in the purchase of landed property, not on marketing or new buildings. The pattern of investment in the 1930s, however, suggests that the flow of funds, traditionally from agriculture to industrialisation, despite the continuing sectoral decline of the former, may have been reversed.

6.3   Population and labour

France was unusual in experiencing no real unemployment before the onset of depression, and very little even then. This was largely a demographic effect, though also in small part a result of structural factors in agriculture and industry which inhibited labour mobility. The relative weight of the small scale family enterprise restricted labour mobility. Overwhelmingly, however, demographic factors were significant.

French population had grown slowly in the nineteenth century and stagnated after the Great War. Although the territorial expansion after 1918 made for a modest absolute increase, the haemorrhage of the war on young men reduced the birth rate thereafter. Thus the population tended to get older. The reasons for a falling birth rate in France have been much debated in historical and contemporary literature. Significantly the science of demography was a French invention. In the interwar years it is evident that influences from the nineteenth century continued to affect the birth rate. A tendency towards family limitation has been attributed to a number of factors: the decline of clerical influence, the perceived need to preserve property, especially farm property, in single units in the face of strict multiple inheritance of the Napoleonic code, a socially 'responsible' behaviour under the influence of Malthus, or physical limitation as a result of TB or alcoholism. All may have had some influence. The latter point about health apart, it is noteworthy that

Table 6.3 French population

	Total	Male	Female	Working population
1891	38.1	18.9	19.2	–
1911*	39.2	19.3	19.9	–
1921	38.8	18.4	20.4	20.1
1931	41.2	19.9	21.3	20.5
1936	41.2	19.8	21.4	19.3

Figures are census figures (millions)

* Pre-war figures exclude Alsace–Lorraine

From B.R. Mitchell (1975) *European Historical Statistics* (Cambridge: Cambridge University Press), p. 30
F. Caron (1979) *An Economic History of Modern France* (London: Methuen), p. 190

a declining birth rate resulted from some form of voluntary family limitation, be it through contraception, infanticide or abortion. Infant mortality was very high in the nineteenth century, far more so than in other industrial countries of Europe, and a decline in the number was a major factor in the modest population growth before the Great War.

There is but a tenuous link between the practice of multiple inheritance and family limitation among peasants. Clearly it was an influence, but family limitation affected all classes and appears to have been a practice first adopted by the bourgeoisie. With a falling birth rate, population growth was maintained in France only by a declining mortality rate and some immigration (Table 6.3).

Both these factors continued in the inter-war years but the demographic impact of the First World War was particularly serious for France and was to have lasting effects for the 20 years which followed. The birth rate showed a small post-war increase, 1919–20, and fell back again thereafter. The political response was double-edged. On the one hand there was a gradual if piecemeal extension of family allowances; on the other, severe restriction of abortion, which remained one of the most reliable forms of birth control. Family allowances had first been introduced by some enlightened, paternalist employers (including Citroën) before 1914. In the 1920s they were extended to some public employees and then in the 1930s further, especially because of growing anxiety at the might of Nazi Germany. Thus the allowances were extended to wage earners in 1932, small farmers in 1938 and were universal by 1939. The latter measures, known collectively as the '*code de la famille*', might have contributed to the small rise in the birth rate from 1938. Alternatively or additionally, it was at this time that the post-war baby generation entered the age of fecundity.

Table 6.4 Age distribution of population

	1911	1936
Under 20	33.5	30
Between 20 and 64	58	60
65 and over	8.5	10

Figures are percentages, showing current boundaries

From J-C. Asselain (1984) *Histoire économique de la France du XVIIIe siècle à nos jours, 2 de 1919 à la fin de l'anneé 1970* (Paris: Seuil), p. 85

Procreation was openly encouraged through various propaganda in the mass media. In the 1930s when the 'problems' became more politically urgent, film was a favoured medium. The other side of the coin brought severe restrictions on the availability of contraception from as early as 1920. At the same time abortion, which had been easily available in Paris before 1914, was outlawed for all but extreme medical cases. It is worthwhile remembering that such political concern was by no means confined to France, though the decline in the birth rate was more serious there. As elsewhere, however, policies and propaganda appeared to have little effect (Table 6.4).

Labour shortages were met with immigration. About two million migrants entered the country legally in the 1920s, principally from Italy (30 per cent), Poland (20 per cent), Belgium (18 per cent) and Spain (15 per cent). These workers usually entered low paid menial or manual work or areas of special shortage. The major single occupation was in farm work, though many Poles specialised as coalminers. This movement helped ensure that labour shortages did not become a major economic obstacle in the 1920s. Slow population growth and mobility, and the large proportion employed in low income bearing farming, restricted the growth of the domestic market. This had a more lasting limiting effect than labour shortages.

6.4 Recession

The international recession affected France a little later than elsewhere. For a time some contemporaries in France thought that she might escape, for there was no perceptible effect before the end of 1930. But the French economy did not prove to be immune from the trade cycle. Indeed it showed no real signs of recovery before the coming of war.

France 'imported' recession as world demand began to collapse from the end of 1929. As an exporting economy France was particularly seriously affected and her export-led boom came to an end. This was especially evident in those areas where exports had been of relatively 'luxury' products with high income elasticity. The market effect was compounded by the suspension of reparation payments in 1931 and their abandonment the following year – for France had been a major recipient of these payments. At the same time outstanding inter-allied debts, where France was a debtor, were written off. More seriously, devaluation of the pound sterling, followed by many other European currencies, and the US dollar in 1933, left the franc relatively over-valued and French goods over-priced. The competitive edge that France had enjoyed in the 1920s disappeared.

Receipts from tourism fell by 90 per cent between 1930 and 1933, textile exports, which had been a staple, declined by 80 per cent between 1929 and 1932, and motor vehicle exports by two-thirds. France had become one of the major iron and steel producers in the 1920s. Now her exports fell by half in 1929–32 and steel production began to decline from 1930. Having enjoyed a balance of trade surplus through the 1920s, France moved into a position of deficit in 1931, which was to persist through the decade.

Total export earnings fell by 29 per cent in 1931, a further 35 per cent in 1932 and by 60 per cent in volume between 1929 and 1935. The decline in sales and profits affected all branches of the economy, bankruptcies mounted and overall investment fell. France entered a period of economic malaise and stagnation reinforced by restrictive government policies and conservative attitudes and practice in business. Unlike other industrial economies in Europe, France appeared to lack an autonomous or politically inspired stimulus to recovery. On the other hand, unlike many of her neighbours, France escaped some immediate effects of recession. Unemployment was never on the scale of Britain or Germany. Figures for those recorded as unemployed, i.e. in receipt of unemployment benefit, jumped from negligible levels in 1929 to 260 000 in 1932 and 426 000 in 1935 – the highest average monthly figures recorded. Although these figures were probably an underestimate (by two-thirds according to Sauvy) they were still low by international comparison.

The reasons for this are easy to determine. As has been shown, there were labour shortages in the 1920s; many of the immigrant workers of that time were sent home in the thirties and new immigration curtailed. (It is well known that illegal immigration continued, particularly for menial agricultural work. By definition this would not figure in labour statistics.) The declining absolute numbers of French workers mitigated upward pressure on unemployment statistics. Further, the agricultural sector, although hard hit by the vicissitudes of the trade cycle, was able to absorb some first generation workers who simply returned to the family farm when they lost a job. Similarly family enterprises in non-agricultural spheres were hardly likely to lay off members of their own family to swell the ranks of the unemployed. Politically, however, unemployment was taken seriously as a real problem in later years; it was serious enough for those who were unemployed. It is significant also that the figures reached a peak when other European states were well on the way to recovery.

France also escaped, or rather was able to postpone, the financial crises that affected most of Europe in 1931. The collapse of confidence led to major bank failure in Austria and Germany, with consequent exchange controls, and the forced devaluation of sterling, in turn followed by a number of minor currencies. France resisted this shock to remain at the heart of the gold bloc (see Chap. 2). The Bank of France had such huge gold reserves that she was able to continue to maintain the gold exchange value of the franc when other currencies could not. In so doing, and in continuing to place the value of the currency above the operation of the real economy after the Depression deepened, French governments contributed to and exacerbated the Depression.

6.5   Government policies (to 1935)

There is little doubt that governments contributed to the contraction in economic activity from 1930. This was little different from most of the rest of Europe, but the policies continued far longer. It was not until the Popular Front government of 1936 that a real attempt at a deliberately expansionary policy was undertaken, and then with questionable success.

Until this time there was little by way of policy save one of protection and a balanced budget. It was taken for granted also that the exchange value of the franc should be maintained. Indecisive action was a result both of uncertainty (all governments after all were working in the dark) and of weakness. Between 1932 and 1935, 11 different administrations were formed, though often with some of the same personnel. All these governments sought to maintain domestic prices as much as possible in a deflationary world. Tariffs were levied on most imports with agriculture being the most highly protected sector. Grain duties were raised in 1929 and 1930; animal and dairy products in 1930 and 1933; subsidies were granted to reduce the area of vine and dispose of surplus wine stocks. Wheat prices, in 1933, and production levels, in 1934, were regulated.

Such measures increased state budget expenditures when receipts were tending to fall, thus making the balanced budget more elusive. But all governments were beholden to their electorates and interest groups within the economy. It is not surprising therefore that agricultural protection in various forms should have been so important as the 'farm lobby' made up such an influential constituency. The small business interest appeared to be similarly influential. A number of chain store groups – Uniprix, Monoprix, Prisunic – had begun to grow in the late 1920s, an area of commercial innovation in the country which had spawned the first supermarkets. Yet these larger shops were deliberately restricted by governments, further branches being prohibited in an effort to protect the small shopkeeper. Such measures were designed to limit new entrants to trade and industry and were not confined to retail outlets. The policy was known as economic 'Malthusiansim', i.e. to restrict production, but with the unintended effect of aggravating and extending the stagnation in the economy.

Import quotas as well as tariffs restricted foreign trade so that a diminishing proportion of imports was bought on any sort of 'free' market. Tariffs were used selectively also to 'manage' trade – a 15 per cent surcharge on UK imports for instance – and there was a substantial shift towards colonial trade (see Chap. 3). Such measures were common to governments of different political leanings, left wing from 1932–34 or right wing from 1934–36. They had a generally restrictive and deflationary effect, which was taken even further by the government of Pierre Laval in 1935. This introduced a strict deflationary policy. Public expenditures were reduced by 10 per cent, rent and price reductions were enforced, civil service salaries reduced. But these policies failed to have the desired effect. Business confidence was not improved and France became increasingly exposed, especially following the Belgian devaluation and abandonment of gold in 1935.

Average consumption was less severely affected. Disposable money incomes fell by about 33 per cent but in real terms this was only 13 per cent. The most extreme fall was for the agricultural sector – 32 per cent – for the extensive government measures had failed to counteract falling world prices completely. The other group to suffer a major fall in income was the unemployed. Wage earners, pensioners and landlords were generally able to maintain incomes in real terms because of the fall in prices. Profits moved variously. Some major companies, like Bugatti the car maker, disappeared, or went bankrupt like Citroën which was taken over by Michelin. On the other hand companies such as Schneider, Menier and Michelin prospered.

It is the perception of economic experience as much as the reality which is influential on behaviour, and people felt themselves to be worse off and threatened. The agricultural lobby continued to be a powerful and sometimes violent influence. Some business leaders and senior government officials became increasingly anxious over threats to social and economic stability and, of course, their own fortunes. Various disaffected groups began to express political views outside the parliamentary process and a number of fascist groups emerged, with crude and overt anti-semitic leanings. Political extremism is nothing unusual at a time of economic crisis and in France there seemed to be no escape from the crisis in the mid-1930s while other states were recovering. In Nazi Germany and Soviet Russia this appeared to be spectacularly successful. The industrial working class in France had been isolated from the political process since abortive revolutionary movements in 1870 (and possibly 1848) and in the 1930s sought political support from parties of the left – Socialists and Communists.

It was in an environment, therefore, of economic malaise, increasing social conflict and political instability (with growing fascist or quasi-fascist support elsewhere in Europe) that the Popular Front of left wing parties was formed. This body was founded in 1934 specifically to fight the election of 1936. It was not a comfortable coalition, unlike the *Cartel des Gauches* in 1924; there were many differences within the Front. The major elements were Socialists, led by Leon Blum, Communists and Radical Socialists, which was a much more bourgeois party than its name implies. The economic programme was radically different from others in that it advocated expansion. The intention was to reverse the policy of deflation, improve incomes and let consumption induce recovery by increasing sales and thereby inducing renewed production. It was in no sense Keynesian – the term was not appropriate at this time – rather the model was the New Deal of the USA. The programme was agreed only in January 1936 for the election in May. Blum became Prime Minister, with Daladier, the Radical leader, as his deputy. The communists refused to join government though their MPs supported the programme.

Agriculture exemplifies well the social attitudes of the French towards economic performance. A principal objective of public policy was the achievement and maintenance of social equipoise. The Méline tariff, for example, was described as an economic regulator as much as a device to protect a vociferous body of producers. The purpose of the policy was both to support and to stabilise prices to encourage autarky and, by the same token, to create conditions of mutual interdependence. Its success was ambiguous, but since Méline was the most active proponent of 'solidarism', which took the habit of social reciprocity into the legislative field, the protection of agriculture was part of an initiative towards rural regeneration. The nineteenth century legacy of rural France was an uneasy amalgam of peasant individualism (viz. suspicion of authority) and communal action. Thus the oft-stated belief that most agricultural transactions were free and unregulated in 1913 was scorned by the Liberals, like the agronomist Michel Augé-Laribé, who argued that the forces of inertia, of complacency, were reinforced by protectionism and the traditional mentality of the bourgeoisie no less than of peasants whereas the impulse to modernise and induce progress foundered on the suspicion of disintegrative capitalism. Change occurred through the effect of rural emigration, by crop selection and converting arable to pasturage or woodland, through tentative mechanisation (and the repartition of farm layouts that it encouraged), but it was piecemeal and geographically restricted, so that the benefits accrued to already relatively advanced districts. The productivity of French agriculture improved between 1870 and 1913, perhaps by one-fifth, but this was a function of the human exodus and the abandonment of marginal arable land. Oddly perhaps, France was less self-sufficient on the eve of the Great War than she had been when the Franco-Prussian conflict broke out. Augé-Laribé repeated the point that by comparison with most of her neighbours, French agriculture was still low in productivity in 1912 in the yields of cereals, milk and carcase meat.

It was a political necessity to protect agriculture, to make peasant electors feel satisfied, however incoherent the policies devised might be, but it was no less incumbent on government not to exalt the role of the state in rural affairs, for peasants were captious and easily offended. So a plethora of communal or quasi-public associations, *comices, syndicats agricoles* and credit unions were set up to energise the countryside. The problem was that these initiatives did not stem the tide; tariff policy produced equivocal results and communal association often reinforced local mediocrity rather than best practice. It is interesting to note that the internal adjustments to French agriculture mirrored changes active in unprotected economies, in Britain and the Netherlands, where a preference for livestock over tillage was impelled by the same structural pressures. The problem peculiar to France before the war was the tendency for peasants to lay out savings and to use a considerable portion of the available agricultural credit on the purchase of land. An active peasant land market alongside one operated in the bourgeois interest seldom formed the conditions that led to *agricultural* improvement, for rustic property, like the ability to live in active retirement off *rentes*, conveyed a social cachet that had little to do with enterprise.

The Great War decimated French agricultural production; good land was destroyed; agrarian communities were desolated. Furthermore, livestock was lost, production was hindered by poor seed, lack of fertiliser and a shortage of labour at seasonal peaks. Governments reacted slowly to the agricultural crisis, but even when extensive regulations were imposed under Clemenceau, the administration was inconsistent. Several measures, especially those dealing with the distribution and export of grain, wine and certain dairy produce, were unpopular with producers, however much the government's hand had been forced. The lessons of wartime intervention were not consoling; the appearance of interference was greater perhaps than the reality, but it was the shadow which disconcerted country people, for government action seemed to produce few benefits that would not have accrued from the play of market forces. The rise in prices was sufficient to enrich peasants who had surpluses to sell, but the good effects of high profits were too short-lived to promote greater efforts at food production given the constraints of labour shortage. When the war was over, politicians observed these peasants hoarding gold or investing in more land – a prudent move considering the gyrations of the currency in the 1920s and 1930s, and especially so because their affluence was brief.

   Governments before Tardieu were aware of problems in agriculture but did little effective about them. Tariff policy was amended in 1928, rural electrification and road building were promoted and the long-standing commitment of the state to improve education and the flow of credit was still pursued with at least rhetorical enthusiasm. Ministers of agriculture tended to be more constant than prime ministers, but most were like Henri Queuille, reluctant to go beyond Méline solidarism. Queuille bespoke agriculture, but as a figurehead, addressing conventions, opening exhibitions, exhorting improvement. After all, the tendencies of the industry after 1921 replicated the decline and adjustment of the pre-war period; the evidence for a radical restatement of policy was not compelling. *Dirigisme*, as often with the Radicals, was a nostrum against big business, a threat to the *Grands Moulins* and the beet sugar-refiners, not a protocol for state intervention. Indeed, fear of big business mediated through peasant suspicion usually resulted in proposals to extend co-operation rather than nationalisation. The socialists had ideas, incoherent, contradictory and still repugnant to peasants, which they could not even try since they were seldom partners in government. André Tardieu began the process of integrating policies for agriculture in the machinery of government activity. His plans were essentially political; they turned upon his desire to give the right wing in France an opportunity of consolidating the peasant vote. They were of course also motivated by economic necessity in the deteriorating circumstances of the late 1920s, but Tardieu had no sure grasp of economic cause and effect. His plans incorporated a kind of stabilisation agency, specifically for wine producers but implicitly for other commodities also. It was never given a serious chance, but almost certainly it would not have worked because the government could not effectively determine production or guarantee prices to satisfy growers, impelled by the prospect of support to magnify their output. Placing a floor under prices in conditions of over-supply implied the drawing of a blank cheque upon the

Ministry of Finances unless, politically impossible around 1930, production was regulated by decree. The tariff was effective in deterring external suppliers from dumping agricultural commodities in France, but the problem of Algeria remained as difficult to resolve about 1930 as it had earlier in the 1920s. The wine trade was undermined by the influx of cheaper colonial produce and there was nothing effective in the Tardieu plan that would have addressed that difficulty. French agriculturists were probably more incensed by colonial over-production than they were about the threat of an external trade war in agricultural products during the early 1930s. It meant at least that all attempts to support prices for arable products were dead letters, which reinforced the reluctance of Queuille to intervene financially in agricultural marketing, despite a fruitless attempt in 1934 to control overall levels of production.

For agriculture the victory of the Popular Front in 1936 decidedly changed the situation. The dominant socialists had powerful political motives to support agriculture. There was a large leftist vote in the countryside which the SFIO hoped to claim and to extend. It was important to befriend the peasantry to harness mass support for policies favouring industrial workers, to obtain rural sanction for assimilation of the working class fully into the political universe of the Republican state. There was, however, another influence upon Blum and his friend, Georges Monnet, the inspiration of the New Deal, which offered lessons in agricultural policy-formation as it did in labour relations. Monnet's principal achievement at Agriculture was the *Office du Blé* (Wheat Board) which may be seen as a fairly conventional, production-centred, statist response to the problem of collapsing cereal prices; it was matched by similar interventions in many countries during the 1930s, most of which were not avowedly socialist. For the first time the Board did intervene in internal marketing. Peasants were appeased by remunerative prices for their wheat, by the power of the state to harass the *Grands Moulins*, and they were also reassured by the Ministry's circumspection in treating with them and their representatives. There is no doubt that Monnet had grandiose plans for a quasi-public regulation of agriculture and the trade in farm products, but the difficulties of the government precipitated yet another crisis in 1937 and the prospects of a French-style AAA* or even of a French *Reichsnährstand* were postponed *sine die*. Monnet's problems were intractable – how to pay peasants in mainland France good prices for their industry while not deterring consumption through artificially high costs for basic necessities. Farmers have a tendency to over-produce, when prices are low to compensate for falling returns and when they are high because the temptation to magnify profits is too great to

---

* New Deal – agricultural adjustment administration.

resist. Achieving equilibrium, very much a French obsession, is therefore exceedingly difficult. Monnet's attempt at an answer was all-round intervention, with the state manipulating output, distribution and pricing. Wheat was the easiest of the major commodities to control, partly because it had been in secular decline as a crop for decades and partly because demand for it was relatively inelastic. Moreover it was already largely monopolised by capitalist flour millers. Even so there were difficulties; Monnet's plan envisaged not nationalisation or centralisation but regulation of retail distribution, touching petty tradesmen as well as big business, corn chandlers as well as farmers. The *Office* was a representative authority but it was dominated by primary producers; in effect it became an agency for fixing remunerative prices for farmers, and tended to protect mediocre agriculturists and to open the way yet again for less suitable land to be reconverted to wheat production. It would have been much more difficult to regulate the meat trade, wine and dairy production, not least because the variety of output in these commodities was not susceptible to state-driven standardisation.

6.6 The Popular Front – 1936–38

Before taking office (the new government formally took over in June), Blum and his supporters were faced with a massive and widespread demonstration of working class strength, or demands, in the form of strikes and factory occupations. These were probably spontaneous and with little trade union connection. Trade unions were numerically weak – they grew in size following the 'success' of the occupations rather than leading them. Government offices, where union membership was relatively high, took little part in strikes. These actions appeared to be demands that the rewards for wage earners would really be delivered. Political negotiation culminating in the Matignon Agreement (named after the Hotel Matignon) brought an end to the protests within days of the new government taking office. And it was thus a political agreement imposed on employers rather than being collective bargaining in the proper sense.

The Matignon Agreement brought average wage rises of 12.5 per cent (the maximum cost that should be felt by any employer; wages went up by between 7 and 15 per cent). Collective bargaining was to be recognised, thus giving a boost to union membership; two weeks' paid holiday was introduced and the working week was fixed at 40 hours. This last measure was aimed at reducing unemployment which, as has been shown, was never on the scale evident elsewhere. In addition there was a genuine desire to improve working class quality of life, as shown by both the introduction of paid holidays and the creation of the Ministry for

Recreation. As male mortality was among the highest in Europe and alcoholism an endemic disease, this was a well-directed move but one that brought hostility from the press and the more well-to-do.

The Blum experiment, as it came to be known, of encouraging recovery through increased expenditure and boosting incomes, is generally regarded as having failed, for both economic and political reasons. The French economy achieved little recovery before 1938. Economic shortcomings were essentially a result of gain in one area being cancelled out by costs elsewhere. Wage increases improved living standards for many, especially industrial workers. An average gain of about 15 per cent in the Popular Front years made up for a similar decline in the preceding years of deflation. However, the extra costs of wages added to inflationary pressures, which were also stoked up by growing public expenditure on welfare, public employment and above all defence. Rising money incomes were offset also by the increasing costs of foodstuffs as agricultural incomes were also supported. On the other hand rents remained low (and housing often very poor and inadequate). The pattern of support for French farmers was extended and elaborated. Yet this support was not sufficient to counter entirely the fall in agricultural income.

Renewed production in manufacturing was actually inhibited by the strict enforcement of the 40 hour week, which stopped people working. There is little evidence that limiting one man's working week provided employment for another. Labour shortages, particularly of skill, developed. Inflation increased, production did not. As Caron (1979) has noted, the French invented 'stagflation'. Increased money purchasing power added to import demand and aggravated the deficit in the balance of trade. Some authorities, however, attribute fewer negative results to the 40 hour week than others, pointing out that this made little difference to the *average* working week. Much more emphasis is placed on what the Blum government did not do.

All European governments resisted devaluation as long as possible; France was able to resist longer than most. No political party advocated devaluation of the franc (Paul Reynaud was the only serious commentator to do so, after 1934). Yet French domestic prices were increasingly out of line with world levels. Devaluation was resisted because of the association with inflation; exchange controls were resisted because of the association with fascist regimes. This omission might be judged as a political mistake with hindsight, for large amounts of gold were moved out of the country. In some cases anxious bourgeois families literally took suitcases of gold and currency across the border.

This might be judged as an expression of lack of confidence; some have discerned a political conspiracy against Blum and his government.

The banks, the bourgeoisie and the press were not happy to see leisure passed to the working class, power to the trade unions, government in the hands of the left and the Prime Minister a Jew. Anti-Semitism was strong and growing in France; Blum, as a Jew, suffered. Whether the main factor was politically connive opposition or economic clumsiness by government, Blum's policies failed to produce the expected recovery. Strikes were renewed in September 1936 as workers felt the lash of inflation; gold continued to leave the country. At the end of September Blum was forced to allow the currency to float with, as a result, an effective devaluation of 25–35 per cent. This partially corrected the effective over-valuation of the franc which had been evident since 1931. But it was not enough in itself to offset stagnation and also represented a political defeat for Blum as devaluation was resisted as long as possible. Those who had exported capital (and thereby helped to bring about the devaluation) saw their worst fears realised. Gold imports as well as exports were now prohibited, ironically as this prevented gold returning to the country. Blum was replaced as prime minister in June 1937, staying on as deputy. In March 1938 he briefly formed a second cabinet but resigned when financial proposals were rejected by parliament.

The economic policies of Blum's first government are generally judged as having failed; the only lasting effect indeed was the *Office du Blé*. Wage increases, together with the strict imposition of the 40 hour week, the introduction of paid holidays and the extra costs of funding social welfare measures, all added to domestic French costs. Despite devaluation in September 1936, prices remained above world levels by about 15 per cent, the effects being partly offset by the domestic inflationary policies. Some contemporaries observed that the limitations of working restricted the ability of France to build up armaments in the face of the growing threat from Nazi Germany. It was in 1936 that German troops entered the Rhineland and that the four-year plan for war preparation was announced. French defence capacity was feared to be significantly weaker; in the same year Germany produced 2880 aeroplanes, France produced 280. Such complaints were clearly exploited for political purposes for, in reality, defence expenses figured highly in the budget. In 1937 31 per cent of government expenditure was on defence, 26 per cent on debt servicing; there was a real diversion from civilian consumption. Here lay the dilemma for Blum: he was rejected by the right for socialism, by the left, especially the communists, for being too timid in economic reform. There was also the politically important factor of non-intervention in the Spanish Civil War.

It is difficult to see very much ideological determinism in the policies of the Popular Front. Nationalisation was limited to 'lame ducks': the impecunious railway companies were rescued and nationalised as SNCF under Chautemps, who succeeded Blum in 1937; Air France had been created from bankrupt companies some years earlier by a conservative government.

On the other hand Blum had brought socialists into government even though their policies were essentially pragmatic. For all its shortcomings, the Blum government made the first real attempts at expansion and government-led recovery. This was a real change from the economic Malthusianism that had been dominant through the previous years.

Blum's second ministry in March 1938 failed to win general support for a decidedly Keynesian programme based on the use of rearmament as an economic stimulus, even though the plan was devised as an attempt to unite the nation in a common endeavour to confront the renewal of depression. Blum was aware that part of the problem could be attributed to Popular Front policies. He accepted the Chautemps government's affirmation of 'social discipline' as a necessary step towards recovery. Strikes and industrial disorder had not been dissipated by the Popular Front, not least because the devaluation of 1936, while it had stimulated recovery for a time, had also provoked inflation. Moreover it was evident that the enforcement of the 40 hour week in a period of expansion merely resulted in irremediable constraints on production. Blum's belief that recovery could be sustained through rearmament required relaxation of the 40 hour week in munitions factories, which was resisted by many of his supporters and others on the left. His answer was to propose an equality of sacrifice for labour and capital by imposing credit controls to reduce profiteering by irresponsible financiers. Moreover, if government could command the disposition of French savings it could direct investment and regulate the national budget. Neither socialism nor economic liberation offered any way out of the impasse in spring 1938; planning, for all its intellectual appeal to French bureaucrats, lacked a proper economic underpinning before Keynes; hence the conversion of Blum's circle of moderate socialists to planned deficit financing and demand management as a way of saving a reinvigorated, morally reformed capitalist system (*moralisation du marché*).

The pragmatic Daladier's Union Nationale which succeeded then began to implement a modified version of the Blum plan, compromised, however, by considerable concessions to the right. The third devaluation of the franc was doubly significant: it encouraged the repatriation of French capital by engineering a sizable profit to speculators; and it also brought a substantial windfall of 16 million francs to the Treasury. Attempts to amend the statutes relating to labour by negotiation, however, failed because employers, sensing victory, were unwilling to meet union demands even half way. In the event, the government moved with public opinion in the enforcement of 'discipline' on the trade union movement.

By the autumn of 1938 Paul Reynaud was strong enough to dispense with most of the Popular Front labour legislation, not by repealing it but through administrative decrees setting its provisions aside.

Reynaud came into prominence in the financial crisis that accompanied Munich. His predecessor at the Ministry of Finance had attempted to reintroduce exchange controls but failed to take his fellow radicals with him. Reynaud's period in office from October 1938 encompassed recovery on a scale not seen since Poincaré, but it was too late to save France from defeat in 1940. He followed Daladier in his attempt to found recovery upon public confidence, which meant bourgeois confidence. He reduced the budget deficit by increasing taxation and administrative reform. Public works programmes were abandoned; the 40 hour week undermined. Rearmament remained a priority, so that labour productivity was a matter of primary concern. Reynaud also accumulated an effective war chest of 48 million francs in the vaults of the Bank, mostly through the repatriation of capital.

All the economic indicators testified to this recovery. Industrial production increased by 20 per cent in those months and unemployment fell by 10 per cent. The trade deficit shrank and industrial unrest diminished, partly because the government abandoned conciliation in favour of repression. Real industrial recovery was underway, largely due to expansion in the strategic, metallurgical industries. Reynaud, for all his liberalism, adopted statist means to achieve his ends wherever necessary and, with war threatening, France had to be prepared. In the drive to bring about recovery, Reynaud and Daladier had disillusioned large sections of the French people, who saw the gains they had made in 1936–37 melt away; it was the reverse of Blum's antagonism of capital.

However, recovery was far from complete and the French economy remained relatively weak. Industrial production and national income remained below the level of 1929 or 1930. Net national product at 1938 prices was 4510 million francs in 1929, 3800 million in 1938. *Per capita* national income in US dollars in 1938 was $300 in France, compared with $500 in Britain and $870 in the USA.

Conclusions

Many words have been written about the French economy in the nineteenth century and the relative retardation displayed. Various factors have been put forward to explain this: shortage of crucial raw materials, population stagnation, commercial and cultural conservation. Although the very emphasis on retardation in France before the First World War has been questioned, it is nonetheless true that the French economy suffered real stagnation before the Second World War and a dynamic resurgence under the Fourth Republic. A question arises as to when the beginning of this post-war resurgence first became evident. How early were the foundations laid? Some, like Caron (1979), have suggested that this was as early as the early 1900s when the 'new industries' of electrical power generation, automobiles and aeroplanes, chemicals and aluminium began. In this scenario the 1930s stand out as the decade of reverse and stagnation; post-war growth was a renewal of a trend evident from the 1920s. The emphasis on the post-war resurgence as a new age, on the other hand (Kindleberger (1964) is an example of this view), is more likely to see the 1920s as the interlude – a period of export-led boom buoyed up by world demand and a cheap franc. The 1930s then saw a return to cultural and structural conservatism evident for many years. It was only with the destruction of the Third Republic and the terrible losses of war that decks were cleared for renewed development.

Wherever it might prove appropriate to place the emphasis, there is no doubting the stagnation of the 1930s; the levels of production recorded in 1929 were not reachieved until 1948–49. Sauvy estimates that national income fell by 10 per cent in 1929–38 and industrial production by 20 per cent. Later analysts, notably Carré, Dubois and Malinvaud, revise this latter figure to a more modest 10 per cent loss, but serious nonetheless.

Despite these data there can be no gainsaying the beginnings of technologically new industries in, or before, the 1920s. But these were overlaid by structural and cultural lags which inhibited the continuance of economic modernisation until after World War Two. In terms of employment, HEP, petroleum refining and distribution, chemicals and pharmaceuticals, and various aspects of engineering were most dynamic; textiles and clothing shared the greatest decline (from 42.4 per cent of active employment in industry in 1915 to 29.7 per cent in 1938), but remained one of the largest sectors.

Structural lags can be seen in the continued and heavy share of the very small, often family-based enterprise, in all branches of the economy. The conservative peasant mentality and insistence on protection is most readily associated with agriculture but small scale was usual in manufacturing as well. It is important to bear in mind that family ownership was by no means inconsistent with commercial enterprise. Major companies like Peugeot, Renault, Wendel and Michelin remained family enterprises and eschewed banks as well as the stock market. Significantly the entrepreneurial, dynamic Citroën went bankrupt and was taken over by the financially cautious Michelin.

Cultural conservatism was strongly influential at times of economic crisis. Various interest groups pressed government for protection.

Nowhere was this stronger than in agriculture. Although agricultural employment fell significantly it remained high by west European standards at 31.4 per cent in 1938, compared with 37.4 per cent in 1913. But this influence extended beyond agriculture, with the effect that new branches of manufacturing and services were limited – chain stores and shoe makers were not able to open new branches in order to protect the interests of existing producers. This economic Malthusianism was not confined to government measures. Industries limited output to maintain profitability but they were only able to do so because of protectionism.

The stagnation was caused also by the objective factors of low profitability, which discouraged new investments. Wages and salaries took an increasing share of NI (43 per cent in 1913, 52 per cent 1938) and wage and salary earnings benefited from reduced working hours and extended social provisions. Above all France had a stagnating, ageing population; the population of working age declined.

Faced with such problems, governments were unable to provide a cure. Competing commercial and political interest groups weakened political attempts at recovery – especially, as we have seen, under the Popular Front. This experiment of Blum's was a failure but the conservatism of his predecessors was no more, probably less, successful. Signs of recovery became evident under Daladier from 1938, a process helped by some arms expenditure, but one cut short by the war and occupation. The relative economic weakness of France was to be exacerbated in the years of occupation. France was still, in 1940, a nation rich in resources, skills and abundant foodstuffs, notwithstanding economic difficulties. It thus proved to be a major economic prize for the invading forces from Nazi Germany. Wartime exploitation was to weaken the economy of France more seriously than the foregoing decade of stagnation.

France was unable to offer great military resistance to German forces which invaded in May 1940. One month later German forces entered Paris (14 June). Reynaud, who had taken over the premiership from Daladier in March 1941, resigned to be succeeded by Marshall Petain, a hero of the First World War. It was Petain who signed the Armistice on 22 June and who led the new government in wartime France from Vichy.

6.7   Further reading

A good basic text on France is F. Caron (1979) *An Economic History of Modern France* (London: Methuen). This may be complemented by a wide ranging book, but one less focussed on economic affairs, P. Bernard and H. Dubief (1985) *The Decline of the Third Republic, 1914–1938* (Cambridge: Cambridge University Press). Both of these have been translated from the French. A similar, but very concise text is J–C. Asselain (1984) *Histoire économique de la France du xviiie siècle à nos jours* (Paris: Seuil). A survey of nineteenth century developments which stresses the real advances of the French economy, especially in terms of *per capita* product, is P. O'Brien and C. Keyder (1978) *Economic Growth in Britain and France, 1780–1914. Two Paths to the Twentieth Century* (London: Allen and Unwin). For an examination of the experience of French development from a rather negative viewpoint see C.P. Kindleberger (1964) *Economic Growth in France and Britain, 1861–1950* (Cambridge, Mass.: Harvard University Press). A similarly negative view of the inter-war years is taken in T. Kemp (1972) *The French Economy 1913–1939. The History of Decline* (London: Longman). The same author has a specialised article (1971) on the exchange rate of the franc in the 1920s: 'The French economy under the Franc Poincaré', *Economic History Review*, **24**, pp. 82–99. Financial affairs are also the focus of M. Wolfe (1957) *The French Franc between the Wars, 1919–1939* (New York: Columbia University Press). Two detailed books provide coverage of the 1930s, but with the emphasis very much on politics and, in so far as economics is analysed, economic policy: J. Jackson (1985) *The Politics of Depression in France, 1932–1936* (Cambridge: Cambridge University Press) and, by the same author (1988) *The Popular Front in France: defending democracy, 1934–1938* (Cambridge: Cambridge University Press). An interesting biography of a central industrial figure can be found in A. Rhodes (1970) *Louis Renault, A Biography* (New York: Harcourt Brace). G. Wright (1974) *Rural Revolution in France* (Stanford: Stanford University Press) is useful for material on agricultural and rural society. Detailed information on the French economy can be found in E. Malinuaud, J.J. Carré, P. Dubois (1962) *La Croissance Française* (Paris: Seuil), L.A. Vincent, 'Evolution de la production interieure brute en France de 1896 à 1938', *Etudes et Conjunctures* (1962), J.C. Toutain (1962) Histoire Quantitive de l'économie Française (Paris: Cahiers de L'I.S.E.A.).

7
Germany

In a sense the experience of the German economy in the inter-war years was the most representative of a common pattern. The problems of readjustment to peace, political reorganisation, the dislocation and physical loss of productive assets were all larger and more extreme than in most other countries. Inflation, a common post-war phenomenon, reached higher levels than elsewhere. After the post-war adjustments the cycle of recovery and, after 1929, recession displayed steeper amplitudes than elsewhere.

Defeat in the war brought in its wake severe losses and humiliation in the peace settlement. The war destroyed the Empire of Greater Germany politically and militarily; the Allies set about destroying Germany as an industrial power, with a will. The attitude was expressed in a crucial clause in the Treaty of Versailles, which held Germany as wholly responsible for the war. It followed, therefore, that the costs of making good the damage were to be borne by Germany. The principle was established in 1919 (though there were historical precedents); the level of reparations demanded was fixed in 1921 (see p. 123). There was a mixture of motives for this imposition; first a crude but simple attitude of revenge, especially evident from France and Belgium who had most obviously suffered from German aggression. But there was also the political need to be seen to punish the Germans by domestic electorates. Clemenceau declared that 'Le Boche payera', which was more calculated to have domestic appeal than to be a full statement of economic policy.

Beyond the attitude of revenge was the motive of weakening German industry for the sake of direct gains to be made by the victorious allies. Thus France reclaimed Alsace–Lorraine and a ready-made iron and steel industry. Britain saw a chance of taking export markets. The seizure of rolling stock, merchant shipping and other assets helped, if modestly, to replenish the diminished stocks of wartime.

Under the Treaty Germany lost all her former colonies, 90 per cent of her merchant marine, 13 per cent of pre-war (European) territory, principally in Alsace–Lorraine (ceded to France) and Silesia and part of East Prussia (ceded to Poland). In addition Eupen-Malmedy was ceded to Belgium and some border territories to Czechoslovakia. Together these areas had previously accounted for 15 per cent of productive capacity and provided 36 per cent of known coal reserves, 72 per cent of iron ore, 63 per cent of zinc ore. The League of Nations took over responsibility for the administration of Danzig, Memel and the Saar, where France had control over the coal supplies. Luxembourg was removed from the German customs union and the major rivers traversing Germany became international waterways. Foreign investments were sequestrated by national governments and the value set against future reparations. Germany was prevented from setting her own tariff levels until 1925. Further restrictions included the demilitarisation of the Rhineland; the area was to be occupied temporarily by French troops but the costs borne by Germany.

The value of reparations was fixed in 1921 at 132 billion (i.e. thousand million) gold marks or £6600 million. This was equivalent to more than double pre-war national income and so constituted an enormous demand on the German economy. Not surprisingly such demands led to opposition within as well as without Germany. For example, there were great differences in the valuation of property seized before 1921: it was put at 7900 million marks by the Allies, 20 000 million marks by the German authorities. In reality, however, reparation payments were far less onerous than the figures above suggest. The immediate demand on Germany was to pay 50 billion gold marks in the form of interest and capital on bonds (in two lots, A and B). Bonds (known as C bonds) to cover the remaining 82 billion marks were to be issued only if Germany could be shown to be able to pay. In practice Germany was required to pay two billion marks annually plus a sum equivalent to 26 per cent of exports. This was nonetheless a substantial burden, especially on the balance of payments. One estimate puts the total cost at equal to 5.4 per cent of national income at factor cost in 1921 or 7.2 per cent for 1925–29. It would inevitably require constraints on consumption at home and buoyant exports. Here was another problem, for German exports could compete with home production in Britain, France or Belgium or in third markets.

Although there were economic problems arising out of the reparation issue the main problems were of a more broadly political nature.

The most notable critic of the extent of reparations was Keynes. He feared that what he saw as exaggerated claims from France and Belgium would weaken the German economy and thereby the fabric of the European economy. A weak Germany would be vulnerable to the threat of Bolshevism – a greater threat in Keynes's view than German revanchism. A weak Germany would leave a political vacuum in central Europe, whereas what was needed was a bastion against the evil force in the east and a vibrant market for the products of western economies. There was much to support such a view. Before 1914 Germany had been at the heart of a European economic system. To weaken Germany, therefore, was to weaken Europe; European prosperity, up to a point, depended on German prosperity. Although the allied authorities were aware of such points there was also the desire to gain exports, by Britain for instance, at Germany's expense. France in particular was noted for intransigence at Versailles. However, this judgement has recently been questioned. The major economic problem facing France was to recover her industrial production. For this she needed inputs of capital, for which reparations were a major source. But they became so only when it had become clear that such aid was not available elsewhere, notably from the USA. As early as 1920 France was prepared to make an easier settlement for Germany but this had been rejected by Ruhr industrialists. On the other hand, French intransigence was understandable: twice within a generation France had suffered German aggression and her anxieties about revived German strength were to be proved correct a little over 20 years later in 1940! In the context of the early post-war years Germany, although seriously weakened, remained potentially strong. Russia (France's former ally) had effectively disappeared from the international arena, and the successor states to the Habsburg Empire were economically weak; France had cause to be concerned.

Reparations were throughout the 1920s a major political issue, though of much less economic significance than was claimed at the time. Yet international hostility threatened the fragile democratic facade of Germany. The Weimar Republic had enemies within as well as without. The former ruling elites resented the move to democracy; the patriotic middle classes felt cheated in seeing the workers gain equal political influence. There were constant disputes between rival political parties; every government was a coalition but the large Social Democratic party remained outside government between 1924 and 1928; no government lasted the full term of four years (in fact the average length was only eight months). The internal weakness of governments was in turn to affect the running of the economy.

7.1   Inflation

Germany was by no means unique in her experience of inflation in the early 1920s, though the rate of hyper-inflation in 1923 was more extreme than elsewhere. There are numerous explanations for the phenomenon, but there is no doubt that the inflationary trends were initiated by the government deficit to meet wartime expenditure. Germany financed the war largely through borrowing; on average through the war years debts were equivalent to 62 per cent of 1913 national income. Many of these loans were from the central bank and were thus printing money. In Britain, in contrast, even though debts were of a similar order (57 per cent of 1913 NI) the City was able to absorb the debt. No combatants were able to raise significant war finance through taxation. Before the war the Reich (as opposed to constituent states) had been unable to levy direct taxes, receiving income from import duties and sales taxes. In the uncertain post-war years there is no doubt that inflationary government expenditure was used to help maintain employment and contribute to social stability. There were also some contemporary suggestions in west European countries (notably in France) that governments connived at inflation to demonstrate the economic weakness of Germany to the framers of the Peace Treaty. Some German nationalists, on the other hand, attributed inflation to the very fact of reparations. This was the impression that governments were pleased to give.

Weimar governments were certainly reluctant to tackle the problem head on – stringent deflation would undoubtedly have caused unemployment and discontent at a politically uncertain time. Not even the stable USA and UK governments were prepared to tackle inflationary pressure immediately after the war, before 1919 or 1920. Further, though the Reich under the Weimar constitution had the ability to raise direct taxes on income and capital, much of this income was passed to, and spent by, the states rather than central government. In Germany it is also evident that there was some business support for inflation, or at least opposition to deflation, through 1920–22, both because employment acted as a social stabiliser and because money profits tended to run ahead of wages. A rapidly depreciating exchange rate made exports cheap and the large industrial producers who could export were able to secure hard currency profits in accounts held abroad. It was the central government (Reich) which paid reparations, not business. Government therefore had no interest in stopping inflation because it showed that they were unable to pay the Allies. There is the further possibility that by such action and visible suffering Germany, like Austria, could obtain a loan from the League of Nations to secure their currency. (This happened to Austria in 1922.)

The real twist to the inflationary spiral came in June 1922. Until that time business profits and exports improved, industrial employment was maintained and real wages probably grew. There was also a net inflow of funds to Germany because foreign held accounts in marks depreciated. From mid-1921 to mid-1922 prices had tended to rise at 17 to 18 per cent per month; from June 1922 they began rising at over 70 per cent per month. Real incomes which had more or less been maintained until now, because of widespread indexing of wages, began to fall. Unemployment increased, but slowly. In January 1923, when French and Belgian troops occupied the Ruhr because of a shortfall in reparations deliveries, the response was passive resistance, which was supported by government paying the workers' wages and continuing other outgoings. This expenditure, when income was falling, was largely financed from the printing press. At the same time the occupying forces took over mines and other basic materials and prevented their moving outside the occupied zone, thus effectively paralysing German industry for a short time. Eventually some cartels made agreements with the occupying forces but the inflationary spiral had been twisted further.

Prices went haywire; currency collapsed. Expectations of price increases fuelled inflation to the point that printing presses literally could not meet the demand for cash. This was the time when legends were made. Housewives went shopping with prams or barrows to carry the money; workers were paid twice a day so that they could buy something. Such a state could not continue for long: money lost value completely; local authorities began to produce their own token money as marks became worthless. The need for some form of intervention became evident before the end of 1923. There was also a social readiness for stabilisation, which was achieved in October of that year.

The effects of the experience were not entirely negative. There were winners as well as losers. Fortunes were made; the 'flight into goods' (a rush to buy something before the price went up) fuelled demand for the goods to be made. The number of businesses increased between 1920 and 1923; stabilisation led to bankruptcies. The main losers were those on fixed incomes or those who could not maintain money wages or salaries to keep pace with prices. These included pensioners or any one living on dividends or interest. And these included the patriotic and thrifty middle classes whose purchases of state bonds had helped finance the German war effort. Debtors meanwhile prospered as the debts became meaningless (the biggest debtor of course was the State itself). Probably everyone suffered in the worst weeks and months of 1923. Shopkeepers found it difficult to replenish stocks; the cost of foreign exchange made it difficult to import anything and export earnings so attractive that there was a real incentive to divert goods to foreign markets, thus aggravating domestic shortages. The social benefits of inflation, which had been real through the first half of 1922, began to disappear as unemployment increased, real wages declined and shortages grew worse.

Stabilisation was achieved in 1923, principally because it was so welcome. There was also now some social acceptance of taxation by central government; higher income tax and a wealth tax were introduced but the redistributive effects were modest. The mark had reached one (German) billionth (million millionth) equivalent value of the old gold mark; it was known as the *Billmark*. A new currency was introduced as a stopgap measure which for some time circulated alongside the *Billmark*. It had no gold or similar support but was presented to the German people as having the backing of the real property of Germany. Despite the logical fallacy of this claim the *Rentenmark*, as it was known, was accepted.

As intended the *Rentenmark* lasted a short time. In spring 1924 a committee of bankers chaired by the first Secretary of the US Treasury, Dawes, negotiated a loan to Germany and reordering of the reparations debts. The purpose of the Dawes Plan, as it subsequently came to be known, was primarily to investigate how much Germany could pay in reparations and to help ensure that she would do so. There was to be no reduction of the total bill but a reorganisation of the payment. A Reparation Commissioner, Parker Gilbert, was enplaced to oversee payment. There was thus effective international control of the Reichsbank. Germany was required to join the new Gold Standard and currency issues were limited. A loan of 800 million gold marks was raised; it provided backing to return to the Gold Standard with a new *Reichsmark*, and also helped German industry recover, in order to provide a tax base for government to pay reparations. Reparation payments were readjusted to 2.5 billion gold marks annually from 1929, initially at a lower level. (Gold marks were used as a consistent measure of value, based on the exchange rates of 1913.) Stabilisation also demanded greater financial discipline than in preceding years. After the Dawes Plan huge amounts of foreign loans, largely from the United States, came into Germany. Most of these were raised by the sale of bonds by local governments and municipalities (the Reich borrowed hardly at all abroad) or, in some cases, by large businesses.

The years 1924 to 1929 saw general industrial growth and much of this was greatly aided by the influx of foreign capital. Thus foreign capital, especially from the USA, helped to modernise German industry in the 1920s. Direct investment (Ford in 1925 and General Motors in 1929 both invested in the motor industry) was often accompanied by up-to-date technology. It is important to remember, however, that much of the borrowing abroad was by German municipal governments rather than by productive enterprises. Reparation payments were fully and promptly paid until 1929 when a revised plan, the Young Plan, was proposed to adjust, and reduce, payments. By 1928–29 payments had reached 3.3 per cent of national income and 12.4 per cent of government expenditure. Between 1925 and 1931, when they effectively ceased, Germany paid 10.8 billion RM in reparations but received 20.5 billion RM in loans. The Young Plan, which was formally adopted in 1930, reduced the final payment to 110.7 million gold marks to be paid by 1987! More significantly the Young Plan reduced the annual payment to 1.64 billion RM (or 2 per cent of current NI at factor cost). However, financial crises meant that the sum was not paid, payments being formally abandoned in 1932, though suspended the previous year. Before the crisis began to bite in 1929 the major problem for Germany was not the payment of reparations as such but the fact that the payment was dependent on further borrowing. The major value of imported capital was in funding a balance of trade deficit. Some went to modernising industry but larger amounts were used for social overhead or welfare provisions by municipal or local governments. City mayors competed with each other, and for the voters' attention, with grand local expenditures. There was little direct connection with reparations. Central government, the Reich, borrowed hardly at all and it was the Reich which had to pay reparations. Nonetheless this borrowing did bring foreign currency into the economy and relieved the economic burden of reparations. Borrowing was valuable in providing liquid assets for investment and other expenditures when domestic sources were so weak. Inflation had wiped out the resources of the *rentier* class and, to a large extent, the banks. There was thus a domestic shortage of investment capital, which was not a function of the need to pay reparations. Their significance was always more political than economic.

7.2   German industry, 1925–29

German industry entered a period of rapid growth in the second half of the 1920s. Overall growth in industrial production for the decade 1920–29 was 7.6 per cent per annum. This was a little lower than in France (7.9 per cent) but far exceeded levels in the UK (2.3 per cent) and the USA (4 per cent). In Germany the late 1920s were years of a real spurt in growth. Germany re-established a lead in chemicals, electrical engineering, optical and precision instruments; she also rebuilt her merchant marine. The steel industry grew so fast that output regularly exceeded agreed quotas of the International Steel Cartel, to which Germany was an initial signatory, along with France and Belgium, in 1926. Thus producers began to look for export outlets in south eastern Europe, reviving the nineteenth century ideas of the *Mitteleuropa* trading area. Another market was to be the USSR, where growth took off as western economies slipped into recession. The high export dependence of the steel industry made it particularly vulnerable to falling world demand after 1929. Germany was helped by the renewed freedom to set tariff levels in 1925. By 1926 she had regained her 1913 level of exports in chemicals and in 1925 the giant combine IG Farben was formed. However, although this company was one of the most successful exporters, some branches of the chemical industry were less export-dependent than before 1914. The main growth areas were in synthetic petroleum and nitrates for fertilisers, for which home demand was buoyant. (Germany also continued to be a leader in dyestuffs but was less dominant than in the pre-war years, partly because of development of the industry in former export markets.) Coal served as both a source of energy and raw material. Coal derivatives such as benzole, which was a basis for synthetic petroleum, were to become major products in future years. Coal exports were vital too and these were assisted by the terms of the International Steel Cartel which gave France, Belgium and Luxembourg access to supplies from the Ruhr. This region became the major supplier of coking coal to those three markets in the 1920s.

The high levels of technical efficiency so long associated with German industry once again became apparent in the 1920s. At first sight there appears to be a high level of investment, helped by large capital imports. This contributed to relative over-production which in turn was a factor in the recession after 1929. This view requires some qualification, however. Harold James has shown that the investment ratio was lower 1925–29 (11.1 per cent NNP) than 1910–13 (15.2 per cent NNP) so the emphasis may not be placed simply on investment levels. More appropriately one should examine rationalisation in industry. However, here again, established views have been questioned. It is clear that the rationalisation movement affected only a few (though important) industries, particularly coal, engineering and motor manufacturing (see Chap. 5).

Rationalisation did not depend simply on new investment but on cost savings through increased efficiency and productivity. The process of rationalisation involved reducing the number of productive enterprises and the numbers of workers employed. Very often also there was concentration in ownership; IG Farben (1925) in chemicals and the giant Vereinigte Stahlwerke (1926) in steel manufacture were both examples. There was also a beginning of some new managerial and productive techniques, imported from the USA. While it is probably a simplification to attribute all such developments to American influence there was, without doubt, some such. German businesses, like those in France, set out to learn from and implement techniques which had been developed in the USA.

Labour productivity in Ruhr coal mines improved significantly, at the cost of employment. In 1913 average daily coal production was 378 695 tons (424 627 employed); in 1929 it was 407 101 tons (375 711 employed). This was very much a result of mechanisation in coal cutting. Similar advances were made in other sectors. In the steel industry, in 1924, 55 plants with 138 blast furnaces produced 1655 tons of steel per furnace per week; in 1929, 45 plants with 115 blast furnaces produced an average 2567 tons per furnace per week. Such growth contributed to over-production in German industry and to growing unemployment. One estimate is that rationalisation lost two million jobs between 1925 and 1930; it thereby contributed to the recession late in the 1920s. This was not, however, a general phenomenon. Very often well-established industries found it easier to raise money from banks than new innovatory ones. Thus it was possible for industries with slowly growing demand to raise finance for investment and new growth in production, contributing to excess supply. Banks, which traditionally had strong links with industry, tended to favour the long-established sectors. It is clear also that some banks had become more closely linked to industry as if by chance. Industrial recession in the mid-twenties had forced some banks to allow short-term credits in effect to become long-term investments. Thus in some cases banks were effectively becoming industrial investment banks, though this was not the original intention. As a result the banks' fortunes were dependent on the fortunes of particular industries. Perhaps this explains other acts of apparent irresponsibility, such as banks continuing to lend to companies even when they were in difficulty, thus compounding the ultimate commercial crisis. Thus structural problems rather than general problems of over-production had developed in Germany by 1929. But the highly cartelised industry contributed to price rigidities when world prices began to fall. Even before this date price rigidities became evident. The export prices of finished goods rose by 1 per cent, 1925–29; those from the USA fell by 11.5 per cent.

In the five years before the recession struck in 1929 German industry grew substantially and re-established itself as an international force. It was not an entirely positive picture, however. Many firms had gone bankrupt or lost large amounts during or after the inflation; these losses were not made good by any state help. The banks had also lost huge amounts during inflation and the extensive foreign loans after stabilisation had been necessary to refinance the banking system, and provide some capital for industry. As we have seen, there had been considerable financial irresponsibility during the inflationary years. A greater degree of financial discipline, deflationary government policies and the effects of the rationalisation procedures in industry all contributed to a decline in the demand for labour. As productivity improved fewer workers were required. From 1926, well before the ravages of recession, there were never fewer than one million unemployed men.

Quite apart from the social cost that such idleness engendered, there was the real cost to the exchequer. Unemployment relief was an unavoidable demand on the state (or municipal) budget, but a source of conflict between government and industry. There was some resentment among industrialists against paying taxes and social insurance contributions which were seen as being used to employ more civil servants. They also added to the cost of employing labour. There was, in short, no real political consensus on the need to raise significant tax revenue. Taxes, and the number of civil servants, were higher in the Weimar period than imperial Germany but, as a proportion of the whole, public employment remained low in Germany. Businesses were consistently opposed to paying unemployment insurance contributions and this became a source of conflict with government. It was anyway inadequate, for the fund was exhausted by 1929.

Wages, as a proportion of national income, were higher in the 1920s than before the War, by about 10 per cent. This was a common development in western Europe. Employers might have complained that trade unions' strength unreasonably increased their wage costs, but these costs remained lower than in Britain, for instance. However, unit labour costs in industry increased quickly, by 2.6 per cent per year between 1925 and 1930, while they declined in the USA by 2 per cent. In Britain there was a steep fall (by 7 per cent 1921–31) but this was mostly in the earlier part of the decade. German real wages increased by 4.6 per cent, 1925–30, which arguably contributed to a deterioration in export competitiveness.

This has become a subject of some controversy among German historians. Borchardt has argued that rising wage costs were a disincentive to new investment in industry and thus contributed to later stagnation as well as the growth in unemployment. Wages increased faster than productivity before 1929. In addition wage costs were further increased by social insurance contributions, as has been pointed out, and by 'wage drift' in overtime as the 48 hour working week was steadily exceeded in some industries. In contrast to these views others argue that wages were not too high; lower wages would have made unemployment worse. The structural problems of German industry led to over-production. Before the crash, however, it is difficult to see this as a general phenomenon, for there was a consistent excess of imports, implying excess demand. There cannot have been excess demand and supply at the same time. On the other hand, there was structural imbalance in the industrial economy, with a tendency towards over-production of some commodities for which demand was growing slowly. With the collapse of demand during the Depression excess supply quickly became apparent.

Trade unions had become stronger in the earlier 1920s than in the days of empire, but they were weakened during the later Weimar years. Unemployment inevitably reduced the bargaining power of labour; union membership declined in the 1920s. With the relaxation of the eight hour day legislation (of 1919), workers could in effect be required to work overtime, particularly in the steel and engineering industries. This planted seeds of conflict between capital and labour. Such conflict was far from being suppressed in the years of the Weimar republic and political extremism was apparent throughout the period.

Agriculture

Agriculture was the traditional low productivity industry of Germany. In the 1920s it remained a weak and costly sector. In 1925, 30 per cent of the economically active population were employed in farming, fishing and forestry; from 1925–29 this primary sector contributed only 16 per cent of net domestic product. That agriculture was a low productivity sector is no surprise but the extent of agricultural poverty and debt is a little surprising. The experience of war, when there were real food shortages, and inflation gave a trading advantage to the agricultural producer. Real assets (food) appreciated during the inflation and debts were wiped out; and yet peasant poverty remained. The anomaly can be explained in a number of ways: for one thing some food prices were regulated so that not all could 'cash in' on inflation; another point is that most small producers were also buying in an inflationary market.

The real difficulties came with stabilisation. Taxes were increased to levels far higher than in 1913. Yet terms of trade had moved against the farmer. Debts mounted again, money being borrowed, very often, to pay the taxes. Borrowing increased so much that the share of agriculture in the national capital stock showed an increase for the only time in German history. The debt position became all the more serious when prices began to fall from 1927. During the Depression, when prices fell through the floor, peasant radicalism increased. The Nazi party found considerable support in rural areas.

The position was complicated by the structure of agriculture. In much of the country farms were small scale family enterprises – the *Bauern*. East of the river Elbe, however, larger holdings predominated. It was here that the Junker estate farmers continued to dominate farming. As government relief for debts increased it was, ironically perhaps, the richest farmers of the east who benefited the most. It is true that the traditional staple crop – rye – suffered the earliest and most severe price fall. The price fall had been delayed by the incidence of tariffs. But protective tariffs had a two-edged effect. First they increased the cost of living for the consumer. Although average real wages improved with price falls, this was moderated. Food continued to be by far the largest item in the working class budget, on average taking 48 per cent of their household expenditure in 1925, and 43 per cent in the cheaper year of 1929. At a mundane level this increased pressure on money wages. Second, state intervention and protection effectively transferred incomes from workers to farmers, the main beneficiaries being the well-to-do farmers in the east. (This was because it was cereal growers who were the most protected. Animal product prices were not protected to anything like the same extent.)

Tariffs also antagonised those who had agricultural products to sell, notably the Netherlands, Scandinavia and Poland, for Germany was a vital export market. However, dairy products were largely unrestricted until the slump. Tariffs did nothing to alter the fundamental economic problems of agriculture, that of over-production. In fact they probably aggravated this problem by providing a protective shield against world market trends. This, however, was short lived. Price recession and protection affected agriculturalists more severely than other producers. Also, the protection afforded to German farmers was in no sense peculiar within Europe. In the German case it exacerbated economic differentiation and social conflicts.

Depression

The causes of the economic Depression were both domestic and international, and are discussed fully elsewhere. Here it is necessary to remind ourselves of the differing arenas of depression: it was clearly relatively severe for primary producers, there was a financial crisis in parallel with a true depression in production, and unemployment reached unprecedented levels. On top of all this the problems arose extremely quickly, within two or three years, and no national government properly knew how to cope with them. It is also evident that within Germany there were domestic factors inducing depression earlier than 1928. Germany experienced a recession in 1925–26, largely induced by contraction in domestic demand and a tight money policy. This recession was quickly succeeded by recovery but the underlying structural imbalances in the economy had not been eliminated. Further, there was increased dependence on capital inflows. Thus there were some structural factors which contributed to economic contraction, before international crisis struck. Although expert opinion differs over the detail of the main causative factors of the international recession (see Chap. 2), there is common ground that there were some factors within Germany and that the recession was not a wholly imported phenomenon. While it is unlikely that this had a determining influence on world recession it worsened the effects of the international trade cycle within Germany and, given the central position of the German economy, in turn affected much of Europe.

As we have seen, falling prices began to affect agricultural producers initially. For a time tariffs protected European farmers but this could only postpone the impact of the international market. Agricultural terms of trade deteriorated from the early to middle 1920s; domestic prices in Germany began to be affected from 1927. However, it was politically unacceptable to allow such price falls to cause economic ruin. All political parties in Weimar Germany courted agrarian support for the sake of the not inconsiderable vote. But there were some inevitable contradictions. Tariffs and price support put up costs for the rest of the community, including the unemployed. The agricultural tariff was little higher between 1925 and 1929 (*ad valorem*) than it had been before 1914, but thereafter it rose rapidly and dramatically. In 1932, when recession was at its deepest, tariffs were equivalent to 3.7 per cent of net national product. Such protective measures, as already noted, continued to transfer income from the non-agricultural population, many of whom were very poor, to the farming community, some of whom were extremely rich. The major beneficiaries indeed were the cereal farmers of East Prussia. Thus Weimar governments found themselves in the absurd position of supporting their sworn enemies – the Junker estate farmers.

Industry

For industry the contracting market of depressed economies produced falling demand and prices, bankruptcy and inevitable unemployment. Falling incomes added to the spiral of falling demand. For the large, export-oriented industrial organisations in Germany there were major problems with finding foreign markets after 1930. Even before this date Ruhr steel companies were over-producing their cartel quota; after 1930 the market difficulties became more generalised. Exports were limited further by tariffs and devaluation elsewhere. The Reichsmark was never formally devalued, which left German exports relatively over-priced. German large scale industry, which was influenced by cartels far more extensively than other producers, was more inclined to respond by restricting output while maintaining prices than by reducing prices. Price rigidities seemed to be built into the system.

A financial crisis struck the German economy when production was already falling and unemployment growing. In 1929 a further and final measure to affect reparations was drawn up. The Young Plan became operative in 1930 (it fixed the payment of 110.7 milliard RM to be paid by 1987; this reduced the bill but at a time of deflation in real terms the charges were increased. A loan of $351 million was made to assist the Weimar government.) In the winter of 1930/1 reparations became the most important issue for the Brüning government. In June 1931 the government issued a declaration that 'the limits of Germany's endurance have been reached.' This was coupled with the collapse of the Austrian Creditanstalt bank which was followed by a run on German banks. It was not clear whether foreign or domestic depositors initiated the run on the German banks. It was difficult to separate them; some of the 'foreign' withdrawals were in reality made by German companies through foreign subsidiaries. This was especially evident in May and June 1931. The suggestion is that financial panic and crisis developed 'independently' within Germany, though it was made worse following the Austrian crisis.

The negotiations between Germany and Austria over the possibility of establishing a customs union had led to financial pressure (the withdrawal of short-term deposits) by foreign banks. This had helped cause the fall of the Austrian bank, but it is evident that there was some domestic panic in Germany as well as foreign pressure. To calm proceedings 'bank holidays' were declared, from 13 July to 5 August, the great banks were reorganised and foreign exchange controls introduced. In June 1932 reparations were finally cancelled, following the Hoover moratorium of the previous year. Exchange controls were an alternative to devaluation. This would have been diplomatically risky in view of international agreements relating to the Reichsmark and politically unacceptable for fear of inflation. All governments imposed deflationary policies, high interest rates and reductions in expenditure. These accompanied downward pressure on wages, thereby increasing consumption falls even further, and some tax increases. It can be seen with hindsight that such policies aggravated the effects of depression. After September 1931 when the pound was devalued and many other currencies followed, the mark was left relatively over-valued and, at this time, devaluation was unlikely to have had an inflationary effect. Earlier, however, it was hardly a political option.

The economic difficulties that became evident in 1930 produced political crisis, growing electoral support for the Nazi party and an end to the Grand Coalition. Brüning began to govern using emergency decrees, by passing parliamentary procedures, because he lacked sufficient support in the Reichstag. There was also growing extra-parliamentary opposition. Business interests were concerned at contracting markets and relatively high levels of taxation as well as the potential political strength of left wing parties. It is quite clear that big business did not launch Hitler to power. Yet the reluctance of business elements to fund additional government expenditures to some extent paved the way for him. Business was consistently opposed to the welfare policies of Weimar; the coalmasters of the Ruhr consistently favoured authoritarian concepts of government, without favouring Nazism directly.

Effects of recession

The measurable effects of the Depression in Germany were more severe than elsewhere in Europe. This is attributable both to the relatively high dependence on the international financial market and to structural aspects of the German economy. The growth of the post-inflationary years was, as we have seen, associated with the concentration of production, particularly in the producer goods sector. Scientific research as well as scientific management contributed to the growth, and re-establishment in world leadership, of the chemical industry. As we have seen, rationalisation and concentration often reduced costs but the customary resort to cartels enabled high domestic prices and, where necessary, export dumping to be maintained. Further, market rationalisation through cartels enabled product specialisation for large works (the steel industry is a good example).

But such rational and cost-effective structures had disadvantages also. The large, specialised unit proved vulnerable to the recession (in contrast the smaller scale, less specialised but higher cost British steel industry was more flexible). Cartels tended to keep prices high so that producer goods prices fell more slowly than consumer goods. In contrast economic theory suggests that in cyclical recession the price of investment goods would fall more steeply, thus encouraging reinvestment and recovery. Thus price rigidities contributed to the depth and prolongation of the Depression in Germany. This phenomenon also suggests that the Nazi party was attractive to some producers because of the promise of markets for producer goods.

Industrial production fell by almost half between 1929 and 1932; national income declined from 75.4 billion RM in 1928 to 45.2 billion RM in 1933. Unemployment accordingly mounted, to over 30 per cent of the civilian labour force in 1932, an annual average figure of 5.6 million. Unemployment was most severe in the major industrial regions of the

Ruhr and Silesia, but was less locally concentrated than in a country like Britain, for instance (there were few single industry towns like Jarrow, Solingen being one of the few exceptions). Nonetheless communist and socialist candidates met with success in the depressed industrial regions.

The elections of July 1932 saw the greatest electoral support for the Nazi party (37.2 per cent of the vote as against 35 per cent for all socialist parties), a position which was marginally reduced in later elections. Even so the Nazis remained the largest single party. Much research has been conducted into the minutiae of electoral support for the Nazi party; one crucial aspect was the support they received in rural areas. From 1930 the party specifically set out to appeal to small farmers and the experience of the Depression, with the fall in farm incomes, made that appeal the stronger. Whatever the detailed causative link there can be no doubt that the Nazi party and Hitler came to enjoy popular and sectional support as a direct result of the Depression and related deflation and unemployment.

The 'moderate' and deflationary policies of Chancellor Brüning proved unpopular on all sides and he was forced to resign in May 1932. Von Papen adopted a slightly more expansionist programme, designed to stimulate business profits. His successor from December 1932, Schleicher, put more emphasis on public works to reduce unemployment. These were insufficient to produce an immediate or magic cure for depression. Hitler was appointed Chancellor in January 1933. By this time there were glimmerings of recovery: unemployment was falling (the 1933 average was 4.8 million or 26.4 per cent). Some of the paraphernalia of state economic management had been assembled by piecemeal means before Hitler came to power: exchange controls, bilateral trading treaties, protective tariffs, agricultural support, public works. These were all to be extended and elaborated later.

7.3 Nazi Germany

Under the Nazi regime Germany achieved notable economic success, particularly evident in the reduction of unemployment. Indeed labour shortages developed before the outbreak of war. In the same years in Britain, for example, unemployment, although reduced, persisted. However, the rate of growth of total production in peacetime Nazi Germany was modest rather than spectacular, especially when compared with the growth of earlier years, or that of her major competitors. In examining the economic history of Nazi Germany commentators have highlighted the ideological and practical peculiarities of Nazi policy and, in particular, the part played by rearmament and war preparation in effecting recovery and growth. On the former point there is a strong consensus that Hitler and his party brought little new to the operation of the economy. The basic elements of policy (work creation through public works, exchange controls and economic protection, control over inflation) were largely elaborations of existing measures. It is important to remember also that recovery had begun before Hitler came to power.

On the question of rearmament there is less historiographical accord. Plans specifying war preparation dated from 1936, by which time unemployment had been largely removed. Further, as we shall see, post-war research suggests that even on the eve of war the German economy was inadequately prepared for war, thus casting doubt on the picture of a well-developed war machine. On the other hand, there is evidence of limited rearmament before 1936. Brüning indeed increased arms spending in 1931; such spending was above the levels earlier in the Weimar period. Moreover war preparation was seen not simply in terms of arms spending, but also in strategic building, road construction, etc.

Nazi economic ideas

Although the full title of the Nazi party was the National Socialist German Workers Party (NSDAP), it is clear that any socialist elements had disappeared long before 1933, and that the emphasis was much more on the nationalism. Before coming to power Hitler had sought support from manual workers; under the Nazi regime manual workers were to gain little. Average real incomes probably declined. The same might be said also for the social stratum most usually associated with support for the Nazi party before 1933, the *Mittelstand* (approximating to middle class, professional and commercial). Much of the early electoral appeal before 1933 was aimed at the middle classes. Nazi propagandists voiced strong criticism against large capital and big business, and in favour of small businesses. In particular they opposed department stores and Nazi thugs often vandalised such premises, especially when they were Jewish owned. On the other hand, little was done to weaken large capital after the Nazis came to power.

There was indeed little consistency in Nazi economic ideas. This might have stemmed in part from Hitler's lack of interest in, or simply ignorance of, economic matters. It was as, or more, likely a pragmatic adjustment to real demands. Different messages were given to different audiences for the sake of electoral support. Rantings against 'big capital' were moderated to distinguish between 'rapacious' capital – or money making money through banking and finance (especially unpopular if there were Jewish ownership) – and productive capital – fixed assets which produced goods. It was quite clear that well before 1933 there was no interest in taking over the means of production in any socialist sense.

There was one clear, consistent element in their thinking and that involved the policy towards agriculture and the social and economic perception of the agriculturalist. All political parties sought peasant support but the Nazis turned the peasant farmer (*Bauer*) into a mythical guardian of Aryan culture. Farming was placed above ordinary productive endeavour. In a radio speech in September 1933 the Reich Minister of food said, 'We need the *Bauer* as the blood source of the nation and we need him as the provider of food for the German people. Therefore it does not matter so much whether the *Bauer* obtains the highest possible price for his produce, so that his enterprise produces the highest possible revenue, but it does matter that the *Bauer* shall be firmly rooted in his soil and receive a fair wage.'

The great surge of political attention paid to the peasantry began in 1928 when Walter Darré joined the party. By 1932 peasant pressure groups had been effectively taken over by the Nazis. In return they were rewarded with large electoral support in rural areas and the food producers were rewarded with elaborate and extensive protection through tariffs and price support. The effect of such policies was to transfer costs to the consumer, the greatest relative burden being felt by the working class.

Nazi economic policy was essentially pragmatic; priorities changed over time. There were, however, some examples of consistency. As has just been pointed out there was a policy favouring farmers; there was consistent unease with 'liberal' economics, with a desire to extend control over resources rather than leave it to the vagaries of the market. There was the further perceived need for territorial expansion to secure resources; the removal (or suppression) of conflicts between capital and labour, the social whole subordinating individual self-interest (though this never meant dispossessing property owners, other than Jews of course); material advance and welfare for people. Hitler was really rather unconcerned with economics. For him economic questions were always to be subordinate to political matters, though it was necessary to compromise on these objectives as policies were pursued through the 1930s. Anti-semitism and concepts of racial superiority were consistent and major aspects of Nazi policy but not primarily of economic significance, though they had economic consequences.

Nazis in power

It is customary to divide the peacetime economy of Nazi Germany into two: the early period, 1933–36, was primarily concerned with removing unemployment; the second, after 1936, with war preparation. Although such a distinction is perhaps too rigid, given that expansion through war was a long-term objective of the Nazis, it remains appropriate to retain such a distinction for the purposes of historical examination. Removal of unemployment was not totally divorced from military or related expenditure. Armament factories provided work and were more attractive work places than older works; building, a labour-intensive activity, usefully employed many people and could have had direct or indirect military use.

Measures to employ the unemployed were an early priority. These took various forms, and most had been introduced in the late Weimar period. Expenditure on public works reached 750 million marks in 1932, for instance. Hitler extended such programmes, though without spending more on direct employment through public works; the Nazi regime did spend money to improve housing and transport and on land amelioration. Altogether about five billion RM or 4 per cent of GNP was used to promote employment. As long as such expenditures were effective investments to increase production and create new taxpayers they were not inflationary. Tax incentives were given to private industry for new investments, with priority to those who would employ more, not fewer, men. There were even tax incentives to employ domestic servants, who were usually women. Otherwise obstacles were put in the way of women taking employment in industry. From June 1933 marriage loans were made available to young couples, to become a grant if the wife did not seek or continue work. Employers were free to dismiss married women if this gave a job to a married man. This was consistent with Nazi values that women should fulfil a role as wives and mothers rather than wage earners. Similarly, young single men (under 25) could be required to make way for married bread winners (135 000 were so affected by 1935). Single women were expected to work. Both young men and women were subject to compulsory labour service on leaving school, in work corps. For women this commitment to work was designed only to last until marriage; they were then to make way for men. Reality did not always follow the design as smoothly as hoped. Women continued to work, especially in what, at the time, were customary occupations, in services, clerical jobs, as well as much work on the land. The restrictive policies were more successful in preventing women entering the labour market, rather than forcing them out. All in all the number of women in full-time employment remained remarkably stable. Indeed, when labour shortages developed later, it proved difficult to recruit women to work.

The reduction of unemployment in Nazi Germany was far more rapid than in other economies in western Europe. Indeed it has been described as miraculous. The combination of expenditure and compulsion was, however, too good to be true. Some of the unemployed disappeared from the statistics but did not reappear as employed. There were two reasons for this: first, the 'nazification' of the civil service brought some incompetent if ideologically sound people into statistical services. As a result a margin of unemployed failed to find their way on to the register; second, and more important, it became harder to register as unemployed. Definitions of unemployment became tighter in that a number of occupations, such as agriculture and forestry, ceased to be eligible for unemployment insurance. By 1935 about four million people worked in such occupations. It is impossible to say precisely how many of the unemployed were removed in this way. It was undoubtedly a minority but could have reached several hundred thousand. It is clear that, however successful the policies of real re-employment, some of the reduction in unemployment, at least before 1936, was a statistical rather than real phenomenon.

The extension of employment, more workers in receipt of wages and growing expenditure would be expected to have had some multiplier effect through the economy, though it was not recognised as such at the time. There was contemporarily more concern with the threat of inflation. In the short run there was indeed some consumer recovery. Consumer goods production increased faster than producer goods; total disposable income in the home market improved; more were employed and many were able to earn overtime pay. National Socialist policies appeared to be paying dividends, though in the very short run, in 1933, the improvement in employment was more the result of the injection of moneys under Schleicher and von Papen in the late Weimar period than the short-term results of Nazism. The upturn in consumerism was short-lived as the political priorities began to shift towards the production of investment goods. This became evident from 1934 and much more so from 1936. Such an adjustment, together with the need to resist inflationary pressures, demanded more controls over the market, especially the labour market.

Trade unions could have no place in the Nazi scheme of things. Storm-troopers occupied the central union offices on 2 May 1933. In their stead a single national body, with compulsory membership, was established, the German Labour Front. Collective bargaining, or even individually negotiated contracts, were prohibited. Local Trustees of Labour fixed wages and conditions. These local offices also kept records of employment of all workers, their skills, how often they changed jobs, etc.

As the re-employment of labour began to succeed, the main thrust of labour policy shifted to the allocation of labour. A Central Administration of Employment Service Board was introduced in 1935 which absorbed the functions of the labour exchange, vocational guidance and placement of apprentices. Like most things, this had been set up in the Weimar period; the Nazis elaborated on it. All such administrative controls are bound to be imperfect. They nonetheless indicate the manner in which the Nazi regime was willing to elaborate and extend such instruments, within an essentially capitalist economy, to allocate and control resources and the returns to those resources. Returns to labour, wages, were governed and limited in order to prevent a diversion from the growing priorities of the regime. These priorities involved an effective diversion of income from labour to capital, from consumption to investment. Wage controls were more effective than those over prices. Real wages probably fell from what they had been in 1931–32 when the Depression had reduced the cost of living. By 1938 they were barely above the level of 1928, as may be seen from the index of real wages:

Real wages
1913 = 100
1928 = 110
1931 = 125
1934 = 116
1938 = 112

Wages and private consumption declined as a proportion of national income.

The pay off for this was, of course, the elimination of unemployment, a reward that was lacking in much of the rest of Europe. As a form of compensation, and as a means of extending National Socialist propaganda, workers became part of the 'strength through joy' programme. This was a means of bringing recreation and holiday facilities. In parallel the 'beauty of labour' campaign set out to improve working conditions. Both these organisations were subordinate to the Labour Front.

Such endeavours were expensive (though less so than armament spending). By 1938 State (Reich) spending reached 33 per cent of GNP against 17 per cent in 1932. Such an increase could only come from greater income, largely from taxation. In 1932 taxes were 25.4 per cent of NI, by 1938 they had increased to 29.5 per cent. In the short run tax rates changed little (and there were some reductions to stimulate employment) but the increase in taxpayers naturally increased the tax take for government. In addition to this was a certain amount of borrowing, some of which constituted deficit spending as borrowing from the central bank, despite the fact that this breached the rules of financial orthodoxy. The means by which this was done was through the creation of bogus companies, which in turn borrowed money from the bank. So-called MEFO bills were issued, as commercial rather than government bills, and as such were legally discounted by the central bank, thereby adding to money supply. (Incidentally they were not redeemed when this fell due in 1938.) These enabled some increase in government expenditure without an increase in income. Government borrowing was not necessarily inflationary, especially as the resultant expenditures added to productive resources. MEFO bills themselves circulated in the banking community. In effect they were a form of money. Total money supply doubled between 1933 and 1938 and other 'non-economic' controls were used to control inflation. It is the 'concealed' government expenditure financed from MEFO bills which leads recent writers, like James (1985), to conclude that real military expenditure was higher before 1936 than has long been supposed (see p. 140).

The balance of payments was at least as pressing an economic problem as any other. Devaluation of the pound sterling and other currencies had left the mark over-valued. Devaluation of the mark was resisted, again largely from fear of inflation. Rigid exchange controls and a series of bilateral trading agreements were instituted, from 1931, and extended thereafter (see Chap. 3). The Nazi government, under Finance Minister Hjalmar Schacht, took up and elaborated such schemes with the 'new plan' in 1934. The purpose of this plan was to minimise foreign currency expenditure by diverting foreign trade, as far as possible, to those trading partners with which Germany had clearing arrangements. Germany was able to effect some marginal trade diversion to these countries (principally in south-east Europe and Latin America) but together they did not make up a complete trading area. It continued to be necessary, therefore, for Germany to trade with other economies in and beyond Europe. Imports from these countries had to be paid for in internationally acceptable foreign exchange. In order to conserve such expenditures all imports required government approval. In this way not only were the volume and value of imports regulated but also their source. Thus government was able to extend control over foreign trade without a direct monopoly or other interference in private ownership or production.

The 'rationing' of foreign exchange was part and parcel of the broader policy of autarky or self-sufficiency. In part this objective was dictated by circumstance – the difficulty of funding imports with an over-valued currency – but this was not the only explanation. Hitler had long rejected the value of the market as an economic regulator and had expressed his ideal of removing Germany from the uncertainties of the international economy. It was, however, clearly impossible to become perfectly self-sufficient. German agriculture was not able to feed the population: imports were essential. Up to a point the clearing arrangements were one way round the problem but it was nonetheless necessary to find some exports to pay for the imports. Further, essential supplies also had to be bought elsewhere – coal from Poland, iron ore from Sweden, oil from Russia and the USA. Germany could not reduce her dependence on imports from states where she had to pay in gold-convertible currencies. Perversely the build-up of armaments and war preparation increased the need for imports and yet made the political and commercial desirability of autarky all the greater.

The four-year plan of 1936

War preparation began in earnest with the 1936 four-year plan under the direction of Hermann Goering. Hitler gave specific orders that Germany should be ready for war in four years. However, in a more general sense it began before this date. This can be seen in an increase in some direct military spending (1.2 billion RM in 1932, 3.6 billion RM in 1934, 5.4 billion RM in 1935) and in related expenditures on building military barracks, roads and communications. Thus there was a clear acceleration in military spending in 1936 but not a sudden change of course. The needs of the plan put great strains on the economy. Shortages of foreign exchange necessitated an ever-widening search for import substitutes. The age of ersatz or substitute production was born. (Schacht, the finance minister who had devoted so much attention to husbanding foreign exchange and trade relations, resigned his post in protest at the anticipated costs of autarky, not because he feared war but rather because he feared inflationary pressures.)

Costs became less important than strategic considerations and import savings. The country was scoured for iron ore; previously uneconomic resources now became worth exploiting. Synthetic rubber and oil plants were extended. This was not an economically efficient process, nor was it hugely successful. Germany did not become self-sufficient; it did become less import-dependent. Some industries benefited enormously, notably IG Farben the chemical combine. This company produced the synthetic rubber (buna), and a synthetic fuel oil from coal. About half of the oil consumed (by 1939) was derived from coal. It was not, however, a perfect substitute for petroleum, being more suitable as a fuel for stationary engines. Iron and steel and engineering sectors also gained enormously from government demands for war preparation. Firms like IG Farben and Krupps became so closely involved that their owners were tried as war criminals after the war. Throughout these years, though, industrial leaders remained subordinate to political. Other industries were less enthusiastic about the plan as their commercial independence was reduced. Import restrictions naturally adversely affected some sectors, especially in consumer goods which had a low priority.

One factor behind the international trading difficulties of the Nazi economy was the failure of the agricultural sector to reach expected levels of production. In common with most other parts of Europe Germany protected its farmers. In 1931, well before the Nazi period, Germany had the highest tariffs on arable crops as well as a 97 per cent wheat milling ratio. The volume of all food imports fell by 38 per cent between 1928 and 1933. The Nazis extended protection to save imports and controls to regulate prices, especially to restrain inflation as prices recovered from the low levels of the Depression. In addition to this was the ideological favour shown in Nazi propaganda to the farmer. It is difficult to judge, however, how far such romanticism was an influence upon, or a rationalisation of, more down-to-earth policies.

In 1933 the government set up the National Food Estate (*Reichsnähr-stand*). This fixed all prices and production quotas for food crops. This is a further example of the extensive controls introduced in the economy. Accompanying this were measures to relieve farm debts and ensure entailed inheritance. In the following year the 'battle for production' was launched, stressing the need to save imports. Evidently this was much more dictated by economic considerations than ideological ones. The four-year plan further stressed priority of domestic production over imports, but with limited success. More potatoes and sugar beets were produced but grain failed to increase. More particularly, there was a worsening deficit on animal fats and vegetable oils. Price support for farmers failed to prevent the drift from the land to better wages in factory work. The income gap between industrial and agricultural work remained.

With the four-year plan for war in 1936 there was a higher priority given to raw material imports over foodstuffs. Food production came under Goering's control. The battle for production was intensified in 1937; the agricultural area was extended by bringing marginal land into cultivation. Hitler also began to stress the need for expansion to find more living space for the German people, partly because of the disappointing levels of self-sufficiency. The battle for production was a qualified success. By 1938–9 Germany had attained 83 per cent self-sufficiency in foodstuffs overall, a high figure but one short of expectations. Thus a margin of import demand remained and the extensive system of trade agreements with European food exporters was perfected to help meet this demand. Controls were less than perfectly effective and, as might be expected, a black market developed. Indeed the need for more productive capacity, for living space for Germans, was one of the factors behind expansion and eventual war.

All these factors raise the question of how successful were Nazi economic policies. It is clear that when war broke out in 1939 Germany was not fully prepared for war. It is also uncertain how far rearmament contributed to economic recovery and growth in the 1930s. War preparation after 1936 contributed only a little to re-employment. Unemployment had by that time ceased to be a major economic problem; in fact, labour shortages developed. In 1937 the four-year plan office took responsibility for labour allocation; in June 1938 a decree enabled the direction of labour to areas of particular importance and in 1939 civilian labour was subject to effective economic conscription (though this was later rescinded).

It is also difficult to see the four-year plan as having had major significance in general economic recovery and growth. Richard Overy (1982) has suggested that road building and the motor industry had a much larger part in recovery, before 1938, than armaments *per se*. Motor vehicles also had a potential military use, though it is difficult to say the same of road building. The first *Autobahns* ran north to south and had no obvious strategic value. Indeed there was much military opposition to these new highways initially. The main point is that building roads was highly labour-intensive and so contributed to the reduction in unemployment. The motor industry showed a big jump in production after 1932 and was encouraged by Hitler's personal interest in 'motorisation' and the extension of popular car ownership. Hitler is said to have given detailed specifications to Dr Porsche over the design of the Volkswagen or people's car. However, the famous Beetle was built only in prototype in Hitler's Germany. Ford and Opel and another 13 motor companies were much more important in terms of production. A stimulus to demand was given in April 1933 with the abolition of car tax. Domestic production increased. By 1934 only 9 per cent of cars were imported compared with 40 per cent in 1928. Vehicle exports grew from 94.5 million RM in 1934 to 260 million RM in 1938. By 1938 also, well over one million jobs had been created directly by roads and cars (Overy (1982) gives a total of 1 150 000). Cars and commercial vehicles were among the fastest growing of industries in the 1930s.

Motor vehicles created demand not only for jobs but raw materials and semi-manufactures and a vast range of related services. Armaments had a limited multiplier effect on the economy. It is nonetheless true that vehicle production was of longer-term military and strategic significance. Car, lorry and tractor production facilities could readily be converted to military purposes; the Volkswagen chassis was used for a military vehicle long before the famous Beetle was sold to the public. It is thus not possible to draw a hard and fast line between industries of military and non-military significance.

At a more general level it is possible to conclude that the German economy under Nazi control was able to reabsorb unemployed labour more successfully than elsewhere but that it was not able to achieve high levels of efficiency, growth of production or productivity. Labour productivity (in industry) grew by only 1.3 per cent per annum 1929–38; over a similar period in Britain (1929–36) productivity grew at an annual rate of 2.5 per cent. Most competing economies developed more successfully. Over the longer period 1913–1937/8, German GNP grew by 36.4 per cent, British by 46.5 per cent, despite the relative stagnation of the British economy in the 1920s.

Thus the Nazi economy grew at the cost of squeezing consumption and real wages and diverting real resources to capital goods, as these index numbers show.

Index of industrial production

1928 = 100	1932	1938
capital goods	45.7	135.9
consumer	78.1	107.8

The reabsorption of unemployment was accompanied by growing domestic controls in the economy, restrictions on labour mobility and liberty and ever tightening protection of foreign trade. Employed workers elsewhere in Europe did better than their German counterparts. Rigid price and wage controls were extensive and proved necessary to restrict the inflationary pressures that built up in the economy, arising from government deficit, coupled with increasing purchasing power in the economy. The stimulus to the economy from growing popular consumption, which was important in British recovery, was much weaker in Germany. In part this can be explained by the disappointing growth in food production. Working class consumption of basic foodstuffs like meat, wheat bread, milk, vegetables and fruit all declined; only rye bread, potatoes and cheese showed an increase. The high cost of foodstuffs limited the discretionary income of workers. Armaments diverted resources from the civilian economy rather than generated general economic development. In 1939 some of these armaments had to be used as exports to pay for food imports.

By the outbreak of war the four-year plan for war preparation had not yet run its course, and it was anyway behind schedule. The plan had been to produce all the nation's oil requirements. The 50 per cent produced was a real technological achievement but was a long way short of the target. Oil imports were very vulnerable to blockade. Similarly the plan had anticipated producing 50 per cent rubber and iron ore and a third of textiles and animal fats from domestic resources. However, it proved necessary to import a third of raw materials, including 80–90 per cent rubber and 99 per cent aluminium. Shortages of raw materials vital for military production became evident. The inclusion of Austria and the industrial regions of Czechoslovakia provided some help – particularly the engineering and armaments industries of Bohemia – but these countries also needed to import. Iron ore imports were largely met by supplies from Sweden; some other supplies of coal, timber, foodstuffs and crude oil were provided by the USSR following the trade agreement of 1939. However, despite such moves, there is something to support the idea that Hitler was forced to risk war in 1939 because of domestic economic difficulties.

For some time there was a view that explained German expansion and eventual war as having been determined by economic necessity – a war of plunder arising out of domestic economic crisis. However, the overwhelming historical opinion favours the explanation that conquest was a political goal and that Hitler wanted the economy to be directed towards that end. Real resistance to German advance and war was a risk in 1939 because the plans for war were by no means complete.

7.4   Conclusion

It is well established and generally accepted that the Nazi regime did not gain power as the result of big business pressure. It appears to be equally true that the regime, in power, was by no means the handmaiden of commerce and industry. Before coming to power Hitler had spoken vehemently against capitalism, especially big capital. In power the Nazis had circumscribed business activity by a host of controls, over prices, dividends, trade and the access to imports. The state itself became more important in the economy through the 1930s, especially after 1936, with the four-year plan for war preparation. Even apart from this the rearmament drive had made all branches of the economy increasingly dependent on demand from the government or armed forces. The market diminished as an economic determinant to be replaced to an ever-growing extent by central decision-making. This has led Richard Overy (1975), one of the foremost scholars on the subject, to draw comparisons between National Socialist Germany and the planned economy of Stalinist Russia!

While it is undoubtedly true that market forces were reduced in the Nazi economy, comparisons with the USSR are exaggerated. There was no dispossession of businessmen or industrialists or other owners of property, because they were capitalists, in Nazi Germany. There was dispossession of Jews and others for racialist reasons; and other property owners or businesses often benefited as a result. Private property and capitalist modes of production remained essentially unaltered, indeed there was some reprivatisation (in banking and other spheres) after 1936. It is appropriate to consider, also, who gained from Nazi policies: as we have seen real incomes were held down and even reduced, if modestly, to 1938. Returns to capital, on the other hand, increased. Business profits showed great increases as recovery and the rearmament programme proceeded. Naturally not all businesses gained equally; some iron and steel manufacturers, for instance, were much concerned at the opening of the Goering, state-owned, steel works in the four-year plan, though these sectors, together with mining, were among the major beneficiaries. IG Farben, the giant chemical combine, also gained considerably. Profits moved from a steady 70 million RM per year 1933–1935, to 140 million RM in 1936 and 300 million RM in 1940.

IG Farben, of course, was hardly typical, but the example illustrates the returns for some businesses in the Nazi economy. Arguably also, all business of any scale made gains from the elimination of trade union activity and effective control over wages. However, it is no more appropriate to see the state as subordinate to the whims of industry than to see the control of the economy as comparable to socialist planning. Ian Kershaw (1985) has examined and explained the complexity of the relationship between business and government with great clarity. Business, including industry and large landowners, represented a cartel of interests in Nazi Germany, one of a number of influential pressure groups, along with the armed forces, the Nazi party and, later, the SS and related police functions. In reality it was often difficult to distinguish between the political interests of government and the commercial interests of industry. IG Farben managers helped to organise the four-year plan, as political leaders were less commercially competent. It was commonplace for there to be a close relationship between servants of the state and directors of industrial enterprises. (To a considerably lesser degree such symbiosis can be detected in earlier periods, in Wilhelmine Germany for instance.) Kershaw (1985) points out that gradually, especially with the preparation for war after 1936, the Nazi and SS police factions gained more influence in decision-making. By the same token there was some decline in the influence of the business/industry group (this can be illustrated by the removal from office of Schacht), though it never became altogether subordinate to the state. Ironically there was more real economic independence for business during the war than before. Thus Nazi Germany was neither a planned economy, in the sense of being subject wholly to political determination, nor a state exclusively representing the interests of big business or 'monopoly capital'.

Nazi Germany was, in economic terms as in other respects, peculiar and distinctive. The characteristics were generated by some degree of historical continuity – the civil service and structure of industry were not short-term creations but had been carried over from the years preceding even the First World War – and the much more immediate response to severe economic crisis after 1929 and the demagogy of the Hitler years which followed.

7.5   Further reading

There is an enormous amount of useful reading available on the German economy between the wars; these can be only highly selective suggestions. General economic history is provided by G. Stolper (1967) *The German Economy 1870 to the Present* (London: Weidenfeld and Nicolson) though it is now rather dated. Much more up-to-date is H–J. Braun (1990) *The German Economy in the Twentieth Century. The German Reich and the Federal Republic* (London: Routledge). K. Hardach (1980) *The Political Economy of Germany in the Twentieth Century* (Berkeley: University of California Press) is a clear historical account. A more quantitative analysis is to be found in A. Sommariva and G. Tullio (1987) *German Macroeconomic History, 1888–1979* (London: Macmillan). The inflation is covered in various works. F. Ringer (1969) *The German Inflation of 1923* (Oxford: Oxford University Press) gives a colourful account of the experience of hyper-inflation. The recent book by P.J. Lyth (1990) *Inflation and the Merchant Economy: The Hamburg Mittelstand* (Oxford and New York: Berg) is a detailed account in one major city. Many years ago a 'monetary' explanation of causes was offered in C. Bresciani-Turroni (1937) *The Economics of Inflation. A Study of Currency Depreciation in Post-war Germany 1914–1923* (London: Allen and Unwin). An examination of causes from an essentially Keynesian stance can be found in K. Laursen and J. Pedersen (1964) *The German Inflation: 1918–1923* (Amsterdam) and a broader economic survey, and up-to-date account, is in C–L. Holtfrerich (1986) *The German Inflation, 1914–1923. Causes and Effects in International Perspective* (New York: De Gruyter). The advent of depression is examined by T. Balderston (1983) 'The beginnings of depression in Germany', *Economic History Review*, **36**, pp. 395–415. This contains a critique of the earlier article by P. Temin (1971) 'The beginnings of depression in Germany', *Economic History Review*, **24**, pp. 240–248. A more general analysis of this question, including the political dimension, is to be found in various works by Harold James. Especially thorough is his book (1985) *The German Slump, Politics and Economics 1924–1936* (Oxford: Oxford University Press). Some of this material is explored in his article (1984): 'Causes of the German banking crisis, 1931', *Economic History*

Review, **37**, pp. 68–87. Financial questions are dealt with in great detail in (1985) *The Reichsbank and Public Finance, 1924–33* (Frankfurt: Fred Knapp Verlag). The background to Nazi power is examined in contrasting ways in I. Kershaw (ed.) (1990) *Weimar: Why did German Democracy Fail?* (London: Weidenfeld and Nicolson) and H.A. Turner (1985) *German Big Business and the Rise of Hitler* (Oxford: Oxford University Press).

The Nazi period is covered in breadth by Ian Kershaw (1985) in *The Nazi Dictatorship* (London: Arnold). This goes beyond economic questions. A good, brief analysis of the economy is R.J. Overy (1982) *The Nazi Economic Recovery 1932–8* (London: Macmillan). He examines specific aspects of the economy in these articles: (1987) 'Unemployment in the Third Reich', *Business History*, **29** and (1975) 'Cars, roads and economic recovery in Germany, 1932–38', *Economic History Review*, **28**, pp. 466–483. Agriculture under the Nazis is well covered by J.F. Farquharson (1976) *The Plough and the Swastika, the NSDAP and Agriculture in Germany, 1928–1945* (London: Sage). Borchardt's controversial views are summarised in K. Borchardt (1982) *Wachstum, Krisen, Handlungsspiel-raume der Wirstschaftspolitik* (Göttingen: Vandenhoek und Ruprecht).

8

Italy and Spain

8.1 Italy

Italy enjoyed a long secular boom in industry and trade between 1896 and the First World War. Giorgio Fuà (1964) has calculated that the value added by industrial production doubled in constant prices between 1896 and 1913, when it accounted for almost one quarter of national income. Certain industries – chemicals, iron and steel, engineering – apparently expanded at an annual rate exceeding 12 per cent. This industrialisation comprehended both heavy investment goods manufacturing and production based on new technology. Growth was much slower in traditional industries such as textiles, leather-working and food-processing, although in 1913 the largest industry in terms of output, capital and employment was still cotton. The causes of the Italian economic renaissance are contested; especially since both parties to the debate, liberal and statist, have right on their side. Stressing entrepreneurial influences is justified by historians such as Alexander Gershenkron and Stefano Fenoaltea in the context of the international business cycle, but it is impossible to dissever market opportunity, innovation, and financial responsiveness as forces for change from subsidisation, protectionism and public contracting after the 1887 tariff reforms. The development of the industrial economy was undoubtedly a 'mixed enterprise', and the argument in essence rages around the rank order of the various influences. The best example of the inter-connection between public and private initiative is the development of hydro-electricity, upon which much of the country's industrialisation depended, in the absence of coal. Engineering firms in Piedmont or Lombardy, reckoned to be uncompetitive because of the cost of imported fuel, gained in confidence as a result of hydroelectrification. Many Italian plants possessed the most modern equipment in the world in 1914.

This was of course a limited field of experience. Relatively few Italian industrial companies compared in size or reputation with German, American, British or French firms. Yet the promise of Italian expansion, when labour was cheap and abundant, had attracted foreign interests, especially in banking. Almost all the larger banks with commitments in industry and trade, like the Banca Commerciale Italiana or the Credito Italiano, founded in about 1894–96, on the ashes of a crash in 1893, were German or Swiss in inspiration, organisation or ownership. French, Austrian and even British financial capital was also committed, through Italian banks, to the new wonder economy. In the same period, between 1896 and 1912, were founded many of the leading Italian industrial combines of the twentieth century, including Fiat, Pirelli and Montecatini. The role of the state was important in the provision of contracts or subsidies especially for strategic manufacturers, and this in particular attracted German investment.

The miracle was flawed, however. If the banks were the engineers of development, they carried uncomfortable weights to handicap their freedom of action. First, the legacy of Italian investment banking before the 1893 crash burdened successor enterprises with much unproductive or politically sensitive capital. Secondly, after 1907, the devious Giolitti and his political circle diverted much investment into projects dear to the hearts of their cronies. Political considerations weighed heavily in investment decisions and this entanglement vitiated the prudent and successful reforms of Sonnino in the field of public finance in the mid-1890s. Thirdly, significant as was Italian industrial development, it was a sectional advance in a still rural, under-productive economy. Almost all the benefits that were not confined to the political elite accrued to the provinces of Piedmont, Liguria and Lombardy where both industrialisation and the provision of social overhead capital were most highly developed. Italy was at a natural disadvantage, having few exportable resources except manpower and certain specialised foodstuffs before the growth of manufactures in the later nineteenth century. Centuries of running backwards since the Renaissance had created a poor environment for internal expansion, except in the north-west. Even urbanisation is no measure of modernisation because in the Italian south and centre most peasants lived in hill cities and worked in the fields round about.

The outbreak of war in 1914 caused tensions in Italian political and business circles hardly matched elsewhere. The industrial base was shot through with German and Austrian influences and the risks of breaking this relationship were considerable; but so also were the potential advantages of sequestration. There was no powerful commercial predisposition towards either the Allies or the central powers. For many businessmen the attractions of neutrality were hard to resist. In the political world also the debate was furious. In the event Italy entered the war on the Allied side in 1915, because that was what an influential group of politicians wanted, but also in fear (and some anticipation of success) of Austria–Hungary.

Italy entered the war half-heartedly. In spite of the pre-war expansion of industry, iron and steel production, heavy engineering and small arms manufacture were still incapable of supplying domestic needs. Italy in 1914, for example, manufactured only about one-third of the steel turned out in Austria and had to import a fifth or more of her needs. Her armies in 1915 were ludicrously under-equipped, and yet by 1918 munitions production had been so successful as to make the army that over-ran the northern Veneto almost careless of its artillery. Aircraft as well as cannons, heavy trucks as well as shells poured out of Italian factories, propelled by hydroelectricity and manned by thousands of recent recruits out of rural Italy. Businessmen became unimaginably prosperous, often by exploiting state subsidies.

Yet the costs were high. The national debt, swollen by a large portion of the 41 billion lire expended on war supplies, pensions and food subsidies, threatened to become unmanageable as annual deficits on the budget multiplied to reach 23 billion lire in 1918–19. The south in particular suffered the financial drawbacks of a war economy concentrated upon the north-west, because its already meagre savings were used to finance industrial investment. Mobilisation was far from popular because it seemed too selective and even partisan. The same bias in favour of pivotal industrial entrepreneurs disturbed the equanimity of the business community. Inflation not only destroyed savings but forced up the cost of living by opening up a wider differential between earnings and prices. Italy was short of capital for investment after the withdrawal of German intermediaries in the banking system. The government eased the flow of credit but at the cost of widening its annual deficits. Expansion in a limited section of the economy was really too rapid after 1917. The banks holding much of the credit available to industry became victims of contested takeovers by industrialists desperate both to obtain credit and to deny it to their competitors.

The economic benefits of the war therefore were segmental and speculative. The minor strategic success and the uncertainties created by unresolved frontier disputes in the post-war settlement were scant compensation for the social divisions and political bombast bequeathed by the experience of war. In particular the war had exacerbated industrial unrest, allowed revolutionaries to find a platform that did not collapse on impact and embittered further the already tense relations between town and country and between rural landowners and their dependent peasants. Had it produced a statesman of wider vision than was provided by the discredited liberal establishment of Giolitti or Sonnino, circumstances might have been different and the rise of mere demagoguery indefinitely postponed.

The crisis that led to the rise of fascism, and might alternatively have favoured another species of despotism, was a compound of political intransigence, short-sightedness and duplicity with intellectual pride and economic instability. Mussolini could not have come to power so opportunely without the ignominious collapse of the liberal state after 1920, but a precipitant of this state of affairs was the severity of the post-war recession in the north.

As elsewhere the war economy was sustained for several months after the Armistice by the difficulties of changing direction rapidly in matters of economic planning. This carry-over spread further into a headlong restocking boom which lulled industrialists and financiers as much as politicians into the belief that prosperity could be maintained. Firms like Fiat, Pirelli, Montecatini, Ansaldo and Ilva amended their production schedules from war to peacetime commodities with little disruption, at the same time as the battle for control of the banks was resumed by the industrial plutocrats of the north-west. Government finances continued in disarray and the balance of payments fell seriously into deficit. Pent-up savings were expended on goods and services not readily available in the domestic economy. In the meantime revolutionary fervour, fomented by opportunism and socialist self-confidence, began to perturb capitalists and bourgeois before the crash late in 1920. In the recession, banks, industrial firms and commercial enterprises failed, while prudent retrenchment by over-exposed business interests was limited by militant opposition to reduced living standards. Various syndicalist organisations sprang up to defend or promote the interests of assorted groups in society. Fascism and bolshevism confronted each other as the politicians, socialists, radicals, liberals and catholics, performed their macabre dance of death in Rome. Unlike Spain, where the salvation of property was engineered in a conventional military *coup d'état*, in Italy the putative strong man who in due course seized control was an outsider, who by the means of his own self-propaganda could be portrayed as both revolutionary and conservator, appeasing the conventional craving for law and order (against anarchists and bolshevists) while embodying in his personality the amoral nationalism of d'Annunzio and the collective urgency of the syndicalists whom he had weaned away from Marxism. Fascism contained a thread of theoretical coherence, but like *Il Duce* the movement shifted with the current of events. Much of the impulse to make change was opportunistic or owed as much to antique fantasy as it did to modern *étatisme*. One result of this is to suggest strongly that the Fascist era, for all its obeisance to planning and technological expertise, built its economic monuments on sand; there is a sense of the provisional and the arbitrary in most of the initiatives associated with Mussolini.

One of Mussolini's economic priorities, so he proclaimed, was to 'ruralise' Italy, which, since Italy had perhaps the largest number of households in the countryside in 1920 in western Europe, was a curious ambition. Fascist agrarian policy was an amalgam of ideals and expedients that was often contradictory. Moreover many of the startling claims of success made by the regime were not only exaggerated but also frequently misleading. Part of the problem was that policy varied according to the prevailing political affiliations of the rural population. Peasants were by no means all Fascist supporters and although some of the old landed elite was left undisturbed by Mussolini's public preference for the peasantry – and was therefore accordingly grateful – the pattern of intervention by the state in agrarian institutions was very variable. Radical, revolutionary peasant communities were broken – for which later the discredited *squadristas* were blamed – and open violence or truculent suspicion between official and local interests in liberal, catholic or even just independent-minded rural communities were widespread, especially in the 1920s. The bitter novels about the Abruzzese *cafoni* of Ignazio Silone are an effective commentary upon Mussolini's friendship for his Italian peasants. Even when peasants were not disaffected they often impeded the agricultural plans of the government. The 'battle for grain' begun in 1925, for instance, made little headway against peasants reluctant to change their ways and to surrender part of their livestock. In general, however, the Italian rural community acquiesced in Fascist agrarian policy. Mussolini courted popularity among the land-owning peasantry, especially among those newly enfeoffed by the state, and he increased his hold upon this influential group further by selective land reform in other districts, usually aimed at the property of his political opponents. The Fascist rapprochement with the Church in 1929 was also greeted with satisfaction in many rural districts, especially in areas where the regime had been regarded with suspicion in its aggressively anti-clerical phase.

Agrarian policy was not comprehensive. The driving force was autarky, but the means to achieve this were necessarily modified through time. The Fascists are celebrated for two 'initiatives': the battle for grain, proclaimed in a typically turgid manner by *Il Duce* in 1925, was the cornerstone of self-sufficiency, although the results were equivocal. The first objective was to overcome Italian dependence upon imported wheat, which had reached embarrassing levels in 1923–24. In the late 1920s, with cultural conditions generally favourable, a concentrated effort to extend the area and impove the yield of wheat in the traditional wheat-growing districts of the north and centre would have been sufficient, for by the mid-1930s the productivity of cereals in the north had increased by at least one-third and already approached the yields expected in northern France. The campaign, however, became obsessional. Wheat displaced many other crops and in the mountainous centre and in the south the programme undertaken by the government caused the loss of much livestock and thus reduced manure available. Yields in the south showed some improvement, but the returns on the arid, barren soils of the region were still very poor by any European standard. The culture of wheat required greater inputs of purchased seed, fertilisers and pesticides than peasants could freely afford and it disturbed the ecological balance of Italian agriculture in at least half the country.

Less contentious was the Fascist policy of reclamation, described as *integrale* because it comprehended drainage, irrigation, land settlement, road-building, and, as a hopeful touch, electrification. Everyone thinks of the Pontine marshes in this context, not least because Mussolini chose to emphasise the success of reclamation in that quarter after the 1928 'Mussolini Law'. The Pontine marshes had been partly drained before 1914, but the Fascists deserve credit for the achievement between 1928 and 1935. The new province of Littoria in 1936 consisted essentially of family farms carved out of the former swamp, settled by veterans introduced into Latium from the Po Valley. In another sense it also exemplified the leader's preoccupation with rural virtues – agrarian *coloni* were to be the backbone of the military state in which he was increasingly interested. In practice Fascist reclamation policy was built upon Liberal precedents, especially in its emphasis upon hydraulic techniques. In districts equally barren or under-populated, such as the southern hill country where more complex irrigation works, reafforestation and terracing were required, progress was very much slower. It is thought that only about 250 000 hectares, costing perhaps eight billion lire, were actually improved in the Fascist era and only about 10 000 landless peasant farmers were given land in the 1930s. There were, however, some other benefits. Malaria was successfully reduced in the country as a whole. Unemployment too was relieved by such grandiose public works, especially in the coastal zone from Tuscany to Campania where a new network of roads was also planned and partly constructed. About one-third of all jobs created by the public works policy of the regime was provided in agrarian reclamation.

Altogether, however, the greatest rural economic problem in the middle years of the Fascist era was the deflation which was precipitated in

1926 and merged with the worldwide Depression after 1929. One symptom of this squeeze was the collapse of several rural, often Catholic, banks. Much of the trade in land that had turned peasants into proprietors in the first quarter of the century was founded upon easy credit. With the burden of debt exacerbated after 1926, not only were many existing landowners embarrassed but new or would-be purchasers of rural property were deterred from the adventure. One estimate suggests that the number of landed estates declined by about 10 per cent in the 1920s, to reach 2.9 million in 1931, and did not significantly increase again in the years up to the war. On the other hand, landlessness was reduced, not only by emigration, by perhaps 1.3 million households in the years between 1925 and 1936. This assault upon the rural population without a stake in the land was organised on several fronts, through leaseholding, share-cropping and other forms of tenancy, even though the products that would have made these minuscule holdings viable – fruit, vegetables, olives, wine – were never subsidised nor officially protected. The incongruity of a policy combining preference for commodities most efficiently produced on good-sized farms and for a numerous 'free' peasantry is plain to see, but it should be understood differently, since Fascist *economic* policies were seldom dovetailed into their social philosophy except by way of rhetoric. Peasants were potential allies when not overbid by the greater claims of rural magnates, but they were also, more importantly, the soldiery upon which the state would depend in its search for glory.

Industry and commercial functions such as banking played a less prominent part in Mussolini's patterns of thought. As the state became more totalitarian and was redefined as a military expression of his imperial ambitions, so all aspects of economic policy were drawn into the network of political control. The close association of corporatism and Fascism needs some qualification, for Mussolini remained for long unenthusiastic about corporative organisations that reflected an establishment he distrusted and despised. Only as *étatisme* became the overriding object of his philosophy, after he had himself become symbolic of the state, could the circle surrounding *Il Duce* readily embrace corporatist ideas and practices. That said, Mussolini had needed to rely upon some established power structures in order to overcome those he believed to be more inimical from the earliest period of his ascendancy. Much of the popular support he received in 1922–24 came from various sorts of conservatives appalled by industrial unrest and the Bolshevist menace. Also, some of the intellectual underpinning of the new Fascist policy was supplied by cartelists among businessmen, by syndicalists among labour leaders deterred by the threat of anarchy and by the romantics who had learnt a great deal from the episode of the Fiume 'free state' in 1920, where ideas later incorporated into Fascism originated. In short, there is no doubt that in 1922–24 Mussolini was riding a tiger. His more fervent supporters were distrusted by the business community for their violence, unpredictable behaviour and amorality. Liberal and Catholic Italy could be appeased by success in turning the revolutionary tide but only if the Fascists themselves appeared to be more responsible to the established interests. Mussolini's dilemma was not resolved until after the Matteotti crisis had passed. Fortunately, however, his political inconsistency could be overlooked in a period of unprecedented boom. When the Red scare had subsided, Italian industrialists and bankers enjoyed five years of rising production and buoyant markets which coincided with the first phase of fascist administration, 1922–26. As in the rest of the world the post-war boom had ended noisily and acrimoniously in depression. The new government in 1922–23 restored equilibrium and set aside many liberal schemes to regulate business in the country as a concession to the industrialists. Those companies like Ansaldo or the Banco di Roma which had faltered in 1920–21 were rescued by the government. De' Stefani, the Treasury Minister, went further by making a severe reduction in the levy on 'excess war profits', by reintroducing private life assurance and by handing back telephone operations to private companies. The index of manufacturing production rose by about 7 per cent per annum between 1921 and 1925 to reach 83 in the last year (1938=100) and the Italian economy was increasingly diversified by new initiatives, including new industries in artificial fibres, chemicals, electrical and automotive engineering. In as much as the government already had a conscious economic plan before 1926 it was already autarkic. The regime encouraged innovations which led to import saving, which had the effect of extending the industrial base of Italy. As such developments in the 1920s could be turned to advantage in the 1930s when Mussolini's attention became fixed upon imperial aggrandisement and the martial state.

The boom inevitably caused inflation, aggravated by a severe balance of payments crisis in 1925–26. The rein over industrial production was tightened and the business community, its good feelings no longer essential to the survival of the regime, was disciplined. Fascist syndicalism was allowed to reassert itself in a major engineering strike in the north-west which roused the spectre of an officially sponsored epoch of industrial unrest. The government went further by creating the Ministry of Corporations. These new political initiatives were complemented by deflationary measures, including the revaluation of the lira at a level (90 = £1 sterling) that was a severe test of Italian business efficiency. Whether it was intended, the effect was to choke off the export boom and force manufacturers to turn ever more inwards to the domestic market. Curiously in face of the balance of payments crisis, no thought was devoted to the prospect of an import boom with an overvalued lira. In any event the cause of the imbalance in 1925, chiefly on account of investment in intermediate goods not available in Italy, was ignored. The risks of a worsening crisis were, however, minimised by draconian measures to support the new exchange rate – higher tariffs, higher interest rates and in 1927 an all-round cut of 10 per cent in wages, all of which effectively reduced domestic purchasing power.

The economy was not isolated from the world Depression in the 1930s. Several *dirigiste* measures adopted before 1929, such as the enforced cartelisation of industries through employers' corsortia, extensive public works and the introduction of certain welfare benefits, were applied with greater enthusiasm in the early 1930s, even though the Government remained committed to deflationary remedies by reducing money supply, cutting wages and fixing prices. The recession of 1931 was fruitful in providing the incentive towards corporatist innovations. Ministries and public agencies proliferated; centrally directed planning became normal and normative; control over investments, profits, dividends, earnings, benefits and work practices was tightened in the interests of the all-seeing State. The Italian banking system, seriously compromised yet again in 1930–31, was totally reformed. The investment functions of bankers were abrogated and replaced by bodies such as IMI (1931) and IRI (1933) which were charged first to buy up frozen assets tied to the banks with money provided out of taxes and then to channel investment in industry and commerce according to priorities established by the government. The banks merely became deposit institutions, although virtually all were clients of IRI. The advantages of this rescue operation were political rather than economic; the government earned public acclaim for saving the deposits and investments of quite humble men. Industrialists at least could count upon the flow of capital from the State into projects that the government approved.

Italy did not suffer especially badly from the Depression even though industrial production declined by about 23 per cent 1929–33. The State took care of the labour force, offsetting any tendency towards disorder and keeping down the level of unemployment at least by statistical means. The experience confirmed Mussolini in his resolve to create a total state based on the co-ordination and direction of various socio-economic, socio-political institutions in which both the collective and individual energies of the Italian people were to be expended in the glorification of the State and its leader. Leaving aside the question whether this design ever could have worked, we can still be impressed by the fertility of imagination in creating such an array of public bodies to articulate the grand illusion. Industrial policy was arranged around syndicalist corporations which did not rationalise all the means of production but ensured acceptable levels of conformity in the workplace. Social policy, welfare, recreation and education were no less *dirigiste*, intended on the one hand to defuse unrest by circumventing the feelings of class solidarity and on the other to create a people worthy of the leader's military ambitions. Such institutions as the *Dopolavoro* (recreation after work) may often have been fatuous but for countless humble families the opportunity for subsidised leisure and communal fellowship was not despised nor despicable. Nevertheless, as in all things Fascist, the thought outran the deed and most of these grandiose plans were either entangled in bureaucracy or sabotaged by the bloody-minded.

The basis of the Fascist economy was autarky. Import-saving was paramount, especially after the invasion of Ethiopia and the imposition of economic sanctions. The exports of the peninsula equally were directed towards the empire, a modest ambition which nevertheless reorientated Italian resources overseas towards Africa. Empire, it should be said, was the first principle of policy-making around which all other initiatives duly revolved. Autarky succeeded in essentials because the *force majeure* of isolationism determined that it should be so. The pressures to restore industrial production to pre-crash levels, achieved in 1938, were immense and cost the government dear in subsidisation and cheap credits. The public works started or completed by the Fascists in roads, railways and hydroelectricity eventually paid handsome dividends, but before 1938 were viewed more soberly in the light of increasing and destabilising budgetary deficits. The Spanish Civil War drew resources out of Italy which were not compensated, except in terms of political prestige. The inexorable passage towards subordination to Germany was of no real assistance to the economy. Indeed by 1939 the government was desperately trying to staunch a flow of capital abroad that promised financial disaster.

Benefits there were. IRI never capitulated to the incoherent bureaucracy of State control; it was a quango but retained much room to manoeuvre. If any institution deserves credit for building up, modernising and promoting Italian industry it is IRI. Fiat, Pirelli, Montecatini, SNIA Viscosa, electricity supply, chemicals, paper, road construction, etc., all benefited from IRI investment and encouragement. Italian industry, of course, gained much from rearmament after 1935, but the efficiency of the Italian war machine in 1939 owed an immense debt to the 'mixed' industrial enterprise established by IRI in collusion with several leading industrialists. Nationalised concerns such as AGIP also did well in an autarkic, militaristic environment. Altogether the Fascist era could show some encouraging economic statistics. GDP had increased by 1.2 per cent per annum since 1922 and manufacturing production by almost 4 per cent per annum. The population had increased by about 0.5 per cent per annum in the same period, so that *per capita* income had improved by a comfortable margin.

8.2   Spain

The modernisation of the Spanish economy after the Restoration of 1875 had been patchy. Most of the peninsula in 1912 remained tied to an inefficient agrarian economy which varied between extreme fragmentation of peasant holdings in the north-west and the traditional exploitation of large estates (*latifundios*) by virtual serf labour in the south. Two-thirds of Spain's active population were engaged in agriculture in 1910 and less than 16 per cent in industry and mining. Moreover political power and social authority resided with the landed interest and their allies in the traditional professions. Some of Spain's older industries decayed in the nineteenth century and cities such as Valencia, Murcia and Segovia could by 1900 be described as disindustrialised. Throughout the peninsula, manufacturing and the related service trades were in the hands of artisans with little capital and conservative instincts. Only in two regions was industrial development clearly evident. In Catalonia agriculture already occupied less than one-third of the population (27.5 per cent) and industry almost one-half. But even in Catalonia most of the industrial and commercial activity was centred upon Barcelona, Sabadell and Terrasa, where its importance in the local and national economy in reality belied its relative backwardness, for neither the textile nor the newer engineering industries were equipped with extensive capital, organised in joint-stock enterprises or aggregated a large workforce in modern factories. Typically, one of the most important of Catalan industries before 1914 was cork-cutting, in which there were still more than 800 establishments in business. As a power-house of industrialisation in Spain the potential of Catalonia was modest, but nevertheless the region did feature very prominently in the process of industrial development between 1914 and the outbreak of Civil War.

More obviously industrial in 1914 was Bilbao, a port with a long established export of iron ore, which after the Restoration turned increasingly to its manufacture. A boom in the 1890s could not be sustained, but even on the eve of the Great War, the Nervion valley stood out as one of the two or three industrial nerve-centres of southern Europe. The iron industry and the related shipping trade were fully capitalist, protected by joint-stock incorporations and well placed to raise investment through the Stock Exchange. One large, consolidated company, Altos Hornos de Vizcaya (organised in 1902), dominated the region, but there were also companies engaged in steel-making, heavy engineering, ship-building, timber and paper-making along the north coast. In both Catalonia and Vizcaya electrification in the towns began early, often under the influence of German firms. In the north the shortage of coal encouraged the adoption of electrical power in industry and this in turn led to the exploitation of hydroelectric energy by the end of the nineteenth century, which was feasible because of the high terrain with fast-flowing rivers, especially those running into the Bay of Biscay.

The First World War generally proved advantageous to the Spanish economy. Industry did especially well, both in the domestic market, from which the belligerents had effectively withdrawn and in which import substitutes were in steady demand, and also in many overseas markets. Almost from the beginning the Spanish were able to exploit the demand, especially among the French, for the materials of war, for metal goods, blankets, leatherware, etc., and as the war dragged on, their opportunities increased in other markets starved of north European supplies, especially in Latin America. Neutrality paid dividends. The war naturally created problems: some raw materials were scarce and expensive; some technically advanced equipment such as machine tools were unobtainable; and inflation eventually caused widespread popular disturbances. Moreover, much of the profit engendered by the war entered into speculative investment in both Catalonia and the Biscay provinces, and some was frittered away in conspicuous consumption by the new rich. Many of the numerous company flotations on the Barcelona Stock Exchange were under-capitalised and short-lived. Nevertheless, Catalonia was transformed into a fully-fledged industrial economy. Between 1910 and 1920 the share of agriculture in the occupational statistics was halved (from 27.5 to 13.5 per cent) and that of industry increased to 62.6 per cent. This was achieved by much rural emigration, from Aragon and Valencia as much as from within Catalonia, towards the urban/industrial complex of Barcelona. Both Barcelona and Bilbao experienced the pangs of rapid, and often speculative, development. In the north industrial develoment spread further, to Guipuzcoa and the Asturias, wherever raw materials and hydroelectric power could be found in conjunction with access to deep water.

Elsewhere in Spain the principal beneficiary of the war was agriculture. The cereal-growers and sheepmasters in particular did well and where the import substitution of other primary produce was practicable the farming community also prospered. Only the Levante gained little. The demand for citrus, almonds and rice was not especially buoyant and Valencia in particular suffered from the economic consequences of the German submarine blockade. Most of the profits in agriculture accrued to the landlords, and with the steep rise in price for grain, oil and sugar, the peasantry, especially in the south and centre, suffered a fall in living standards sufficient to provoke unrest.

One measure of the windfall character of wartime prosperity is disclosed in the foreign trade statistics. From a perennial deficit, averaging 85 million pesetas in 1911–13, the economy achieved a surplus throughout the war (1916–18, average of 480 million pesetas), only to fall back into deficit again after the war. Indeed in 1920–21 the imbalance averaged about 1300 million pesetas, which caused alarm in the government, although most of the deficit was accumulated in buying investment goods or in rebuilding inventories run down before 1919.

The self-confidence of the northern business community was reinforced by their success in the war. Holding to the belief that Spain should be remoulded in the image of Catalonia there was much agitation to invest war surpluses in major development schemes such as the privately organised project to harness the falls of the Duero, capitalised at 150 million pesetas. The Madrid government tried to restrain the enthusiasm of the northerners and in 1917 a political crisis arose over a proposal to dedicate excess war profits to the modernisation of agriculture. The upshot was a compromise in which the political establishment accepted the necessity of combining agrarian and industrial/commercial development in public planning, and although the particular arrangement did not endure, the principle was absorbed into the system and found expression again in the 1920s, 1940s and 1960s.

If Spain had prospered in the war, the country suffered as much as any other from the post-war recession, out of which, as in Italy, there came a dictatorship. The continued disruption of markets and the stock-building which followed the war provided every country with industrial capacity and agricultural surpluses, with the comforting expectation of continuous prosperity. In the autumn of 1920, in Spain as elsewhere, the bubble burst. The uncompetitiveness of much of Spanish industry aggravated the recession, which in any event was made still worse by social disorder. The slump destroyed the illusion of industrial success: it caused textile mills to close; shipping to stand idle; euphoria on the Stock Exchange to subside into truculence, as banks suspended payment, quoted companies collapsed and half-realised development schemes were indefinitely postponed. Even in Bilbao and Oviedo iron ore exports plunged from about 2 million to 0.5 million tonnes in 1919–21 and ship-building virtually ceased.

Social unrest threw Spanish business into double jeopardy. The insurrection began in the countryside, where many districts endured three years of turmoil as the poor peasantry rose against their enemies, demanding land reform and decent wages, fulminating against inflation, indifference and squalor and promising themselves the fruits of revolution (*el trienio bolshevista*). Many of the same grievances affected the urban poor, especially those drawn into employment in the new factories. By 1919, Catalonia was embroiled in vehement labour unrest and the disaffection spread. Around Barcelona the workers' grievances were exploited by the anarcho-syndicalist CNT (Confederacion National de Trabajo) which engaged in savage guerrilla war with the employers' associations and held out defiantly even when a formidable new governor was appointed to suppress the tumult. In fact political initiatives were confused and the orthodox political parties seemed bankrupt of ideas. A change of government in April 1922 which attempted *détente* with the CNT outraged Catalan businessmen and the moderate socialist trade union organisation. A demand for the restoration of order provoked a military coup in September 1923 which brought General Miguel Primo de Rivera to power. Primo turned the tide against revolutionary socialism and began his dictatorship with a surprising degree of popular support.

The first Spanish dictatorship lasted from 1923 to 1930. Its economic policies were often incomplete or contradictory but the will to modernise the creaking economy of rural Spain and at the same time to encourage established business interests was apparent from the start. Primo repudiated his promises to Catalonia because of the entrenched opposition to provincial autonomy among his Madrid supporters. He actually abolished the regional council, the Mancomunitat, in 1924 and provoked immense ill-feeling among the business elite of Barcelona. The regime also failed in its attempt to reform agriculture, again because it could not afford to offend the oligarchy of Castile and Andalucia; even the notorious *latifundios* of the south were left untouched. Policy tended further to favour the inefficient producers of cereals even when supplies were plentiful. Although much state money was invested in public works in the countryside, the results except in the relatively advanced regions of the east and north-east were disappointing. Irrigation, above all in the Ebro valley, was the marvel of the Primo rural works programme. Rural electrification, peasant resettlement and marshland drainage had little impact before 1930.

The regime, however, viewed development in a broader perspective. Internal communications were still inadequate in 1920 and were regarded by almost everyone as essential to the creation of a national market. Road and railway construction, together with electrification and the building of docks, industrial plant and the urban infrastructure, entered the plans of the Primo government in its palmy days before 1928. Since much of this enterprise would of necessity have to be underwritten by the state, the key to its success rested in the hands of the Finance Minister, Jose Calvo Sotelo, who showed great ingenuity in devising fiscal means of support, including the idea of state monopolies in essential commodities such as petrol, organised by CAMPSA in 1927. Calvo's success was limited by the nearly universal assault upon his projected income tax from the rich and powerful. Income taxation was to be the means not primarily of redistributing wealth but of paying for the scheme of public works, but that did not make it acceptable.

Nevertheless the results were not unimpressive. New roads and railways were built in the 1920s. Irrigation schemes offered a livelihood to farmers well placed to exploit urban and industrial demand in the northeast and this in turn benefited manufacturers dependent upon the home market. Electricity generation increased by 50 per cent between 1926 and 1929 to reach 2.43 million kWh. But in the early 1930s Spanish consumption was still far below the rest of western Europe and the chief beneficiaries of the programme were Catalonia, Navarre and Biscay where the industry had started.

The dictatorship reaped the gains of a general boom before 1928–29 in which the business interests, though perhaps not satisfied, were able to feel that the anarchy of 1919–23 had passed and would not be repeated. Foreign trade remained in deficit, but its volume increased threefold before 1929; the ore trade was especially buoyant, with output doubling to 6.5 million tons in 1929. Moreover, profits in general were back at levels not far short of the wartime boom by 1927. Technological change, on a narrow front and in few localities, was unprecedented, with new initiatives in chemicals, automotive engineering, rayon and cellulose able to strike sickly roots in a protectionist environment.

By 1930 the two provinces of Barcelona and Vizcaya were as much industrialised in terms of employment structure and investment as any part of southern Europe. But even French industry did not depend on so backward an agriculture as Spain, where production for the market was either limited to commodities originating in the sub-marginal *latifundios* – bread grain and wool – or to the produce of intensely cultivated but minuscule peasant holdings in the east (Murcia, Valencia, the Ebro Valley) – olives, fruit, vegetables, corn and wine. Even the wool trade was no longer a source of large overseas earnings and the commerce in citrus fruit, almonds and olive oil from the Levante was subject to increasingly effective competition from other parts of the world after the First World War.

The collapse of the dictatorship in 1930 was followed by a period of turmoil and uncertainty that had scarcely any adverse effect on the economy. The political outcome was a republican constitution with comparatively dispersed or discrete powers, which turned out to be inappropriate to a policy of reform and modernisation. Primo's government had begun with a great degree of popular support, which had evaporated within five years. The socialists in the early 1930s were not really better placed to solve the intractable problems of Spain.

The Second Republic was doomed from the outset by political discord. The socialists who came to power in the spring of 1931 were dependent upon other republican factions. The government strove for two years with bourgeois support to enact a moderate reform of blatant economic abuses. Catalan acquiescence was obtained through devolution of regional autonomy, although in the province the revolutionary left were never dependable allies of the moderates and once the reform ran into heavy weather the pretence of a broadly-based republican–socialist coalition was abandoned in partisan recrimination.

Two strands of moderate policy gained wide support on the left, land reform and the secularisation of civil institutions, marriage, divorce, burial, education and social welfare. This assault upon the Church, however, was ineffectual. It did not destroy its power and it rallied conservative opponents of the regime around an issue that was not in essence sectional, unlike the defence of the military and of the landlords' interests. Land reform failed for more complex reasons. First, of course, there were the still considerable powers of the *latifundistas*, who could delay or divert proceedings, intimidate officials or peasant beneficiaries of the new order and use the Church in their defence. Secondly there was an increasing dissociation of expectation and achievement; slow progress embittered the peasantry, divided rural communities and caused political disorder. Thirdly, the problems of redistributing land and creating rural employment were more intractable than the planners believed, since investment trailed well behind expropriation. Fourthly, as planning was increasingly described as bourgeois, theoretical or insensitive, it irritated many activists for whom ends amply justified means.

Quite apart from the disagreements that impeded the progress of reform, the contemplated changes occurred against a background of increasing international depression. Spain might have emerged from the crisis without too serious wounds, had not the political upheaval become so bitter and implacable. The disenchantment of the far left with a compromising coalition government was exacerbated in November 1933 when elections brought in a less reformist, less sympathetic administration, which eventually fell under the ideological sway of a Catholic corporatist movement influenced by Mussolini and Dollfuss. The ultra-conservatives were not much appeased, however, since the government did not disavow either its republican credentials or the concept of gradual reform inherited from its predecessor. The pace slowed; some contested changes were not effected; and the various revolutionary factions, including the CNT, were excluded from policy-making. This obviously provoked the anarcho-syndicalists into violent reaction, not least in order to exorcise the spectre of Dollfuss, who had destroyed their counterparts in Austria. Separatism in Catalonia was obliterated by direct intervention of the government in Madrid. The bitterness engendered by the authoritarianism of the radical coalition lingered and in the election of November 1936, it was replaced by a popular front pledged to restore and extend the policies of reform of 1931–3 and to suppress the growingly confident movement of the anti-republican right. The polarisation of Spain, serious in 1934–35, became critical in 1936. The confrontation of anarcho-syndicalists and communists against the falange made the Civil War virtually inescapable.

This play of force in the foreground of history masked an action that was related to but somehow disjointed from the melodrama. The Great Depression could not be ignored by Spanish governments, but it could be afforded a lower priority than in countries more heavily dependent upon foreign trade. In Bilbao, the crisis was acute, since shipping, iron and steel were reliant upon world trade. Yet in 1934 the Bank of Spain observed: 'The complete and closed nature of our economy, our limited industrialisation, . . . our totally rudimentary system with its small-scale financial institutions and businesses [have] brought about our relative isolation from the Capitalist world and contributed to make the crisis more superficial'.

Whereas in most developed countries unemployment reached a peak of between 23 and 45 per cent of the labour force in 1932–33, in Spain the highpoint did not exceed 13 per cent. In Catalonia, insulation from overseas trade ensured that the peak of unemployment fell in 1936, under conditions of political turmoil, when it was calculated at only 6.5 per cent, or at about one-third of the level in the Nervion valley. Un- and under-employment were endemic in the agrarian south, which displayed yearly averages greater than in the north-east, and despite the attempt at land reform Andalucia, Extremadura and neighbouring provinces were bedevilled by the lack of opportunities for work throughout the 1930s. In general, agricultural unemployment frequently accounted for 60 per cent of the recorded total, 1932–36, perhaps chiefly because of impediments in the way of emigration into the country towns or to Latin America.

Foreign trade may not have been vital, but it suffered a sharp decline nonetheless. From a peak in the late 1920s of about 5000 million pesetas, exports and imports valued together fell to less than 1500 million in 1935–36. Industrial output per head, which had risen by around 1.75 per cent per annum, continued to increase until 1932. The fall was swift but shortlived – 1913, 100; 1930, 133; 1933, 111; 1935, 129 – until the outbreak of war. Much of the decline occurred in the north and north-west.

Catalonia was scarcely affected by the *economic* crisis, not least because its industrial structure was actually strengthened by the movement towards autarky pursued during the Republic. Catalan textile industries supplied home demand and benefited extensively from cheap labour, cheap raw materials and, in the crucial years, from bumper cereal crops which enlarged rural spending power. Only after 1933 did matters deteriorate since both falling agricultural exports and a round of wage-cutting depleted domestic demand.

There was no serious financial or banking crisis, and the government felt no powerful urge to restrict public expenditure in order to balance the budget. Some investments were postponed in 1933–34 but it is difficult to dissever political from economic decisions in this respect because it coincided with a decline of enthusiasm for agrarian reform and modernisation. In the north the problems of the iron and steel industry did affect capital formation, in hydroelectricity as also in steel-making plant and equipment, but the boom of the 1920s had tended to produce excess capacity which reduced the need for new investment in the 1930s.

Spain was so troubled with industrial unrest in the early 1930s that a sense of impending crisis belied the economic equilibrium. The militancy of organised labour was primarily political in motivation and owed little to the apprehension of social catastrophe, as the experience of prosperous Catalonia clearly attests. The strike was still a weapon of political protest or intimidation in republican Spain; indeed for many labour leaders it was the principal lever of revolution.

However well Spain survived the Great Depression the country fell into desperate straits from 1936 onwards. Once the Civil War had become unavoidable, rational economic policy was more or less abandoned. The aims of economic production were necessarily directed to the war effort and the two sides in the conflict were concerned to satisfy as much of the military and civilian needs of their subjects/supporters as they could. The failed coup of 1936 had left the Republic with about half the territory and half the population of the country, but Madrid controlled almost all the industry and commerce, most of the valuable raw materials and an agricultural base largely free of *latifundistas*, but with a productive bias towards pastoral and horticultural commodities that had to be adjusted to provide the bread of the people. Burgos was securely in command of the agrarian west and south, not short of foodstuffs but devoid of manufacturing and commercial outlets. Consequently the nationalist drive to conquer the industrial north in 1937 was crucial to the outcome of the war. After Bilbao had fallen, the territory of the Republic was gradually overrun until the process was complete in 1939.

The nationalists benefited from the military and logistic support of the Italians and Germans, which was more effective than Russian and international support for the Republic, not least because the ultimate costs of fascist intervention were not great. The Germans took what they needed in raw materials, the Italians very little. The nationalists also gained from the co-ordinating powers of a military despotism. The Republic had to reconcile too many conflicting interests, not least often incompetent international interference. Collectivisation and sovietisation of regions or institutions under republican administration were pursued with conviction by an increasingly centralised revolutionary left, especially in Catalonia: but this alienated bourgeois and radical adherents without yielding benefits in the form of enhanced output. It was not always clear whether the defence of an increasingly embattled state or some form of permanent revolution was the priority, which undermined the resolve of the Republic as a whole.

From an economic point of view the Civil War was disastrous. It caused duplication of economic institutions across an unbridgeable but inconstant divide, diversion of manpower and resources and destruction of capital. Armies commandeered, despoiled or wasted marketable commodities. Peasants and bourgeois fled or hid their savings; workers were distracted from the business of production and the commercial interests stood appalled before the shifting conflict as a toxic waste of their enterprise. The autarky of the Spanish economy was wrecked by 1938, although neither side could easily afford to replace the shortages with imported commodities. Nevertheless, once the fighting was over, the economy rebounded rapidly. The falangists introduced policies to support business and land-ownership, to encourage investment and to obliterate militant radicalism. The Second World War, however, provided as great a stimulus since neutral Spain profited both from the preoccupation with total war of the belligerents and also from German mastery of western Europe.

8.3 Further reading

Italy

A good general economic history, however unexciting, is S.B. Clough (1944) *The Economic History of Modern Italy* (New York: Columbia University Press). More interesting and sound on economic issues is Martin Clark (1984) *Modern Italy 1871–1982* (London: Longman). Giorgio Fuà edited and co-ordinated a three volume history and analysis of Italian economic development, which has not been translated and is difficult to read for non-econometricians. A brief statement of his findings is contained in G. Fuà (1964) *Notes on Italian Economic Growth*

1861–1964 (Milan: I.R.E.I.). On the fascist economy, R. Sarti (1971) *Fascism and the Industrial Leadership in Italy* (Berkeley: University of California Press) is worth reading. More comprehensive is G. Toniolo (1980) *L'Economia dell'Italia Fascista* (Bari: Laterza) which is fairly even-handed in its treatment of controversial issues. Two other books were used by the author, V. Lutz (1963) *Italy: a study in economic development* (Oxford: Oxford University Press) and J. La Francesca (1972) *La politica economica del fascismo* (Bari: Laterza).

Spain

Three books on economic development in Spain are indispensable: Nicolas Sanchez-Albornoz (1987) *The Economic Modernization of Spain 1836–1930* (New York: New York University Press) which contains several first-rate articles on various aspects of economic change; J.R. Harrison (1985) *The Economic History of Spain in the Twentieth Century* (Manchester: Manchester University Press); J. Nadal *et al.* (eds) (1987) *La economia española en el siglo XX* (Barcelona: Ariel), chs 4, 5, 9.

Political history is well treated by Raymond Carr (1982) *Spain 1808– 1975* (Oxford: Oxford University Press). Other studies in English of considerable value are: R.H. Chilcote (1968) *Spain's Iron and Steel Industry* (Austin: Texas University Press); G. Jackson (1965) *The Spanish Republic and the Civil War, 1931–39* (Princeton: Princeton University Press) and, above all, E. Malefakis (1970) *Agrarian Reform and Peasant Revolution in Spain* (New Haven: Yale University Press).

9

The Low Countries

9.1 Introduction

The Low Countries in the early twentieth century were divided economically by more than the fact of Dutch neutrality and Belgian prostration in 1914–18. Memories of the unified state before 1830 remained green for generations and the Belgian ruling elite in particular could not be brought to consider commercial co-operation except at the most perfunctory level, even in the 1920s. The Scheldt Question, which turned upon the rivalry between Antwerp and Rotterdam to the disadvantage of the former, was still a live issue even after it had been formally resolved. The Antwerpers' sense of grievance, as much as Brussels' fear of Dutch dominion over the two kingdoms, held back the rational impulse towards customs union. It was essentially divisions in Belgian society that determined the relationship of the two nations, since 1831 had ensured the victory of French and of the French-speaking professional classes in the government of the new state, just at the time when economic development also favoured Wallonia. Distrust between Walloons and Flemings was not recent, but it had flourished in the nineteenth century when the French political establishment, French business and French culture were set on course to inundate the Dutch sections of society. The economic powerhouse of Belgium in about 1880 was in Wallonia, in a narrow band of country between Liège, Mons and Charleroi, thanks to ample stocks of coal and early enterprise in engineering and textile production. The fact that the chief industrial resource of the Netherlands, Limburg coal, was found just across the frontier was itself a bone of contention, for the southern provinces of the northern kingdom (south Zeeland –

172

'Staatsvlanderen', north Brabant and north Limburg) belonged, in irredentist opinion, to Belgium.

The diplomatic barriers were formidable, but the economic differences between the two states were little more conducive to rational collaboration. Belgium was held to be an industrial state by 1913, whereas the Netherlands, despite some progress since 1880, was still in essence agricultural, but with a large and impressive mercantile presence in the world. This, however, did not supply the means of co-operation, since each economy had developed with little consideration of the other; the industrial south of Belgium had more in common with north-eastern France than with the Rhineland or the North Sea economy to which the Dutch inclined. Moreover, Belgium was industrial only to a limited extent, since it possessed a large peasantry producing crops that did not complement the agriculture of the Netherlands. Rural Flanders had a sentimental attachment to the north that was not matched by the perception of common economic interests, and rural Wallonia, when not engaged in supplying the needs of nearby cities, more closely resembled the peasant economies of Luxembourg, the Eifel and the French Ardennes than any part of the Netherlands except Limburg.

Both states possessed distracting colonial interests. The Belgian Congo was a principal source of the wealth of the ruling family, but it also influenced the way in which the national economy had evolved before 1914. Nevertheless the Belgian Congo was probably the least integrated colonial empire in Europe. The Dutch Empire, especially Indonesia, played a more significant role in Dutch commerce, not least because many of the products of the East were well suited to the still largely craft-based manufactures of the home country, where the processing of tobacco, spices, coffee and many other 'colonial wares' were more important than heavy industry.

There were, of course, things in common. The two states set much store by their exports. Neither embraced protectionism, especially agricultural protection, with much enthusiasm, because of this exposure to export markets. Both states enacted liberal covenants with their citizens, their peasants and industrialists especially, in which law, good housekeeping and social policy combined to encourage enterprise and self-help, and in both it was the great financial intermediaries, the merchant banks, that led the course of industrial development. However different, Belgium and the Netherlands had a reservoir of savings ripe for investment that was about equal in 1910–14. Even by European standards their people were rich in the resources necessary for industrial and commercial development. Colonial proceeds contributed something to this state of national wellbeing, but in Belgium (and Luxembourg) the legacy of industrialisation before 1850, and in the northern kingdom

(Holland and north Brabant specifically) remaining accumulations from a glorious economic past (which had ended before 1780), were more important to the composition of national income and wealth early in the twentieth century. In this respect the similarity of the two economies is misleading: Belgium, rather like Great Britain, resting upon laurels hard-won a generation or two before, was slow to adapt to new economic opportunities, 1880–1920, whereas the Netherlands, on the principle of *reculer pour mieux sauter*, was in vigorous development at the same period.

In all of this Luxembourg played little part. The Grand Duchy possessed an agriculture more backward than either of its northerly neighbours, a rudimentary commercial organisation and an industrial structure almost entirely dependent upon coal and iron. Before 1920 Luxembourg belonged essentially in the sphere of Germany, part of the Zollverein, to which it might have remained economically attached had not insensitive German behaviour in the war and the defeat of the Axis in 1918 driven the state into new paths. The Belgo–Luxembourg Economic Union of 1921 was a compromise that neglected problems of industrial integration, but it succeeded chiefly because the monetary and mercantile relations of the two states rapidly became bound inextricably together. The immense importance for Luxembourg of the iron and steel industry was not put at risk by BLEU. Luxembourg production continued to increase throughout the 1920s. The losses of the war – output down to about 25 per cent of 1913 levels in 1919 – were quickly made good, with production in 1929 amounting to 5.6 million tonnes against 4.0 million tonnes in 1913. The output of the two countries was surpassed only by three or four other countries at that date – the USA, Germany, the USSR and Great Britain. That, however, was virtually the sum of the economic importance of the Grand Duchy.

9.2   Belgium

The Belgian economy had grown satisfactorily in the quarter-century before 1914. The rate of expansion was not as great as that of more recently industrialised economies, but there is no evidence of stagnation as the industrial sector attained maturity. The essential division between the heavily industrialised provinces of Hainaut and Liège, dependent upon mining and metallurgy with a more recent interest in chemical manufactures, and the agrarian and still rather under-developed region of Flanders (but no less the Walloon province of Luxembourg) persisted into the inter-war years, despite the revival of Antwerp in the later nineteenth century. The Flemish territory contained an efficient but fragmented agriculture which was adapted quite successfully to new lines of production under competition from the New World without recourse to stringent tariffs. Flanders and Brabant were also the seat of the ancient, but partly modernised, textile industries of the kingdom – linen, fine woollens and cotton – which were under pressure from national policies of import-saving, but were adapted to new patterns of demand by an emphasis upon skill and superior design. Belgian exposure in export markets in 1913 mirrored that of Britain, coal, iron and steel, steam-powered engineering products, heavy chemicals, cotton and other textiles, with the addition of small arms, foodstuffs (raw and processed) and specialities such as diamonds, tobacco, coffee and craft goods. The Congo played a small part; in 1913 only about one per cent of total trade was with the African dependency.

Except in the Ardennes agriculture was well adjusted to the urban–industrial society of this overcrowded country. Commerce was still largely disaggregated in small, inter-personal enterprises. The French political and economic elite held the levers of power in Brussels and Liège where a small number of wealthy and influential mercantile or financial institutions existed in the late nineteenth century. In Antwerp and Gent there were similar capitalist combinations, characterised by the Antwerp shipping interests. Perhaps 10–12 per cent of the gainfully employed were engaged in the commercial sector, many as small dealers.

The Belgians were forced into war in 1914 and suffered severely from the consequences of German depredations. Plant and machinery were sequestrated, part of the labour force was deported and both raw and manufactured commodities were diverted to German use. No less important, however, was the direct damage inflicted by the war, the number of people killed and disabled, the loss of much highly productive land in Flanders (about 125 000 hectares) and the destruction of houses, workshops and factories in the path of armies contesting a moving front. Belgian statistics are not very trustworthy but it is evident that both industrial and agricultural output fell sharply, by perhaps one-half in critical periods, between 1913 and 1916. By 1917 the economy was on the verge of breakdown. Inflation caused by the combination of dearth and excessive money supply became rampant in 1916, at least in part under German direction. Overseas trade foundered and internal communications were so badly disrupted that the delivery of goods became haphazard and intermittent. Even the Germans found it difficult to divert Belgian assets to the home country in such chaotic conditions. The Belgians, as in 1940–45, certainly concealed materials from their hated overlords in the First World War but it is impossible to conclude other than that the war was a disaster.

It was not an irredeemable disaster. Several deficiencies were quickly made good, especially the waste of agricultural land in the war zone. The result was not a rapid return to pre-war levels of output, but in spite of the international agricultural depression of the decade, Flemish farmers regained much of their nineteenth-century prosperity before 1929. In general the boom of 1919–20 was strongly marked in the country. On the face of it this is curious, for, quite apart from the physical dislocation of the economy still apparent in the aftermath of war, the Belgians felt disappointment and chagrin at the outcome of the peace settlement. Business confidence was buoyed up by the promise of reparations but also because the scarcity of commodities raised prices and profits to unaccustomed levels. The short-lived nature of the boom, moreover, was masked by a programme of reconstruction and new investment. This stimulus was enhanced by a sustained revival of overseas trade. Antwerp was busier in 1922–23 than in 1912–13 and the Congo, almost for the first time, was rationally exploited for its raw materials, copper, tin, palm oil, coffee, cocoa, copal. In industry, a short break in recovery in 1921 passed without too much strain on business confidence or labour participation. Thereafter the trend was upward. Textiles, coal and metallurgy all overtook pre-war levels of production in 1923–24. New industries such as oil-refining, rayon and cellulose, photographic materials and wireless telegraphy were established securely by 1922–24 and had already begun to attract external interest, by the Dutch AKU or Philips for example, before the decade was over. Electricity generation, averaging 1500 megawatts in 1913, was devastated in the war, but by 1922 had been re-established; in 1927 output exceeded 3240 megawatts and the heavy metal-working industries had been modernised to take account of electricity.

The chief problem was monetary. The Bfr. was under pressure from outside and inside the country by 1921. One problem was the soaring national debt which increased more than tenfold in the decade after 1913. Reparations from Germany added 7 billion Bfr. to the economy before 1924, but this was offset by the Belgian policy of taking excessive German marks, a legacy of the occupation, out of the economy, which cost 7.6 billion Bfr. Devaluation was inevitable, but was conceded reluctantly. In 1921 the pound sterling bought 50.3 Bfr. In 1925 the government tried to restore the Gold Standard at a parity of 107 Bfr. to the pound. This failed, and a year later the rate had to be fixed at 175 Bfr./£ sterling.

The result was gratifying despite internal inflation. The recovery of the early 1920s was translated into a hectic boom in 1926–29 as the economy benefited from an under-valued franc. Had not others followed suit the boom would probably have gone higher. Even so, by

1929, the economy was working almost at full capacity and the government, hoping to produce a technical correction, attempted to slow down expansion, but with the financial institutions virtually autonomous the dose was difficult to administer. The October crash had a sobering effect but the economy possessed enough resilience to withstand the worst consequences of recession until 1931. Because much of the expansion had been floated upon easy credit the Belgian Depression was characterised by a failure of public confidence in the financial institutions that had promoted the *hausse*. Their role is therefore crucial to our understanding of the difficulties of the 1930s.

One feature of the Belgian economy that increased in importance in the 1920s was the part played by the banks in the possession and direction of industrial and commercial enterprises. The Société Générale (SG), the oldest and largest of these financial–industrial undertakings, set the course followed by others. All the main banking groups had by 1925 extensive portfolios of investments, especially in manufacturing industry. To some extent the First World War acted as a solvent in the process. Thus the Société Générale acquired holdings in 85 enterprises between 1917 and 1930, increasing total investment in industry from 227 million Bfr. to over 2000 million Bfr. in the same period. Joint ventures between bankers and industrialists were also widespread. Thus SG coordinated the development of several companies operating in the Belgian Congo, the evolution of Petrofina (founded in 1920) and of Sabena (1923). Almost all the new industries in Belgium after 1920 were promoted by financial capitalists, when not the direct consequence of foreign investment. Although the financial establishment in Brussels had long been suspected of bias in favour of the French in Belgium, the pattern of investment was similar in both Dutch and Walloon regions. Leading Brussels houses, in addition to the Société Générale, such as Lambert and the Banque de Bruxelles, were complemented by Antwerp enterprises, especially the Algemene Bankvereniging, which was in an especially expansive phase of development in the mid-1920s. In detail the banks did not necessarily distinguish Walloon and Dutch in their choice of investments, but it is nevertheless true that Antwerp extended its financial involvement in the economy chiefly in Dutch-speaking areas, whereas the Banque de Bruxelles (which acquired the Crédit Général Liègeois in 1927) dominated Wallonia.

Not all the cartels were controlled by the banks. A few industrial complexes diversified into finance in the early twentieth century, notably Solvay, the chemical conglomerate, but the sense that the Société Générale represented Belgium Inc. was difficult to disavow by the end of the 1930s. The power of the banks was increased by amalgamation and the spread of branch operations, so that the four greatest corporations were more or less national enterprises by 1928 when the merger movement passed its peak.

But the banking system was over-exposed by 1930. The interconnection of financial and industrial property-holding resulted in a conflict of interest between the banker as industrialist and the banker as trustee of public liquidity. Deflation after 1931 reduced the value of the banks' share portfolios, increased their losses on outstanding credits and induced many to freeze overdrafts. Public confidence foundered and most banks were subjected to a run upon their deposits. A few suspended payments. They were subsequently reconstructed, after transferring frozen assets, in all amounting to 1900 million Bfr., to a new state corporation established to provide credit for industry. This was not intended to replace the banks' functions in industrial investment, for the government believed that relief from their insupportable burdens would stimulate fresh activity. However, in order to prevent a recurrence of the crisis the banks were compelled to dissociate deposit and investment operations. Thus the Société Générale was transformed directly into a general holding company while the Banque de la Société Générale was founded to manage its deposit business.

Banking reform restored public confidence, but it did not resolve the wider economic crisis. Between 1931 and 1934 the government hoped the disorder was self-correcting and concentrated essentially upon the support of agriculture through tariffs. In 1934 the crisis had become so severe that further intervention was necessary. The deterioration had been aggravated by the over-valuation of the Bfr. after 1931, since the government adhered to the Gold Standard, at least in part to maintain public confidence in the institution of banking. Policy-making was therefore rather restricted. The government engineered an expansion of credit at low interest to relieve the burdens on industry, agriculture and mortgages of property, which was matched by rent control and tax reductions. Wages, pensions and the general level of public expenditure, however, were also reduced. The results were disappointing. Economic recovery was not achieved and social unrest multiplied in step with the discomforts of unemployment and austerity. Support for both socialists and quasi-fascist groups increased; the desire for collective policies of one kind or another was widespread, but it was hardly more coherent than the craving for strong leadership.

A turning-point occurred in March 1935 when the government abandoned the Gold Standard and devalued the Bfr. by 28 per cent. Devaluation did not exactly do the trick, but the economy revived in 1936–37 on the strength of better trade figures. Even at the peak of the cycle, however, the indices of production, employment, incomes and profitability did not equal the level attained in 1929. The ensuing recession in

1938 was psychologically disturbing, but it proved relatively mild because Belgian manufacturing companies were already engaged in preparation for war. Another important contribution was made by the Congo which experienced a rapid expansion of mineral production, and offered a good market for Belgian exports, after 1935. By 1937, 8 per cent of Belgian imports and 11 per cent of exports were exchanged with the Congo. A system rather like imperial preference had been established to enlarge the field of self-sufficiency.

Belgium suffered very badly in the Second World War. The German administration proceeded to confiscate possessions, practise enforced deliveries, deport labour and persecute Jews and dissidents. Cut off from overseas trade, the economy was repositioned towards the east. As in the Netherlands and Denmark, the German authorities seized Belgian industrial capital and otherwise interfered with the investment decisions of Belgian entrepreneurs and banks. The statistics disclose the dire effects of the Occupation, but should be read with caution, for the Belgians understandably disguised production and diverted resources from the occupying government. Iron and steel output was about halved between 1935–39 and 1940–44 while food production measured for statistical purposes fell by a greater percentage. Rationing was introduced to conserve falling food and raw material stocks. Daily calorie intake fell from 2400 to 1200 per day, although the thriving black market increased the 'official' figure by a substantial if unknown quantity. Inflation was out of hand before 1943, by which time general prices were ten times higher than in 1936–38. When the fighting reached the country in 1944 there was a sudden further dislocation of industrial production. The effects were short-lived, not least because many economic installations, notably the port of Antwerp, were captured undamaged.

9.3   The Netherlands

Dutch neutrality in the First World War had an equivocal effect on the economy. Dependence upon international trade and services made the Netherlands vulnerable to the outbreak of hostilities. Foreign trade, which had almost doubled in value between 1900 and 1913, collapsed in the war. Imports fell from Fl. 3.9 million to Fl. 0.97 million, 1913–17, and exports from Fl. 3.1 million to Fl. 0.82 million. Blockade, import saving and enforced austerity in several traditional markets disrupted trade in primary produce, shipping and insurance, while the potential growth of industrial exports was limited by deficiencies of capital and raw materials for manufacturing. On the other hand, part of the explanation for the decline of foreign trade lies in increasing autarky. Diversion of resources into domestic production and consumption was inevitable but it was encouraged also by a swelling flood of opinion in favour of internal development. However, the emphasis upon development was heaviest in the latter part of the war when economic conditions were unfavourable. The war falls into two parts. Until 1916 the benefits of neutrality tended to be positive. National income, in real terms, rose during the years between 1913 and 1916 by about 20 per cent. Thereafter it fell back and by 1918 was considerably lower than it had been in 1913. In 1917–18 the blockade became serious; raw materials were everywhere scarce; and inflation undermined purchasing power. Business opinion was becoming restive by the autumn of 1918. Peace brought relief but no clear sense of salvation. Yet 1919 was a good year. The apparently critical scarcity of the previous year was replaced by full production and the satisfaction of pent-up demand. More perhaps than in the belligerent countries, it was as if a brake had been released. Materials flowed promptly into industry and nearly all the barriers to trade, diplomatic and political, were removed. Government quickly dismantled the apparatus of control. As in the rest of the world the boom worked its way out through 1919 to 1921, but while it lasted it was headlong and profitable. The Dutch even more than in the war benefited from the legacy of wartime neutrality in supplying the unrequited demand at home and abroad for both merchandise and commercial services.

Recession, severe in 1921, followed from the end of the re-stocking boom, and was aggravated by inflationary pressures carried over from the war. The government that had not been unduly perturbed by money supply in 1918 presided over an even greater emission of currency in 1919–20, not least out of a desire to maintain its liberal credentials in a period of decontrol. Slack monetary policy redoubled the difficulties of manufacturers and importers who could not absorb the excess liquidity by their supply of commodities. The failure of several businesses and especially the bankruptcy of the Rotterdamsche Bankvereniging brought about an adjustment of policy. The Depression, however, was destabilising; trade and shipping suffered, unemployment rose, stocks in hand increased abruptly and had to be financed at high cost and the general burden of debt, extended freely in the post-war inflation, became a drag upon recovery in 1921–24.

Recovery, however, was clearly evident only in 1925. The economy emerged from the slump with few burns, none of them serious. Anxiety about the balance of payments continued throughout the decade, because, although the Netherlands had been accustomed to deficits on visible trade for a long period, there were additional problems in the 1920s. Home sales for manufactures were buoyant between 1923 and 1930 and they proved notably more reliable than exports hampered by protectionism in overseas markets. Moreover, domestic demand also drew in imports, particularly from countries with under-valued currencies. The response was not unimpressive, but it depended upon the exploitation of new opportunities. On the negative side, agriculture, a pillar of pre-war prosperity, became a problem in the mid-1920s. Insurance, brokerage, banking, shipping in foreign trade grew more slowly in the period than in the later nineteenth century, because of the rising tide of nationalism even in the service sector, at a time when international commerce was rather stagnant.

Agriculture was not unprosperous, except for a few years around 1931, but it failed as an engine of growth in the 1920s. Few farmers foundered, but their profits floated essentially upon the home market. Agricultural exports were stuck at about Fl. 700 million (1920, Fl. 710 million, or 41 per cent of total exports; 1930, Fl. 690 million, or 40 per cent), but then fell abruptly in the 1930s (Fl. 354 million, or 33 per cent in 1938). Gross production, however, increased by a quarter in the 1920s and by a further 10 per cent between 1931 and 1938. Employment also rose between the wars. The number of farms and manpower both increased by about 10 per cent. Support for agriculture by the government was introduced, in the teeth of much liberal opposition, in 1930. The subsidisation was piecemeal until 1933, when a statute, the *Landbouwcrisiswet* (Agricultural Crisis Act), was enacted in order to co-ordinate policy. Loans, grants and a discrete system of price support were added to regulations controlling output and the trade in agricultural produce. Import quotas played a major part in this policy. Once they had been accepted for agriculture it was inevitable that other sectors would demand similar protection.

By the mid-1930s the government was drawn into measures to control foreign trade in the national interest. The most striking initiative in a country so dependent upon shipping was the creation of a body to provide credits to sea-going businesses – the Maatschappij tot Behartiging van de Nationale Scheepvaartsbelangen (Association for Support of the National Shipping Interests). In 1933 carriers on the inland waterways were regulated by compulsory cargo sharing. This emphasis upon the sharing of diminished opportunities was as characteristic of Dutch economic policy as direct financial support. Given that opportunities for industrial and commercial rationalisation were restricted in a state where modernisation and cartelisation could play little part in raising productivity, the allocation of resources under public supervision was the best means of mitigating the depression which hit the Netherlands hard.

One option the Dutch did not choose was to abandon the Gold Standard. This posed serious problems since the guilder had not been undervalued even before 1931 *vis à vis* gold. Dutch policy was to maintain the value of their currency as much on ethical as on commercial grounds. This limited the scope of deficit financing so that increased government spending had to be accommodated within a more or less balanced budget. The 1933 agreement between seven European states to defend the Gold Standard as it then existed brought relief but no long-term resolution since the value of the various currencies in relation to gold was not in equilibrium – the guilder was badly placed by comparison with the Belgian, French and Swiss francs and the Italian lira. The agreement was not stable and the economies had little in common.

In this context Dutch economic planning turned increasingly towards the reduction of internal prices, the so-called policy of adjustment. There was a group of economists who favoured devaluation, especially in 1935–36, after the Belgians had amended the value of their currency, and one Minister of Economic Affairs resigned over the issue, but for months the conservatives held the line. An austere policy of retrenchment was mitigated only by *pro rata* reductions of taxation. A revenue not expanded by higher taxation or from a greater reservoir of taxable income could not support a coherent policy of enlarged public expenditure. The relief provided in 1930–34 was envisaged as strictly temporary and the government was implacably opposed to the accumulation of all but provisional deficits.

The role of government in economic affairs expanded in the 1930s, but in a rather curious way; it was co-ordinating rather than innovative, intermediary rather than propulsive, and although a central planning bureau was established under Jan Tinbergen, it had scarcely accomplished its first objectives before war broke out. Dutch resolve to defend the Gold Standard eventually failed. Dutch vulnerability to the flight of capital, one of the reasons for adhering to gold, was demonstrated without equivocation only days after the French and Swiss devalued in 1936. Faced with disaster the Prime Minister, Colijn, still professed an unshakable belief in sound money – he should probably be commemorated as almost the last statesman in Europe to trust in pre-war commercial verities. Nevertheless, once the decision was taken, inhibitions about interventionism relaxed, even though no self-confident *étatiste* emerged to pose as the saviour of his people.

On the face of it the severity of the Depression in the Netherlands, particularly in social terms, presided over by a conservative/liberal administration, could well have provoked serious disturbance. The craving for order, orderliness and communal responsibility, however, were subsumed in both socialist and Christian constitutional thought. A moral debate about unemployment, deprivation and inequality of suffering did take place. Economic *dirigisme* was an option, not an ideology, in Dutch terms. Most leaders of opinion attempted to square the circle by assimilating into their ethical calculus the Dutch obsession with *sound* business practice, and thereby largely exonerated both government and plutocracy from the charge of class greed. Dutch policy, rather like British, was a succession of gradual or compromise measures to deal with particular demands or particular emergencies.

The government adopted a scarcely more active role in financing social policy in the 1930s. Unemployment, which had averaged over 6 per cent of the workforce in 1925–29, rose steadily thereafter to 16 per cent in 1931, 29 per cent in 1933 and to a peak of 35.2 per cent in 1936. It then fell rapidly to 28 per cent in 1937, which illustrates the adverse effects of a high guilder and fiscal conservatism very clearly. The government was reluctant to intervene to create employment, except very indirectly, and although agriculture could absorb some of the excess employment in industry and trade, as in France, the results were insubstantial. Some political parties trifled with corporate solutions, including institutional trade organisations for business and labour, but the plural character of the Netherlands constitution and the dispersion of economic forces along confessional lines hindered any coherent policy of corporatism. The socialists rather belatedly adopted the proposals of the Belgian De Man Plan (their *Plan van de Arbeid*) in 1935, but the scheme of widespread public works and indicative planning was not even considered in depth until the first socialist entered the Cabinet in 1939, by which time it was too late. The social impact of the Depression was severe, yet *laissez-faire* by government was justified in part by public opinion and in part by the strength of traditional social institutions providing assistance or communal amenities. They were inadequate, but social tensions in Dutch society were moderate throughout the 1930s and the government was confronted with no sense of urgency.

The Netherlands had little time to reap the benefits of recovery in 1937–38 before the outbreak of war. The Second World War was disastrous in the Low Countries. Invasion of the Netherlands was compounded by plans to convert the economy into a German dependency. The Dutch economy, which even in the 1930s had maintained an open outlook upon the world, was wrenched out of shape by Nazi despoliation. Raw materials, foodstuffs and manufactures were seized as early as May 1940 and transported to Germany. Within a year Dutch factories were made dependent upon German orders, Dutch workers were deported to other parts of the Reich and part of the capital equipment of Dutch industry was expropriated. German eagerness to seize Dutch assets was, however, thwarted by passive resistance and industrial sabotage. Furthermore the Dutch were governed by a civilian administration for much of the war and the structure of the pre-war civil service was largely held in place. The Dutch were able to ensure their survival, not least because the bureaucracy efficiently controlled the rationing and price of scarce commodities, and conspired with business interests to impede German depredation and exactions. Because of the blockade, the diversion of resources to Germany and the often deliberate interruption of production, general conditions deteriorated in the latter part of the war. In 1944 dearth rapidly developed into crisis. The 'hunger winter' of 1944 marked the depth of this crisis when prices for unobtainable commodities climbed steeply, rationing collapsed and production largely ceased because both labour and raw materials were so scarce and the machinery of economic management virtually seized up amid a spiralling budget deficit. The effects of fighting on Dutch soil merely aggravated already impossible conditions of crisis. The prostration of the Dutch economy at the end of hostilities was in some ways more absolute than in France, Belgium or Denmark. Material damage, for instance, was estimated at 26 000 million guilders, almost as much as the national assets in 1938 (Fl. 28 700 million), although this figure was not expressed in constant prices.

For a small country, the Netherlands had a high profile in certain developing branches of the economy. Its principal industries were controlled by large corporations, some of which had international ramifications by the 1920s. The most important were the Royal Dutch Petroleum Company, the Algemene Kunstzijde Unie (AKU), and Philips Gloeilampen nv. The cartel known as the Margarine Unie dominated a section of Dutch industry which had a significant future and in 1929 joined forces with Lever Brothers Ltd to form Unilever. Coal mining and the railways were state-directed monopolies and in 1918 was founded a national firm to produce iron and steel, the Hoogovens Ijmuiden, which not only possessed a monopoly but, like all the greater Dutch manufacturing and most of the commercial corporations, developed substantial international interests (in Germany). The profile of the Dutch economy stood out in sharp relief because of these great enterprises. They were obviously not the sum of manufacturing and mining production. The Netherlands was still the home of countless small or medium-sized businesses, most of which offered no prospect of enlargement or expansion. Unlike the Belgian or British economies the Dutch was modern, technologically advanced and rationally organised in the 1920s and 1930s. This did not prevent trouble in the economy at large, but Dutch industry and commerce were able to maintain an international presence out of proportion to the size of the national product largely because of the versatility and affluence of the great enterprises. All maintained subsidiaries or deployed investments in other European economies. Belgium was a preferred target, but Germany, especially in the 1920s, was also attractive to the Dutch. Nevertheless the two largest international combinations were with Britain, Royal Dutch Shell and Unilever. Philips and AKU represent most fully new industries grown large and prosperous by the seizure of new market opportunities, in radio and other electrical appliances, and in rayon and viscose textiles. Hoogovens Ijmuiden, which only began production in 1924, soon found that the size of the domestic economy constricted growth, and the company turned to export markets, which was difficult in a period of dumping and cut-throat competition. Thus the company moved into the purchase or foundation of subsidiaries behind rivals' tariff walls. The Dutch economy was generally in deficit on visible trade throughout the period, and yet the international or export-based impulsion of its leading components was as strong as any in Europe. Industry was drawn by export markets, because of the small size of the Dutch domestic economy, but also because the Netherlands retained a commitment to liberal policies longer than almost any other nation state. The Dutch Empire, although indispensable to the national economy, especially as a source of raw materials, was never conceived as an autarky. Britain, Germany and the United States were the principal trading partners, supplying both materials and manufactures and also receiving Dutch products; France, Belgium and Scandinavia were also of importance. For certain technically-advanced products as much as for diamonds, butter, margarine and horticultural commodities, the Netherlands held a worldwide lead in the later 1920s. The Netherlands was not an industrial society, but certain towns such as Eindhoven and Tilburg were as industrialised, speaking of their social structure, as Mulhouse or Clermont Ferrand, Karlsruhe or Kassel by the later 1930s. Limburg, which spans the frontier with Belgium, with coal deposits on both sides, formed a northerly extension of the Liège-Hainaut industrial belt in the southern kingdom. Nevertheless the status of the Netherlands as a major producer of industrial goods in Europe was not achieved before the 1950s when growth of the economy was comparable with that of the West German 'economic miracle'.

Industry may not have been insignificant, but it was overshadowed in macro-economic terms by Dutch interests in commerce and finance. Banking, insurance, shipping and entrepôt trade had made the international reputation of Amsterdam and Rotterdam. The mercantile elite was especially influential in public affairs, deflecting too inquisitive intervention by government and iterating the virtues of sound money and commercial probity. Dutch financial institutions were much less implicated in industry than their Belgian or German counterparts, for they adhered as firmly as the British to principles of liquidity in banking. Circumstances changed slowly from the 1930s, because government supervision was more difficult to resist after the banking crisis of 1931–32, but the financial institutions retained most of their operational independence. Even in the war, under Nazi occupation, Dutch banks and insurance companies succeeded in thwarting several German attempts at direct regulation or confiscation.

9.4   Further reading

Belgium

There is no up-to-date history of the Belgian economy between the wars in any language. An expert economist who lived through the period and brought to bear on it a clear understanding was Francois Baudhuin whose (1944) *Histoire economique de la Belgique 1914–39* (Brussels: Bruylant) and (1945) *L'Economie Belge sous l'occupation* (Brussels: Bruylant), although scarce, are indispensable. For anyone who can read Dutch there are four excellent chapters on Belgium in volume XII of the (1958) *Algemene Geschiedenis der Nederlanden* (Antwerp: Standaard). Other subjects on which there are good books include the Solvay undertaking: J. Bolle (1963) *Solvay, L'inventeur, l'homme, l'entreprise industrielle, 1863–1963* (Brussels: Institut Solvay); A. Florquin (1972) *Société General de Belgique, 1822–1972* (Brussels: Lambert); B.S. Chlepner (1956) *Cent Ans d'Histoire Sociale en Belgique* (Brussels: Institut Solvay). For the Customs Union see especially W. Robertson (1956) 'Benelux and the Problem of Economic Integration', *Oxford Economic Papers*, 8/1, pp. 35–50.

Luxembourg is the subject of an excellent economic history by Raymond Kirsch (1971) *La croissance de l'économie Luxembourgeoise* (Luxembourg: EUL) and there is a chapter by A. Calmès (1958) in the *Algemene Geschiedenis*, vol. XII (Antwerp: Standaard).

The Netherlands

The best detailed account has regrettably not been translated: I.J. Brugmans (1961) *Paardenkracht en Mensenmacht. Sociaal–economische geschiedenis van Nederland, 1795–1940* (The Hague: Nijhoff). Johan de Vries produced a brief but effective economic history of the present century in 1973, *De Nederlandse economie tijdens de 20ste eeuw*, which was translated (1978) as *The Netherlands Economy in the Twentieth Century* (Assen: Van Gorcum). His (1973) 'From Keystone to cornerstone. Hoogovens Ijmuiden', *Acta Historicae Neerlandicae*, vol. 6, pp. 112–45, is also worth reading.

The other works consulted in writing the chapter are all in Dutch, of which the most important texts may be mentioned: five chapters in the *Algemene Geschiedenis der Nederlanden*, vol. XII; J.A. de Jonge (1958) *De Industrialisatie in Nederland tussen 1850 en 1914* (Rotterdam: Elzevier); J. de Vries (ed.) (1968) *De Jaren 30* (The Hague: Nijhoff).

10

Scandinavia and the Baltic

10.1 Scandinavia

The Scandinavian economies displayed generally favourable trends of growth and increases in *per capita* income over the inter-war years. By no means, however, did they escape the effects of the trade cycle; but the most extreme consequences for countries to the south and east were avoided by combinations of good fortune and political maturity. There was little political extremism; governments remained essentially moderate and centrist. Social democratic parties came to power in Denmark, Norway and Sweden in majority or coalition (with radicals in Denmark, agrarians in Norway and Sweden). The basis of their programmes was liberal rather than socialist, encouraging state intervention to protect large agricultural populations and to try to deal with unemployment. Despite the existence of Quisling's party in Norway and a small faction in Denmark, there was no real threat of fascism. Finland was something of an exception, in that her national independence from the Russian empire, following the 1917 revolution, was borne into civil war and instability. A right wing and strongly nationalistic regime saw the prohibition of the Communist Party in 1923 for fear of Soviet penetration. It was only in Finland that fascist sympathies, under the leadership of the savagely patriotic General Mannerheim, could be identified. In the early post-war years the ravages of inflation were greater in Finland than in other Nordic countries; recovery and growth far less certain. Unlike her neighbours Finland remained predominantly agrarian in employment throughout the inter-war years. In 1930, 70 per cent of the labour force was employed in agriculture compared with 30 to 40 per cent elsewhere.

In all cases unemployment was a chronic phenomenon. Depression brought an increase in numbers but, unusually, years of recovery and growth of employment continued to be accompanied by high unemployment figures. There were clearly strong seasonal factors in explaining this, though they were less obvious in Denmark. A further factor was the closure of the USA to migrants after the First World War. Large numbers had migrated there before 1914; the biggest relative outflow had been from Norway, which had shown the highest loss of any European country apart from Ireland. The perceived need to rationalise production in the face of competition in the 1920s had the effect of adding to unemployed workers in manufacturing where alternative employment, most obviously the service sector, was insufficient to absorb them. The persistence of high unemployment was problematical, especially at times of deflation. However, the political experience provided the basis of relief measures which were to be of value in later years.

With the exception of Finland, Scandinavian countries had achieved relatively well-developed industrial bases by the end of the Great War. Sweden made gains in the war years with the accumulation of overseas balances; Finland established her political independence for the first time. All these nations had a history of high levels of education and other social provisions. The educated population were receptive to technical and other innovations. Scandinavian industry came to be characterised by high cost but technologically sophisticated products. The Scandinavian economies were well known for relatively high social overhead expenditures. Educational advance contributed to the readiness to be flexible and adaptive to exploit market opportunities; and the markets were large. As 'peripheral' economies the Nordic countries had grown very much on the expanding markets to the south. As industrial and urban demand in western Europe expanded the Scandinavian economies were able to serve that demand with exports of foodstuffs, shipping services, timber, paper and engineering products. That Finland had for so long been tied to the Russian market was one major reason for its relative backwardness at the beginning of this period.

Sweden was the most industrialised of the Scandinavian economies. Denmark had comparable *per capita* income (GDP) but this was based on higher value agricultural exports. Danish industry had developed much more to serve the home market and this continued to be the case in the inter-war years. Norwegian industry had perhaps the shortest history, being based very much on the recent development of HEP and related high energy manufacturing of aluminium. More traditional industries were associated with servicing fishing, sea faring and forestry. Before 1900 Norway was poorer than her immediate neighbours, resting on fishing, farming and shipping with little manufacturing. One commentator has gone so far as to refer to Norway as the 'Sicily of the North'.

Denmark

Denmark was less affected by the First World War than many European neighbours, but in common with the rest of the continent suffered severe inflation. This demanded deflationary policies through the 1920s. For much of her history Denmark had been closely linked to the British market for agricultural products. The importance of agriculture to her export economy had stimulated industrial and technological developments to assist that sector. A number of developments in the dairy industry had provided a basis for innovations in refrigeration and other electrical goods. The diesel-engined ship was a Danish invention and ship-building was a growth industry in the 1920s. There were declining sectors also: textiles were adversely affected by imports in this decade.

Norway

As in Denmark, governments in Norway followed conventional deflationary policies in the 1920s. As economically necessary as they might have been, they aggravated social conflicts and labour discontent. Pent up demand from the First World War had been released into a flood of imports and resultant trade deficits. This in turn produced falling exchange values of the krone, which had been removed from fixed exchange at the outbreak of war in 1914. It was eventually stabilised at par in 1926, formally returning to gold in 1928, some time after Sweden and Denmark. The cost of this stabilisation was constraint on domestic consumption and investment. However, the re-establishment of confidence in monetary values attracted foreign capital investment. American capital flooded into Europe in the 1920s; Norway was attractive to German, British and American companies. American and British companies brought up the major part of the aluminium industry, IG Farben of Germany took a large share in Norsk Hydro, the chemical concern; Unilever moved into margarine and soap manufacturing; British companies took over beleaguered pulp manufacturers and mining enterprises. As a result, these and a good many other under-capitalised companies were taken over, often at a fraction of their nominal value.

One of the major problems of Norwegian industry was the relative over-supply of staple products (forest products and fish) and shipping services. Aluminium and other non-ferrous metals did not fall into this category. In an over-supplied world market Norwegian producers had difficulty competing on price (Greek shipping lines could always undercut Norwegian, for instance). In two traditional areas, however, Norway was able to exploit technical innovations to her commercial advantage. In whaling, factory ships and new oil separating processes, together with radio communications, enabled long, productive absences in the Antarctic. In freight shipping, Norwegian owners were prepared to pump in substantial amounts of capital on new steamships, concentrating on special cargoes rather than cheap mixed freights. Thus Norwegian lines became one of the major shippers of oil and refrigerated cargoes, demanding quality, reliability and technical competence rather than simply a low price. There was also an increase in passenger liners, especially on transatlantic routes, to meet the growing demand for international travel.

Sweden and Finland

Sweden was the most industrialised country in Scandinavia, Finland the least, but each grew at a similar rate in the inter-war years. Already by 1913 Sweden was ranked 12th in the world table of manufacturing output – in *per capita* terms in 6th place, above a major industrial nation like France. But unlike France, and other combatants, Sweden enjoyed an industrial boom in the war years. She was by no means insulated from inflationary pressures but was able to stabilise her currency and return to gold (1924) earlier than elsewhere. The favourable economic circumstances for neutral Sweden in the war enabled her to build up foreign credits and pay off debts, so that she became a net capital exporter during the 1920s. This was in marked, and short-lived, contrast to the long-term import of capital which had characterised Scandinavian economies before this time.

As a primary exporter, especially of paper and pulp, Sweden was adversely affected by falling relative demand but tackled deteriorating terms by diversification and rationalisation. Engineering, high quality forest products and iron ore were vital exports in the 1920s. Domestic rationalisation improved productivity and contributed thereby to the smooth and steady development of the economy in this decade. But it did nothing to alleviate chronic unemployment; perhaps it even made it worse by reducing the demand for labour in manufacturing. Further, the deflationary policies pursued in Sweden as elsewhere forced a reduction in wage payment for public works schemes, which had long been in operation in Sweden. This can only have had a negative effect on aggregate demand.

It was in the 1920s also that commercial banks developed a more direct role in company ownership. Before the end of the nineteenth century, Swedish banks had moved into share ownership following the German example. Legislation (1909) to restrict banks' share ownership had little effect. Following the boom of the First World War a number of companies collapsed and their shares therefore passed to banks as their major creditors. As a result bank ownership of companies increased. It is difficult to judge how far such a development had favourable results for industrial growth in this decade; it probably encouraged the process of rationalisation. Direct banking interest did not inhibit industrial competition – the banks themselves were oligopolistic competitors. But banks were a major source of investment capital and could thus service demands for that capital from Swedish industry. However, the direct links between banks and industry induced political distrust, and commercial banks were again forbidden to acquire commercial shares in the 1930s. They were not required to sell at a loss those shares owned from the 1920s. Further, to circumvent the law, large banks set up small companies to buy industrial shares. Thus banks were able to retain control without formal ownership.

Although growing at a similar rate overall, Finnish industry was much less advanced than in Sweden. Finland remained primarily an agricultural economy. Land reform after independence in 1917 extended the number of smallholdings. The total arable area was increased also, with the purpose of allowing more land settlement. Agriculture retained a social and political importance as well as being the major employer. In contrast to an economy like Denmark, it remained a low income sector in Finland. In Sweden agriculture had been overtaken by industry in share of GNP before 1914 and in share of employment during the 1920s. Finnish industry was dominated by forest products. Paper and pulp exports increased year by year, though they tended to be at the cheaper end of the market than those from Sweden (more cardboard and cheap paper than Sweden) with a lower level of technical sophistication (chemical processing was introduced in Sweden whereas mechanical processing continued in Finland).

Finland's historical links with the Russian market had left her in a weaker position at the opening of the 1920s than her more powerful neighbour, Sweden. This was not totally disadvantageous, however. Finland had developed the largest paper producer in Scandinavia, Kymmene Aktiebolog. This company had exported paper, principally to Russia, before 1917. Swedish and Norwegian companies, on the other hand, had exported pulp for processing into paper in Britain, though Sweden exported more paper than Finland in total. With the loss of the Russian market the company was forced to fight for export markets elsewhere. There were great improvements in efficiency through rationalisation – labour productivity doubled in the 1920s – growth which was to help the industry withstand the effects of recession at the end of the decade. Labour productivity doubled again after 1933 so that by 1938 Finland had become the largest paper exporter in Scandinavia.

Depression

The economic history of Scandinavia in the inter-war years is dominated, as everywhere, by the Depression. However, in many respects the economies of the Nordic countries were less severely affected than many other European nations, except for the high levels of unemployment. These economies were highly dependent on foreign trade, and in particular on a limited range of export commodities. Inevitably, therefore, they were adversely affected by the general contraction in world trade in the years of depression. The advantages for these economies, however, was that they were exporting goods for which demand remained relatively buoyant in staple markets. Nonetheless, any barriers to exports were vital; the devaluation of the pound sterling in 1931 and the imposition of exchange controls in Germany in the same year were of greater immediate impact than the international crisis which followed the crash in 1929.

Denmark

The Danish economy did not suffer greatly in the years of the Depression. GNP continued to grow at a healthy rate through 1929 and 1930, at 6.7 per cent and 6 per cent respectively. The only year that there was negative growth was 1932 (–2.6 per cent) and growth for the decade as a whole (1929–38) averaged 2.5 per cent per annum. In contrast to her neighbours to north or south, Denmark experienced relative social and political stability in these years. The story was far from altogether positive, however. Unemployment, a chronic problem, reached a peak of 32 per cent in 1932 and rarely fell below 20 per cent for the remainder of the decade.

Despite the heavy reliance on agricultural production and exports, Denmark's terms of trade improved during the Depression. Price fall was greatest for raw materials and basic bread grains. Danish staple exports – pig meat and dairy products – were less seriously affected. Falling wheat and cereal prices in fact resulted in cheaper animal feed and bigger profits for pig farmers. There were, nonetheless, difficulties with exports as the major markets, Germany in 1931 and Britain in 1932, introduced protective measures. Denmark followed Britain in devaluing her currency in 1931 (by 24 per cent) but even so was limited in the amount she could export to Britain. The 1933 trade agreement was a virtual lifeline for Danish exporters, yet restricted access in the face of effective priority to imperial suppliers (see pp. 34–6). In 1934 Denmark signed a trade treaty with Nazi Germany which involved settlement through a bilateral clearing arrangement. Mutual trade remained generally in balance. The state took an increasingly interventionist role, limiting production of pig meat and other commodities in 1933. Such measures, national and international, helped secure market stability but did nothing to foster growth or expansion.

Industry had always been more oriented to the home market than exports so was not faced with export competition. However, it proved necessary to extend protection, especially after 1931. The government employed quantitative import restrictions as well as tariffs. But in doing so they protected relative inefficiency as often as employment. Average productivity grew slowly; there was little change in structure. Added value in manufacturing, after negative years in 1931 and 1932, recovered quite quickly to a peak of growth in 1935, after which the rate of growth declined again, but always remained positive.

All in all the 1930s were characterised by stability rather than staggering growth. The access to the British market was a mixed blessing; Denmark earned a trade surplus in this market but it was limited by agreement and by slow growth in demand. In common with other Scandinavian economies, there was increasing interventionism by the state, in a regulatory rather than directive or prescriptive role.

Norway

Though smaller, the economy of Norway was similar to Denmark's, being dependent on a small range of primary commodities to earn its living internationally. In common with Scandinavian neighbours, a high proportion of Norway's GNP was earned in foreign trade. She was also peculiarly dependent on the British market. In the 1920s over a quarter of Norwegian exports went to Britain. This close relationship to the British market inevitably meant that the Norwegian currency followed sterling in devaluing in 1931. Indeed the devaluation of the krone continued, so that when joining the sterling area in 1933 the Norwegian currency was 10 per cent lower in real terms than before 1931.

Norway had been highly dependent in international markets on fishing, shipping and forestry and related industries. Each of these major sectors was affected differently in the recession. The recession followed a pattern similar to elsewhere, with troughs in production in 1932 or 1933, recovery to pre-slump levels only in 1936. Unemployment reached a peak in 1933 at 33.4 per cent of the insured population or 110 000 men. The figure had been as high as 25.4 per cent in 1927, 15 per cent in 1929, before recession. Full employment was not achieved before the Second World War.

Government played a small part in bringing about recovery. Despite the election to power of labour governments, financial policy was orthodox, though there was some monetary expansion. In addition, continued protection for farmers and subsidies to export surplus production continued. Legislation was also introduced to protect small fishermen by discriminating against foreign trawlers: they were prevented from landing any catch in Norway. Forestry was in a different position in that, as an industry, it was organised on a larger scale than fishing. Cartel and monopoly marketing organisations were developed without any government assistance, but without government resistance either. Even so both fishing and forestry contracted in exports in the 1930s. The major export earner was commercial shipping, accounting for over 50 per cent of export earnings. Despite contracting world trade, Norway's merchant marine was able to continue such high earnings through market manipulation, in particular through an international cartel whereby shipping tonnages were pooled for marketing purposes. The commentator Fritz Hodne (1983) concludes that recovery was not export-led, however. Most shipping earnings were spent abroad (new ships in the inter-war years were largely foreign built), thus limiting the direct stimulus to the home market. It would be a mistake, nonetheless, to dismiss the importance of this large earning capacity altogether.

If government policy was largely neutral and shipping exports limited in effect, what of other explanations? The first point to make is that recovery was limited, as witnessed by the continuing high levels of unemployment through the 1930s. Manufacturing increased its share in total production and in exports, albeit at modest levels. Metals, chemicals and ores increased production. Membership of international cartels (as for example for steel and nitrates) helped secure a share of the international market. Cartelisation was characteristic of industry domestically as well as internationally. There were 73 cartels in 1923, over 100 by 1928 and over 500 by 1960.

There was more growth in the home market, with a considerable variation in the pattern of demand. Increasing real incomes and technological innovations fostered an expansion in the demand for durable consumer goods such as synthetic fibres, household appliances (associated with the increase in supply of electricity) and radio. Domestic industry was able to meet a large amount of this growing demand and Norwegian companies established a place for themselves in the production of electrically-powered consumer durables.

Swedish recovery

The Swedish recovery experience in the 1930s has aroused a great deal of interest because of the apparent success of government policies of deficit financing and other Keynesian measures. Alternatively, the Swedish recovery, which was real enough, can be attributed, with equal validity, to autonomous demand growth, particularly in export markets. Sweden had the objective advantage of having been relatively mildly affected by the recession, except for the level of unemployment which, as we have seen, was a chronic phenomenon in Scandinavian economies. Indicators of national product and industrial production fell less steeply in Sweden than elsewhere in Europe (the USSR alone being excepted). Recovery therefore involved a shorter journey than for many other states. Another point of consequence, not one peculiar to Sweden, but evident for most smaller economies in Europe, was that measures that would be consequential from a great power had little international effect if taken by a small nation. Thus, for example, British devaluation in 1931 was followed by a great many countries, including Sweden. However, a further devaluation by Sweden (the krona cut from 18 to 19.5 to the pound in 1932) was undertaken without any retaliation elsewhere. The improved foreign exchange position enabled a cheap money policy at home.

Unlike the British case, there is no doubt that the cheap money policy was deliberately designed to achieve recovery and re-employment. Public works policies – the deliberate creation of employment – were well established in Sweden (and indeed in much of Europe; a nineteenth century practice). There was nothing Keynesian about such measures. What was new in this context was the extension of existing schemes and the addition of state subsidies for building, together with an unorthodox system of financing such expenditure. In this there was clearly some influence from the new economic thinking which Keynes represented and was later to typify.

The Swedish economists, B. Ohlin and G. Myrdal, advocated more state intervention and expenditure to increase demand. Their ideas were adopted by the Social Democratic party and, in particular, Ernst Wigfors, who became finance minister in 1933. In 1932 a coalition government, in which the SDs were the senior partners, had come to power. (This represented a real change in domestic politics and in the political attitude of the SDs, who now had power for the first time. In the 1920s they had supported financial orthodoxy and wage cuts.) Wigfors' policy included redistributive taxation as well as deficit spending. A budget deficit was to be balanced over a number of years (3–4) rather than year by year. The extra income generated by public expenditure in the initial year could provide increased government revenue in subsequent years. This was the real economic radicalism. It is noteworthy that such policies could be undertaken without the hostility and opposition from high income groups and financial interests (especially the banks) which were evident elsewhere in Europe (notably France under Blum).

It is at best uncertain, probably doubtful, however, how far such public expenditure influenced recovery directly. Such measures were too late to prevent recession. A long strike in the building industry, 1933–34, also hampered their effectiveness. H.W. Arndt estimated that direct public investment made up about half the deficiency in private investment, which suggests that the measures were counter cyclical to a point, though in themselves insufficient to bring about recovery. Nonetheless there was some marked reduction in unemployment from 189 000 in 1933 to 50 000 in 1935. Domestic policies, therefore, appeared to have an impact from 1934.

By this time, however, recovery was already under way in the export sector. The major explanation for Swedish recovery lies with the boost to export demand rather than public works at home. They were not entirely separate, of course; cheap money and devaluation aided investment and export sales. The major stimulus to demand came from growth outside rather than inside Sweden. Iron ore exports to Germany increased dramatically. Total exports grew from 3 million tons in 1933 to 10.2 million tons in 1936 and 12.5 million tons in 1939. Over 70 per cent went to Nazi Germany and rearmament. Britain continued to be the major single market. The UK building boom provided a vital outlet for timber; the UK also took 25 per cent of steel exports in 1939. Timber, however, declined as a proportion of total Swedish exports, Finland making up the difference. Paper and pulp increased by 40 per cent between 1929 and 1937.

Budgetary policies cannot be seen as solely responsible for Swedish recovery, though they clearly had some counter cyclical effect. The major stimulus was export demand – only Sweden and Japan were able to increase their export ratio in the 1930s. In agricultural policy Sweden remained conservative and protectionist (government was a coalition of SDs and agrarians). Agriculture remained a relatively retarded sector, though to a lesser extent than for her Finnish neighbour, rather more than in Denmark. However, agricultural protection did enable the maintenance of agricultural incomes and therefore home demand.

Finnish recovery

Finland recovered production in the 1930s at a rate similar to that of Sweden but without favourable interventionist policies of the same order. Like Sweden, however, Finland did follow a cheap money policy. However, Finland remained throughout essentially an agricultural economy (in 1930, 70 per cent were employed in agriculture compared with 30–40 per cent for her Scandinavian neighbours) and the domestic economy was accordingly affected and restrained in recovery. Politics were dominated by pro-agrarian governments throughout the period. However, as an exporter she was less severely affected than others, such as Denmark and Norway, because the commodity terms of trade for timber and timber products moved less adversely than for foodstuffs. Similarly, income elasticity of demand for timber was relatively high (compared with foods) and export demand grew quickly in the 1930s, for reasons similar to those affecting Sweden. The improvements in labour productivity in the paper and pulp industry in the 1920s provided a modest cushion against the worst effects of recession at the end of the decade. In the 1930s productivity was doubled again. Finland was therefore able to offer effective competition to Sweden and become the leading paper exporter in Scandinavia by 1938. However, this success did not apply to industry generally. Structural rigidity characterised much of Finnish industry, with the result that many saw mills became bankrupt, iron works were forced to amalgamate to survive and so on; unemployment persisted. Britain was Finland's major single market, accounting for 40 per cent of total exports by the end of the decade.

10.2 The Baltic States

The Baltic republics of Estonia, Latvia and Lithuania established their independence, briefly as it turned out, after the Russian revolution. In many respects they are similar to the new and successor states of eastern Europe. In contrast to the states which emerged from the Austro-Hungarian Empire, the Baltic States broke away from the Russian Empire, and in this respect bear some resemblance to Poland and Finland. Within the Russian Empire the Baltic regions had been in many ways more highly developed than much of the rest of the country, though considerably less well developed than most of western Europe. Levels of agricultural productivity exceeded the Russian average and there were regions of highly developed industry, in Estonia and Latvia rather than Lithuania. There were, further, cultural differences from the Russian centre, with different religious backgrounds (Lutheran Estonia and

Latvia, catholic Lithuania), higher educational standards, and different land holding and property relations (concepts of property based on Roman law obtained in the Baltic; they had no roots in Russia proper). The cultural history in many respects bears a closer resemblance to Finland and Sweden than Slavonic countries. This is more clearly so for Estonia and Latvia than Lithuania. The traditional Russian commune had no place in this region; there was more individual peasant ownership and a larger landless labouring class. Many of the large estate owners in Estonia, and, to a lesser extent, Latvia had been German or of German origin while in Lithuania they had been Polish.

Thus the new states had some economic base and a great sense of national identity, in language, culture and religion, on which to build. Land reforms to redistribute the most vital resource in favour of the ethnic peasantry, from alien land-owners, were quickly introduced, in a manner similar to many nations of eastern Europe. They were more extensive in Estonia and Latvia than Lithuania. All three states were relatively heavily dependent on agriculture for income and exports and all three had to undergo profound economic reorganisation after independence. This involved reorienting trade and completely restructuring (or constructing) the financial system.

The loss of the Russian market, previously a vast home market, was most important. Although poor in *per capita* terms, Russia had constituted an enormous market for the products of the Baltic and the most important source of supply for basic foodstuffs and raw materials. Now such trade for the first time would be conducted across political boundaries. These new states were born into a position of high foreign trade dependence. Yet little of it was to be with Russia. Though the treaties signed with Soviet Russia (1920 or 1921) contained trade clauses, there was little turnover with the former motherland. Throughout the inter-war years Britain and Germany were major trading partners of all three states. They traded little with each other, as their trade structure tended to be in competitive rather than complementary goods. The loss of the Russian market was more serious for the more industrialised economies of Estonia and Latvia than Lithuania. Some losses could never be made up. The Knoop owned textile factory in Krenholm, Estonia, had been the largest in the Empire (indeed it was claimed to be the largest in the world, with 5000 looms operating) before 1914. The major market and source of raw material had been the Russian Empire. Faced with the need to find new markets the company set out to diversify products and pursue new markets in Scandinavia, eastern Europe and Germany. Further, it used its influence with the Estonian government to secure protective tariffs and formed a cartel with the only other Estonian textile producer of any consequence. Last of all the company set up manufacturing plants, by dispersing some of its own superfluous capital equipment, in neighbouring Latvia and Memel (Lithuania) to cater for those, protected, markets. In this way the company adapted to new circumstances and survived until the Soviet annexation after 1939. It was never able to recover its former position, however. In Latvia the metallurgical and engineering sectors, including ship-building, were particularly badly hit. Such losses were made all the greater by the Russians stripping factories of equipment in their retreat, as they had done in Poland.

In the 1920s timber and related industries - plywood, paper, pulp – came to the fore in Estonia and Latvia and Estonia developed a shale oil industry. There was, by contrast, little industrial development in Lithuania, and most was concentrated in the Memel region, formerly German and ceded to Lithuania. Such manufacturing as there was in Lithuania was predominantly in small scale and handicraft enterprises. Only 1 per cent of the enterprises classified as industrial in Lithuania at the end of the 1920s employed more than 75 people. In 1930 the proportions of the labour force employed in manufacturing in the three countries were as follows: Estonia 17.4 per cent; Latvia 13.5 per cent; Lithuania 6 per cent. Latvia, with Riga, and Estonia (Tallinn) had well-developed commercial centres and ports; Lithuania's only effective commercial outlet to the sea was the ceded port of Memel. Riga and Tallinn had been major ports before 1914, though in the new commercial environment their functions were adjusted to serving general import and export needs of sovereign states rather than more specialised tasks. The new states needed to import basic foodstuffs as well as such tropical goods as coffee, tea and sugar, and nearly all fuel (coal, coke, mineral oil; Estonia had shale oil and all continued to use wood as fuel). Major exports were timber and flax, and their derivatives, and increasingly bacon and dairy products. The latter agricultural specialisms were fostered through a system of co-operatives in turn encouraged by governments. These, together with shale oil from Estonia, were the fastest growing exports in the 1920s. Britain and Germany were overwhelmingly important markets, taking over half exports and providing about three-quarters of imports in this decade. In general a trade surplus with Britain financed a deficit with Germany.

In common with the new states elsewhere in Europe, the Baltic countries faced problems with establishing new currencies upon independence. For some time old Russian and German paper money was used as a medium of exchange. The issue of new currencies faced the familiar difficulties of deficits of government revenue, shortages of gold and foreign exchange and inflation. In general stability was achieved in 1922 in Latvia and Lithuania, though with more difficulty in Estonia. This country was the first to begin issuing its own currency (the Estonian mark) but this was badly affected by inflation. Eventually a new currency was issued (the krona) in 1928, following re-financing with

Table 10.1 Index of industrial production in the Baltic

	Estonia	Latvia
1932	79.3	75.7
1934	97.7	119.8
1936	121.6	131.5
1937	140.5	147.8

1930 = 100

international loans in the previous year. All the currencies were linked to gold (until 1933).

The Depression

As small economies, heavily dependent on international trade and borrowing, the Baltic States were inevitably radically affected by the international recession after 1929. In all cases foreign trade contracted, import restrictions were introduced, gold exchange abandoned. Further government played an increasingly active role in the economy and, politically, there was a general shift towards totalitarianism, away from the democratic principles on which the states had been founded. This had been evident as early as 1926 in Lithuania and from 1934 in Latvia and Estonia. However, all three nations were neutral in 1939 when their independence was crushed.

As they were the more trade-dependent, Latvia and Estonia suffered more from the collapse of the international economy (see Table 10.1). Lithuania's economy did not escape either. Indeed Germany was the most important market for Lithuanian exports in 1929 and the contraction of German trade therefore had severe effects. Restrictions over imports, import substitution and exchange controls followed. Gold was abandoned in 1933. In an attempt to save imports Latvia and Estonia increased their production of bread grains and other cereals (the annual average area under wheat virtually doubled between 1926–30 and 1931–5; Lithuania showed a more modest increase). Lithuania was in a weaker position to pursue import substitution in industry because of her poorly developed industrial base. To have begun production would have been hugely expensive in terms of imported capital equipment. In most respects industry remained negligible in Lithuania. One exception was in beet sugar. By 1936 Lithuania had two sugar factories operating, producing an annual average of 12 800 tons of sugar, 1931–35. Production before 1930 had been negligible. In Latvia, by the same date, there were four such factories, producing 31 500 tons annually (compared with the

Table 10.2   Distribution of foreign trade

	Estonia			Latvia			Lithuania		
To	Germany	UK	USSR	Germany	UK	USSR	Germany	UK	USSR
1930	30.1	32.3	4.5	26.6	28.4	35.3	59.9	19.5	1.6
1932	26.2	36.7	0.4	26.2	30.8	38.4	39.1	41.4	3.5
1937	30.6	33.9	4.1	14.1	14.7	2.5	16.5	46.4	5.3

Figures are exports, per cent

From RIIA (1938) *The Baltic States* (Oxford: Oxford University Press), pp. 151, 165

previous quinquennium, 2900 tons per annum). As a result, imports of sugar into these two countries fell to negligible levels.

These sugar factories had been built with government aid; government intervention was to characterise the 1930s. In a pattern consistent with the rest of Europe political agreement was to influence foreign trade also. The major trading partners remained Britain and Germany. Indeed the two powers engaged in a virtual trade war in the 1930s, competing for the Baltic markets. As Britain continued to buy and sell with a freely exchangeable currency, while Germany did so more and more on a clearing basis, Britain was the more attractive partner, especially as an export market. Germany remained a more important source of imports for Latvia and Estonia (see Table 10.2). Latvia (in 1932) and Estonia (in 1934) signed clearing agreements with Germany and all three signed bilateral trading deals with Britain in 1934. These gave access for agricultural and timber products in return for guaranteed imports of coal (see Chap. 3).

As demand for their exports recovered, so too did production. The fortunes of the Baltic were directly linked to recovery in Britain and Germany, notwithstanding attempts at greater self-sufficiency. Latvia and Estonia in particular benefited from the building boom in Britain, with exports of plywood and other timber. Nearly all trade was handled by state monopolies or government offshoots (including co-operatives). In Latvia and Estonia, especially, there was significant recovery and growth of manufacturing in the 1930s, but this could not protect the nations from the vulnerability of geography. Following the German invasion of Poland in 1939, all three states were annexed by the Soviet Union, and were later invaded by German forces.

10.3   Further reading

This is an area much less well covered in English than many other parts of Europe. The book by T. Derry (1979) *A History of Scandinavia*

(London: Allen and Unwin) is useful but not detailed on economic affairs. Two recent specialised volumes, F. Hodne (1983) *The Norwegian Economy in the Twentieth Century* (London: Routledge) and H. Johansen (1987) *The Danish Economy in the Twentieth Century* (London: Routledge) fill many gaps in this subject. A. Montgomery (1938) *How Sweden Overcame the Depression* (Stockholm: Akademisk) is something of a classic examination of specific economic policies and progress. There is very useful, if dated, material in *The Baltic States* (1938) published by the Royal Institute for International Affairs (Oxford: Oxford University Press). More recently R.J. Missiumas and R. Taagesen (1983) *The Baltic States. Years of Independence* (London: Hurst) has some limited material on the economy.

11

Central and eastern Europe

The special circumstances of the economies of central and eastern Europe after the First World War were largely influenced by their infancy as nation states. Redrawing the map of Europe by the great powers of the West (Britain, France and the USA) resulted in the break up of the old Habsburg Empire and the carving out of this multinational community and portions of Imperial Germany, Russia and the remnants of the Ottoman Empire, new nation states often with fragile economic foundations. The new and successor states, Austria, Hungary, Poland, Czechoslovakia, Romania, Bulgaria and Yugoslavia had little in common in culture, language, history or economic characteristics. Austria and Hungary were the successor dual imperial powers of the Habsburg Empire. (Since 1867 Austria and Hungary had exercised power and control over their respective territories. Previously power had centred on Vienna, with Hungary subordinate to Austria.) The 'rump' states were thus deprived of great internal markets and sources of supply. Austria in particular became a small economy and nation with a vast capital and state bureaucracy that had grown to serve the needs of empire. Typically the former Austrian territories were the more likely to have some industrial base with consequent higher incomes. In the former dual monarchy Hungary had tended to be the more unified kingdom, within which minorities had been subordinate. In former Austria national minorities had enjoyed more cultural freedom.

Poland had the immensely powerful unifying force of language and national consciousness, which had sustained the Poles as subject peoples since the eighteenth century. But the newly drawn national boundaries embraced Polish areas from Austrian Galicia, German Silesia and Russian Poland with very different economic backgrounds. The former

German territories were the more developed. Poland did have the advantage of substantial coal resources and some industrial development. This was some way behind Czechoslovakia, however.

Czechoslovakia was by far the most industrial of the states of central and eastern Europe, with industrial regions in Bohemia comparable to those of western Europe. She was to retain this position of industrial supremacy in the region throughout the inter-war years. National unity was weaker than in Poland, Bohemia and Moravia – the Czech lands – having formerly been in Austria, and Slovakia – a more backward agricultural and lower income region – in Hungary. Although Czech nationalism and consciousness was established in the nineteenth century it was, perhaps, weaker than in Poland. There was no history of independent national existence for the state as a whole. Cultural as well as economic differences between Czech and Slovak remained. Apart from Czechoslovakia, Yugoslavia was also created as a 'new state'. The other countries within this region were (or in Poland's case, had been) established nation states, though with much changed frontiers and populations.

The most complex of the new states was Yugoslavia, with catholic, orthodox and muslim inhabitants; former Austrian territories (Slovenia, Dalmatia), Hungarian (Croatia, Bosnia), independent Serbia and Montenegro. Traditional conflicts, such as those between Serbs and Croats, persisted, and were exacerbated by contrasts in economic fortune. Slovenia was one of the most economically advanced regions; Bosnia and Herzogovina remained backward by comparison, displaying social and economic characteristics more reminiscent of Asia than Europe. The old kingdom of Romania was enormously enhanced and extended with the addition of Russian Bessarabia, Hungarian Transylvania and Austrian Bukovina, to treble in size. Bulgaria lost some territory to Greece.

The redrawing of boundaries left anomalies, the most politically sensitive of which was to prove that of national minorities. German speakers in Poland and in Czechoslovakia, Hungarians in Romania and Yugoslavia were to be, in varying degrees, foci of discontent in later years. This was made the stronger because, in order to create a nation, the new states emphasised liguistic and ethnic identity and induced an element of nationalism which extended into economic life. Nationalism was stronger than any other shade of political ideology, affecting both left and right. Radical revolution in Hungary and the short leadership of the communist, Bela Kun, was succeeded by a severely reactionary regime wherein resentment against national losses at Trianon (the post-war treaty affecting Hungary) was the central theme. In Bulgaria, a peasant-socialist government under Stamboliiski was violently overthrown in 1923 by a more nationally defensive regime. The uncertain early years of the revived Polish state were brought into order under the quasi-military rule of Marshal Pilsudski (1926). The seeds of fascist sympathies of the 1930s were, in many cases, implanted in the nationalism of the post-war years. Only Czechoslovakia remained as a liberal democratic regime, but even she did not escape the overtones of protective economic nationalism.

The economic base of most countries in this region was weak also because they were highly dependent on agriculture. The proportion of the population dependent on agricultural incomes was as follows (the figures referring to 1930–31, except for Bulgaria, 1921): Bulgaria 75 per cent, Romania 72 per cent, Yugoslavia 76 per cent, Poland 69 per cent, Hungary 51 per cent, Czechoslovakia 33 per cent. In this context agricultural incomes were lower than in industrial or other occupations. Yet because of the important role of agriculture and the value of land to the population, nearly all states instituted some form of land reform shortly after the First World War. There were, in most cases, political reasons for such moves also – to cement national identity by dispossessing alien landlords in favour of ethnic peasants, and to provide a source of income to the many returning fighting men. Strict economic considerations were not always to the fore in drawing up such reforms. As a result a great many smallholdings were created, sometimes lacking proper commercial viability, often lacking sufficient capital equipment. It must not be supposed, however, that smallholdings were necessarily relatively inefficient. This was far from the case. Smallholdings were usually better suited to intensive production of livestock, fruits, vines etc. In some cases also they had better grain yields than larger farms. However, a large proportion of newly formed small farms were undercapitalised, forced to borrow and therefore became heavily indebted at a time when terms of trade for farmers were deteriorating. In some instances the reforms were still being put into effect when the crisis broke in Europe, after 1929.

It is perhaps of greater consequence that there was a great demand for land as property among the peasant populations of central and eastern Europe. This demand was met extremely unevenly. Broadly speaking reforms were extensive, with substantial redistribution of landed estates in Romania and Yugoslavia, modest redistribution in Poland and Czechoslovakia and, for particular reasons, negligible redistribution both in Bulgaria and Hungary. (In Romania some 6 million hectares were redistributed by 1929, with great regional variation in detail.) In Bulgaria peasant smallholding predominated and there was little reform as such. In Poland land distribution favoured peasant smallholdings in the eastern areas but a great many large farms remained also. In Czechoslovakia there was some expropriation of large *latifundiae* but much to the benefit of medium-sized farms. In Hungary, after the overthrow of the communist leader Bela Kun, reform plans were reversed so that agricultural structure remained extremely inequitable, with large estates and a landless labouring class. Despite the importance of agriculture in the economies, few governments paid great attention to the development of the productive potential of this sector in the short run, instead putting more emphasis on industry. Thus there was a common tendency to favour those sectors of the economy which did not have a comparative advantage, for the sake of import saving or national autarky. Such trends were reinforced by the experience of economic recession but were already well established before the end of the 1920s.

11.1   Austria

Austria was relatively well industrialised from the beginning of the period, in many ways comparable to Czechoslovakia. Similarly, she was highly trade-dependent from her rebirth in 1918. Unlike Czechoslovakia and other economies in the region, however, the major problem facing Austria was sources of supply rather than markets. Austria had been at the heart of a great trading empire; now she had to import the bulk of her food, fuel and materials. In the short run there were critical shortages, verging on famine, which required international intervention. This was succeeded by rapid inflation, international loans and the creation of a new, stable currency, the schilling. In this respect the experience of Austria was as comparable to Germany as much as to other successor states.

The inflation period provided a stimulus to production, as it did elsewhere; agricultural output recovered 1913 levels by 1923 (for the principal grain crops; sugar beet exceeded pre-war levels). By 1924 the economy was developing quite favourably; manufacturing industry by this time provided 79 per cent of exports, most imports being of food, fuel and raw materials (59 per cent together). But there was a constant trade deficit. This was the result of both the inelastic demand for food imports and the high import content of manufactured exports. Despite this (or perhaps because of this import dependence) governments pursued liberal tariff policies until 1927. The deficit was to some extent made up by invisible earnings (financial services and, increasingly, tourism) but more particularly by foreign borrowing and credits. The reliance on foreign borrowing, often short-term, was to leave the economy particularly vulnerable in the recession, in a way similar to Germany and far more so than Czechoslovakia. Of course this could not have been foreseen, though it became clear with hindsight. On the other hand, the tendency among Viennese bankers to borrow short, abroad, and lend long, at home, was less than prudent.

In the favourable growth environment of the late 1920s Austrian industry boomed, growing at a rate comparable with Germany, though from a lower post-war base. Also as in Germany, there was a considerable degree of rationalisation of production. The savings of labour which resulted produced similar unemployment, which remained at over 10 per cent throughout the decade and before the recession. From 1927 there was a renewal of protectionism; agriculture was fostered to reduce the level of imports. The area under major crops (barley, wheat, rye, potatoes and sugar-beet) and all yields increased. Thus the generally favourable picture of the 1920s was moderated by foreign indebtedness, some financial irresponsibility, and a move toward autarky in the later part of the decade. Austrian industry showed impressive growth rates, but a large share was the result of import substitution; exports were restrained.

11.2 Czechoslovakia

As we have seen Czechoslovakia was the most industrialised economy in the region. A large proportion of Czech industry was in metallurgical and engineering branches with a small, but growing, chemical sector. These industries increased their share of the total modestly in the 1920s. There was a similar modest fall in textiles and mining. In the 1920s Czechoslovakia had the highest rate of growth of incomes. This economic success was based on three factors. First was the indubitably crucial one of natural resources. The major industrial regions of the Habsburg Empire lay within Bohemia; Pilsen became one of the major industrial cities in Europe, with well-developed engineering and armaments works (including Skoda) as well as brewing. Second, much of the industrial capacity escaped wartime damage or destruction, in contrast to neighbouring Poland, for instance. The third factor might be termed economic management: Czechoslovakia achieved monetary stability early, in 1919, after a modest rate of inflation. The new currency was also relatively undervalued, giving exports a competitive edge. Between 1920 and 1929 exports grew by 155 per cent to increase their share in national product (GDP) from 18 to nearly 31 per cent. Such earnings made Czechoslovakia into a capital exporter, a unique position in the region. Industry grew by 9 per cent per annum in this decade, agriculture by 5 per cent, GDP by 5.9 per cent.

This growth was a remarkable achievement and all the more so as Czechoslovakia faced the great disadvantage of loss of markets. The vast home market of the Habsburg Empire had now become a number of protected nation states. It would be a mistake therefore to suppose that Czech industry was able to prosper on the basis of some 'natural' comparative advantage. This was certainly true for some export sectors (such as glassware) but not for all. Textiles, machinery and metals did not enjoy such comparative advantage yet were important export sectors. The dependence of Czech industry was inevitable and necessary; the growth of the 1920s was export-led. There was also some reorientation towards markets in western Europe rather than the 'natural' markets of the other successor states. Czech industrial exports faced protective tariffs in neighbouring economies.

Of course Czechoslovakia also introduced tariffs, but the effect of these was more to favour domestic agriculture, effectively redistributing income in favour of the less efficient producer than supporting industry. Agriculture remained an important sector in Czechoslovakia, particularly for employment in Slovakia and Ruthenia (formerly Hungarian). In these regions there was little established industry and the development of the 1920s had virtually no impact. The agricultural protectionism of Czechoslovakia was as limiting on the growth of international trade as that followed anywhere else, though arguably as necessary to protect the low income regions of the east. The major agricultural exports, especially hops, malt and sugar, of which Czechoslovakia was a major producer, came largely from the Czech lands of Bohemia and Moravia.

11.3 Poland

Poland, by comparison, suffered general stagnation over the inter-war period. Stabilisation was slow after one of the most severe rates of inflation (the zloty was introduced in 1926). Although Poland had industrial regions in Silesia, with valuable coal resources, she remained essentially an agricultural, low income economy. Yields of the major crops stagnated, total production growing slowly through some extension of sown area. Output of grain *per capita* actually declined. Polish industrial resources were weakened by the war. There had been a certain amount of direct damage in the war but the major losses were inflicted by dismantling. Production had been stimulated by wartime demand in Prussian Silesia (to become western Poland) but areas further east were adversely affected by the dismantling of equipment by Russian forces and the German and Austrian requisitions. Of the war-time 'damage' to the industrial base of Poland, only 4 per cent resulted directly from the fighting, the remainder from systematic dismantling (52 per cent by Germans, 22 per cent by Austrians, 18 per cent by

Russians). Such losses contributed to the slow development of Polish industry in the 1920s, the slowest growth in the region. Thus Polish industry remained narrowly based on coal and lignite deposits. Coal remained the major export earner; structural change was negligible.

There was one outstanding exception to this sorry tale, the port of Gdynia. As Danzig (Gdansk) became a free port, and not Polish territory, so the Poles built a new port at Gdynia, from a small fishing village. This port became the second largest trading port in the Baltic, after Copenhagen. Further, railway extensions were newly built to carry coal for export to the port. The driving force of nationalism, to establish a Polish port, was no doubt an important contributing factor to this success.

11.4 Hungary

Industry in Hungary grew slowly, but faster than in Poland. *Per capita* incomes, however, increased at a rate exceeded only by Czechoslovakia. However, the maldistribution of farm resources in the new Hungarian state did little for the income of the agricultural population but provided a means of producing an export surplus. The major problem facing the country in the 1920s, therefore, was the loss of markets rather than productive capacity. Before 1914 Hungarian agriculture had been a dynamic and large export earner, and the major industries in Hungarian regions had been linked to agriculture. She had become the world's largest exporter of wheat flour, for example, and was in the forefront of flour milling technology, even exporting equipment to the USA. The much reduced Hungarian territory, left with a third of her pre-war area, retained a higher proportion of productive capacity – over half of former industrial production. There was thus a basis for the development of Hungarian industry (though it must be stressed that Hungarian regions had been less industrialised than Austrian). Given the reduced size of the country there was some overcapacity in flour milling in particular. Food processing (flour milling principally) declined as a proportion of total industrial product in the 1920s from 42.4 per cent (post-war territory) in 1913 to 35.7 per cent in 1929. Metallurgical industry and engineering declined also from 30 per cent to 21.5 per cent; consumer goods as import substitutes increased in proportion.

11.5 The Balkans

The Balkan economies of Bulgaria, Romania and Yugoslavia displayed some rapid growth in industries in the 1920s, but this was from a low base so that industry had a minor part to play in their economies. Bulgaria, having been allied to Germany and Austria in the First World War, was required to pay reparations (to neighbouring states) thereafter. These, coupled with outstanding debts, were a great burden to the economy (at five times the pre-war level of debt), until reduced in 1923. Currency stabilisation and gold exchange (effectively in 1926, formally 1928) were achieved at the cost of swingeing domestic deflation, in accordance with contemporary orthodoxy and the dictates of international loans which provided the backing for the currency. One aspect of policy was support for industry, under an umbrella of high domestic protection. Although industrial production grew quickly, artisan output grew faster than factory production. Manufacturing was predominantly in food processing and textiles, and very much concentrated around the capital, Sofia. In contemporary terms, therefore, Bulgaria remained industrially undeveloped, with a limited and low income home market.

Agriculture remained at the basis of the economy and export earnings. The peasant smallholding structure did not inhibit growth but there were undoubtedly some politically disappointing expectations. The peasant leader, Stamboliiski, had ideas of Bulgaria emulating Denmark, with a highly efficient agrarian economy based on family smallholdings and systematic co-operative marketing. Thus he encouraged the formation of co-operatives. His leadership came to a bloody end in 1923 and subsequent leaders were more enthusiastic in encouraging industry, with mixed results as we have seen.

Romania trebled in size as a result of the post-war peace settlement. In terms of natural resources it was blessed not only with a rich agriculture but also with oil. Industrial production recovered by 1925 but remained a small sector. There was some real growth in the consumer goods sectors in the 1920s, very much as import saving, though oil remained the major industrial export earner. International demand was growing rapidly for oil and it was exploited very much as an export commodity rather than as a raw material for Romanian industry. However, through the inter-war period, nearly all was refined in Romania, rather than being exported as crude oil. The oil industry was very much an enclave development with only a limited impact on the economy as a whole. Thus Romania experienced industrial growth but did not become an industrial economy, rather remaining a land of peasants; wheat and maize continued to be the major products.

Yugoslavia's major economic problems lay with the great regional variations and lack of cohesiveness. The country lacked even a single railway system. In addition Serbia had been a battle area in the war and had suffered much damage, probably greater than any other nation. Further she had also felt the effects of dismantling and requisitioning of equipment in the war. Early state sponsorship for industry, through tariffs, subsidies and so on, had only a minor effect, yet agriculture was almost neglected. The 1925 tariff was designed to protect infant industry first and foremost, while agriculture continued to provide the mass of employment and exports. Thus Yugoslavia in the post-war decade had a history similar to other Balkan states, with virtually no structural change in the economy.

11.6 Depression and recovery

The economies of central and eastern Europe were brought into the Depression after 1929 through two major forces, their high trade dependence and the general level of indebtedness. As exporting economies, principally of foodstuffs or other primary products, these small economies could not escape the effects of a general contraction of world demand; terms of trade moved to the disadvantage of primary producers worldwide. For these countries there was the additional factor of dependence on foreign loans. Nearly all government debt in the Balkan countries was to foreign creditors; in Poland, in 1928, 60 per cent of capital stock and 40 per cent of industry was foreign owned, in Hungary the respective figures were 50 per cent and 25 per cent.

The loans raised by the new nations in the 1920s naturally placed them in debt to foreign banks (and governments). However, some of these loans were, in effect, needed to service old ones; further loans were raised in the 1920s to repay former debts. One problem, as was the case in Germany, was that much of the borrowed money had not been used to finance means to repay the debt. In Hungary, for instance, only 20 per cent of loans were used for productive purposes, a further 15 per cent for building (much of which was of a prestige or luxury nature); 40 per cent was used to repay old debts. The position in Romania and Yugoslavia was probably similar, though in these cases records do not allow such an accurate assessment. On top of this it was necessary to resort to further loans during the worst years of recession (1929–32) in order to meet short-term obligations. Even Czechoslovakia, the least dependent of all on foreign loans (a capital exporter in the 1920s) had to borrow abroad in the years of crisis.

Much of such borrowing was short-term. In 1931 one half of the Hungarian national debt was in short-term loans; in Austria one quarter; in Yugoslavia only one sixth. The recall of such loans, or the failure to provide further short loans, was one of the main contributory factors in the crisis and international illiquidity. A general moratorium of debt payments for one year, proposed by President Hoover, eased the position but did not remove the problem. Hungary stopped paying foreign debts and interest from late 1931 (foreign assets could be taken only in pengos and used in Hungary); Austria introduced strict exchange controls in 1931, later relaxing them and formally devaluing in 1934; Romania (by 38 per cent) and Yugoslavia (by 28 per cent) devalued currencies; Czechoslovakia avoided this until 1934. Uniquely, Poland neither devalued nor had exchange controls, with a resultant loss of gold holdings, until 1936 when it was forced to introduce controls. Outstanding debts made it all the more difficult to raise new capital in the 1930s when recovery began to get under way. Thus these small and poor economies were forced to rely increasingly on their own capital resources, an especially difficult problem for economies like Romania and Yugoslavia.

The mountain of debt was all the more difficult to climb because of falling export-earning opportunities with the closure of markets. Difficulties of foreign trade were felt particularly by agricultural exporters as their earning power was the more seriously affected. On the other hand, industrial exporters (Austria and Czechoslovakia) found it hard to secure markets, especially as their export prices fell less drastically than those for agricultural products. As has been shown above (Chap. 3) the majority of European states turned to bilateral trading treaties in the 1930s. The most significant of these were the treaties negotiated by Germany, which involved payment through clearing arrangements rather than with foreign exchange. In 1931 Germany signed such treaties with Hungary, Bulgaria, Yugoslavia and Romania; they were later renewed by the Nazi regime, much to its own advantage. By offering a market to the primary producers of south-east Europe, Germany was able to extend political influence in this region; the countries of the region sacrificed a degree of political independence for the sake of short-term commercial gains. Austria, Czechoslovakia and Poland became less dependent on the German market, though a proportion of trade was conducted on a similar clearing basis. Clearing arrangements, indeed, became commonplace between various countries and without necessarily involving Germany. Only Germany used them for systematic political purposes, however.

The collapse of multilateral trade also induced states to pursue policies of self-sufficiency, and so seek to minimise trade with neighbours. Thus Austria and Czechoslovakia, for instance, supported agriculture while Bulgaria, Romania and Hungary sought to increase their industrial output. Foreign trade turnover tended to recover more slowly than total production in the eastern regions of Europe as in the west, in part as a result of nationalist policies. These can easily be seen as misplaced with the advantage of hindsight, but it must be remembered that the economies of eastern Europe were in a defensive position. They were too small, alone, to influence the world market and therefore had to respond to the crisis. In the absence of a lead from the more powerful national economies, or international co-operation, they were bound to seek import substitution and export promotion. Thus all these nations, to some extent, became more defensive and autarkic in economic policy in the 1930s.

Austria

As an industrial economy Austria, like Czechoslovakia, benefited from the improvement in terms of trade in the recession. On the other hand, as her industry was so heavily export dependent, she suffered from the decline in trade. Austria was further, and spectacularly, affected by the fall of the Creditanstalt Bank whose collapse signalled financial crisis throughout Europe. The response to this was conventional, in that the government introduced exchange controls (1931) and resisted devaluation for some time. (The state also rescued the Creditanstalt.) Effective devaluation (by 22 per cent) was permitted in 1932 and formalised in 1934. This encouraged recovery up to a point but it was here, as elsewhere, an incomplete process, for export markets remained restricted. On the other hand, the tourist industry grew significantly, adding to export earnings. Visible trade was faced with difficulties; that with neighbouring Czechoslovakia was reduced, for instance. Germany became the major trading partner, though German trade penetration never reached the levels that it did in the Balkans. However, German economic interests were manifest also in other ways. German capital came to dominate much of the engineering industry; the Austrian metallurgical conglomerate, Alpine Montan AG, which was the largest industrial concern in Austria, fell into the hands of the Vereinigte Stahlwerke, the German steel combine. Although foreign capital ownership was by no means new, in this case it proved commercially damaging. In the recession, production was transferred to Germany; the Austrian blast furnaces were closed in 1932 and 1933. In this way the burden of economic contraction was shifted to the Austrian branch of the business.

In other respects, German trade expansion, as in the Balkans, worked against Austria by excluding her from some markets. One response was to extend trade links elsewhere; the Rome protocol of 1934 opened some modest opportunities in Italy and Hungary. The increasingly right wing political leadership in Austria was evident in such deals; Austria continued to trade with Italy, in breach of League of Nations sanctions over the war with Abyssinia. A trade treaty with Czechoslovakia in 1936 was rather too late to secure any substantial growth in trade turnover.

Nonetheless, the Austrian economy displayed rapid recovery in the years from 1932 to 1937 (as is well known, in 1938 Austria was united with Germany and ceased to function as a separate economy). Growth was comparable with Germany, and faster than in Czechoslovakia. Although *per capita* income remained well below levels of western Europe, it was comparable, again, with Czechoslovakia. There was particular success in agriculture as a result of deliberate import-saving measures, just as agricultural economies were taking measures to reduce industrial imports. The import dependence of all agricultural products was reduced and there was sufficient growth in the dairy sector to provide an export surplus.

Czechoslovakia

Ironically the Czechoslovak economy, which had been the strongest in the region in the 1920s, was one of the least effective at recovery in the 1930s. The Czechoslovak economy followed a pattern very similar to that of France: boom in the 1920s, stagnation in the 1930s. It was severely affected by the closure of export markets in the 1930s, competitive devaluation and 'beggar my neighbour' policies. The devaluation of the pound sterling in 1931, and subsequent devaluations in much of the rest of the continent, left the Czech crown overvalued and Czech exports disadvantaged. The Czech authorities resisted devaluation until 1934 but at a cost of domestic deflationary policies. This restricted economic activity, and state aid was directed to the least efficient sectors of the economy.

By 1929 exports were 30 per cent of GNP; the loss of export outlets was inevitably to have a profound effect on the economy. The main sectors to suffer in Czechoslovakia were in heavy industry, especially as neighbouring economies both developed their own industrial sectors and had difficulty funding imports. Between 1929 and 1933 exports fell by nearly two thirds. The virtual closure of export markets severely limited recovery, though Czechoslovakia contributed to the general malaise itself by extending protective tariffs in 1933. Perversely, as it might seem, the state put resources into subsidising agriculture and agricultural exports even though these had no comparative advantage and discriminated against agricultural exporters which might otherwise have provided export markets for Czech industry. Agriculture, however, was the major sector in the economy of Slovakia – industry was virtually confined to the Czech lands; all governments had to protect the interests of their own peoples. In Czechoslovakia unemployment persisted and recovery was slow and imperfect. Unemployment was also higher in the German speaking regions, which later came to be labelled 'Sudetenland'. This added to the social discontent of a national minority which was exploited by Nazi leaders in Germany. However, average *per capita* income was probably higher than in neighbouring states. Net national income *per capita* in 1938 (at $US 176) was higher than in Hungary ($US 112) or Poland ($US 104) and very much higher than in the Balkans. Further, added value in agriculture, though below income generated by industrial activity, was higher than that earned in agriculture in the 'agricultural' economies elsewhere in the region.

As exports stagnated the home market became more important in absorbing production, though never sufficiently to induce full recovery before 1938. As elsewhere, there were autarkic tendencies in Czechoslovakia, supported not only by protectionism but also by state-sponsored cartelisation. In 1933 the Cartel Act required registration of all such agreements. This revealed 538 cartels in that year; by 1938 the figure had reached 1152. Thus there was some erosion of the liberal market economy even in Czechoslovakia which, throughout the interwar years, had maintained a position as a parliamentary democracy and liberal capitalist state. The state introduced strict exchange controls and controlled the largest monopoly trading organisation, the Czechoslovak Grain Company. Apart from an unplanned period of deficit financing in 1931 and 1932 the government retained a strictly orthodox financial policy. Devaluation in 1934, and then again in 1936, came too late to have a major effect on international trade. By 1937 exports had recovered to two thirds of their 1929 level; industrial production did not recover fully before the loss of Sudetenland to Germany in 1938, and occupation in 1939.

Poland

Poland suffered one of the worst recessions of the region. Industry achieved some real recovery after 1936 but the agricultural sector, which was particularly large in Poland, continued to suffer. Recovery after 1936 was accompanied by extensive state intervention in the economy. Government had helped to extend the effects of recession before this date by resisting devaluation and refusing to introduce exchange controls. Poland remained a member of the gold bloc until 1936, and suffered restricted recovery. Financial openness demanded stringent domestic deflation and restrictions of demand. Capital imports had to be paid for by a surplus on visible trade. This was achieved between 1930 and 1935 but at the cost of falls in domestic consumption.

The agricultural producers suffered the most severe price fall in the Depression. By the low point of 1935 their prices were, on average, 30–35 per cent of the 1928 level, a much steeper fall than their costs. The poverty of the peasants, especially in the eastern regions of the country, in turn further restricted the home market. There was some marginal shift to livestock farming in response. Government intervened by buying up produce for export at below cost, all to maintain an active trade balance.

Other areas of direct state intervention, such as direct ownership of a number of enterprises, are more noteworthy. An investment plan for industry was introduced in 1936, at the same time as a programme to modernise the army. These two objectives were not always wholly compatible as they competed for funds. The four-year investment programme was more evidently successful than the six-year military project. The industrial investment scheme was actually over-achieved and ahead of schedule by 1939. Even so, it made only a modest difference to the overall industrial structure and performance of the economy. By the end of the decade, on the eve of war, the state owned 100 major industrial enterprises, including 80 per cent of the chemical industry, 40 per cent of iron and steel, 95 per cent of merchant shipping and all air transport and railways.

The direct stimulus to industry came too late to have a profound effect on the economy, though there was real growth from 1936 to 1939. How far this was the product of state intervention or of the expansion of total world demand (and aided in this context by a devalued zloty) is difficult to judge. It is unlikely that state action was the only factor responsible. Even so, 1939 output only approximated to 1913 levels, at about one fifth of those in Britain. The Polish economy and army were poorly equipped to face invasion in 1939.

Hungary

As an agricultural exporter Hungary was badly affected by the steep price fall. Between 1929 and 1933 her agricultural exports declined in value by 60 per cent. Domestic agricultural production had done badly in the 1920s: yields had remained stagnant and livestock numbers were never able to reach the levels of 1913. Yet the farm sector continued to provide a vital source of export earnings. Export difficulties had serious short-term consequences. The financial crisis of 1931 left the treasury short of gold and foreign exchange (£8 million worth of gold left the country between May and July) with a need to borrow heavily. The level of debts would have taken half total exports had the position not been alleviated by international moratorium (see p. 25). Devaluation would have made exports cheaper, but increased the effective level of debts to the exchequer in domestic currency. As an alternative, government had strict exchange controls and paid variable premia to exporters. In this way exporters could receive payments, in pengos, additional to the official exchange rate in return for their foreign currency earnings.

Futher, these premia varied according to the currency earned with the highest rate (a premium of 50 per cent) being paid for exports to the sterling area, countries in the gold bloc or countries outside Europe. Even so, it was necessary for the government to negotiate a series of clearing agreements as a basis for the greater part of its foreign trade. Those with Germany were the best known, but by no means the only ones. By 1935, 63 per cent of trade was conducted through clearing arrangements. The clearing system enabled government to influence the pattern and structure of foreign trade and thereby restricted imports of certain protected products – the textile industry is a good example. In the German case it was the Nazi government that was able to exercise the greater influence and subordinate much of the Hungarian export economy to German needs, especially towards the end of the 1930s. Even though the terms of trade for agricultural exports were improving later in the decade it was difficult for Hungary to escape German trade agreements, the terms of which were rigorously imposed in Germany's favour. Thus, although such trade deals were advantageous in the short term in providing a market for Hungarian exports, in the longer run they were of much less value to the Hungarian economy.

The major source of growth in the 1930s was industry, yet industrial output grew by only 1.5 per cent per annum. Public utilities and consumer goods were the fastest growing of all. Coal production and iron and steel remained with under-utilised capacity throughout the interwar years. There were some sectors with a more favourable performance, however, though with limited impact on the economy as a whole. A significant development came with the discovery of bauxite in the 1920s; in the 1930s most of this was processed into aluminium, largely for the export market. There were other examples of relative technical advance. In Ganz a diesel locomotive industry had success with exports. There was even some manufacture of diesel-powered ocean-going ships for export – a noteworthy achievement for a landlocked country! Without doubt the major growth industry was textiles. It was developed by private entrepreneurs, but behind tariff walls, in the 1920s, using second-hand machinery bought in Britain. By 1938 production was four times the pre-war level. The growth of these industries was real, even spectacular, but misleading, for the overall performance of the economy in the 1930s was modest. Growth was one of the slowest in Europe.

Romania

Romania achieved real industrial growth in the 1930s but it was inefficient and highly dependent on protection. Agriculture remained the major employer and, as elsewhere, the peasant producers were particularly hard hit in the recession. An index of agricultural prices fell by 55 per cent from 1929 to 1934, and did not recover before the outbreak of war. Average costs of industrial products used in agricultural production declined by less than 20 per cent (the low point in this case being 1932). There was some recovery in trade aided by access to the German market, though similar qualifications about the utility of this privilege apply to Romania as to Hungary. Indeed by 1939 commercial agricultural production was almost totally geared to the German market. Wheat and maize remained the principal export crops throughout the period but increased quantities of soya (for IG Farben), sunflower (for Solagra) and flax (for Sudostropa) were grown directly for German commercial interests.

Total agricultural production actually declined relatively in the 1930s because of the more rapid growth of industrial output. The state encouraged industry. In 1936 imports of machinery were allowed if they were to be used for import-saving production. High domestic prices in a highly protected market fostered the growth of import substitutes, especially in textile and food processing, to the extent that over-capacity developed in some sectors. The only significant industrial exports were in timber products and oil. Oil production showed a steady increase up to 1936, and a small decrease therefter. Nearly all was refined before export, though the industry retained characteristics of enclave development with limited broader linkages in the economy. By 1938/9 industry produced 31 per cent of national income, agriculture and forestry 38.5 per cent.

With the ready international demand for oil, Romania was less beholden to the German market than some of its neighbours. However, an extraordinary degree of dependence on this single market for agricultural exports did develop. Further, after 1936 a programme of rearmament was initiated, with Czech arms manufacturers taking a central interest. When Czechoslovakia was occupied by German forces in 1939 this sector of Romanian industry fell into German hands.

Bulgaria

Bulgaria had the fastest rate of growth of industry in the region, and one of the fastest in Europe, in the 1930s, at 4.8 per cent per annum. As in the Romanian case, much of this was a function of import substitution. Food processing was the major sector. There was, however, little effect on employment, as artisan production grew at a faster rate than in factories. Agricultural production underwent some marginal shift to higher value crops. Industrial crops (tobacco, sunflower and cotton) increased at a slightly faster rate than agricultural production as a whole, though fruit, vine and vegetable production increased most of all (see Table 11.1).

Table 11.1   Gross agricultural output *per capita* in Bulgaria

	1931–35	1936–38
All crops	109	122
Industrial	95	107
Grain crops	109	118
Vegetables	144	175
Fruit and vine	124	130

1926–30 = 100

From J. Lampe (1986) *The Bulgarian Economy in the Twentieth Century* (London: Routledge), p. 85

The state assisted agriculture by encouraging cheap credit and investment. As a result, yields improved and total production increased. Yield improvements were particularly notable on small farms. There was no correlation between size and productivity in this context (small farms were more suitable for labour-intensive crops like vegetables and fruit). At the opposite end of the productive process, the government intervened further in marketing. In 1931 a government grain monopoly was established and helped to subsidise, or dump, exports. The state also established or 'encouraged' cartels for the marketing of sugar, tobacco, fruit and other products. Such measures had no direct influence over production but rather sought to regulate sales in a peasant economy. This example was a long way from the dream of emulating the Danish model. However, it demonstrates that small scale peasant household farming was far from being essentially inefficient. Indeed, as we have seen, the main problem was over-production. Bulgaria became more dependent on the German market, which by 1939 took 68 per cent of exports.

Yugoslavia

In contrast to Bulgaria, industry in Yugoslavia developed slowly. In the inter-war years there was only a 5 per cent shift from agricultural to non-agricultural occupations. In industrial terms Yugoslavia was one of the least developed economies in Europe by 1939. Despite state encouragement for industry it remained a poor, peasant economy. The great regional imbalances remained, Croatia and Slovenia having a far higher level of development and *per capita* income than the rest of the country.

In common with other Balkan economies Yugoslavia was drawn into the German commercial orbit, and this may have restricted industrial development. Within the Nazi concept of Europe, Yugoslavia was seen as a supplier of food and raw materials, not manufactures. Principal exports were timber, crops and minerals. In 1937 she produced 350 000 tons of bauxite, but only 300 tons were processed into aluminium in Yugoslavia. The balance was exported as a raw commodity. With the invasion and occupation in the Second World War, Yugoslavia was dismembered and ceased to exist as a nation state, the economic components being subordinated to German demands.

There were real economic developments in the new and successor states of central and eastern Europe in the inter-war years. They were, however, moderated and limited by objective factors, the international trade cycle and influence of the market. The secular shift of trade in international terms from before the First World War left most of the agricultural producers and exporters at a disadvantage; the cyclical depression after 1929 worsened the position further. Thus recovery was accompanied by, and dependent upon, elaborate defensive and protective measures, import saving and general moves towards economic autarky. Ironically, it was the most industrialised economy in the region, Czechoslovakia, which endured one of the most prolonged recessions in the 1930s; industrial recovery, or very often new growth, was stronger in the least industrialised economies of the Balkans because they started from the lowest levels. There was a widespread adoption of sub-optimal policies where national governments favoured and supported those sectors in their economies which were weakest in terms of comparative advantage. Thus, as we have seen, Czechoslovakia supported the agricultural producer, Balkan states actively promoted industry despite high cost and low levels of efficiency. Such nationalist policies in turn hindered broader international economic exchange and recovery. However, in all this, these small states were merely microcosms of a similar pattern of political economy which was going on throughout Europe.

There are two broad conclusions. In all cases the states of east and central Europe were relatively weak as independent entities and readily fell under the influence of the expansionary Nazi state at the end of the 1930s. This was manifest in a variety of ways: annexation (Austria, Bohemia and Moravia); conquest (Poland, Yugoslavia); political alliance (Slovakia, Hungary, Bulgaria, Romania). Further, despite the varied and sponsored economic changes and developments, relative levels of production and national and *per capita* income changed little over the inter-war period. The Balkan States remained the poorest, as they had been in 1918, Czechoslovakia and Austria the most advanced.

11.7 Switzerland

Switzerland was unusual. Though small and vulnerable, with virtually no natural resources, it had become, even before the First World War, one of the most industrialised countries in Europe, in *per capita* terms. In this respect the country bore some similarity with Sweden: a high-income, high-cost economy very much export-oriented. Swiss industry specialised in good quality, high added value products. The most famous example, clock and watch making, exemplified the high ratio of skill to raw materials. Other well-developed industries included chemicals, both dyestuffs and pharmaceuticals, textiles and confectionery, especially chocolate. Other branches of food processing were able to exploit domestic material inputs, from the highly productive dairy sector in particular. With a small home market, exports were necessary to exploit economies of scale and fund essential imports of food, raw materials and fuel. The Depression thus affected Swiss industry severely, because of relatively inelastic import demand. Like France, Belgium, the Netherlands and Poland, the Swiss remained on gold when other economies devalued in the 1930s, eventually devaluing in 1936.

The social consequences of depression were the more serious because of the heavy regional concentration of some industries. Textiles were concentrated in the north-east cantons, chemicals almost exclusively in Basel. The most hard-hit town was St. Gallen, centre of the embroidery industry. This industry had already been badly affected by falling demand in Germany and Austria in the 1920s. Between 1910 and 1930 employment fell by over 3.5 times (117 000 to 32 000). Thereafter St. Gallen became a ghost town and the countryside round about was worst affected of all. Much of the industry was carried on through out-work, so farming families were doubly affected on top of the agricultural recession. Agricultural incomes fell far less than in many other European countries, however. Swiss farmers specialised in dairy and other animal produce – hence the milk-based products that figured in export markets. The prices of animal products fell far less steeply than field crops in the Depression. Further, Swiss farms were relatively efficient, producing higher yields than many of their neighbours to the east. Among manufacturing industry, clocks and watches were nearly as badly hit as textiles because of falling demand internationally. The newer industries, chemicals and dyes, suffered far less than the traditional sectors, though they accounted for a very small portion of industrial employment: 3.1 per cent of the total in 1929.

11.8   Further reading

There is an excellent general history of eastern Europe in H. Seton-Watson (1945) *Eastern Europe between the Wars* (Cambridge: Cambridge University Press). It pays only scant attention to major economic issues, however. These are more comprehensively addressed in I. Berend and G. Ranki (1974) *Economic Development of East-Central Europe in the 19th and 20th Centuries* (New York: Columbia University Press). More thorough and detailed material can be found in M. Kaser and E.A. Radice (eds.) (1975) *The Economic History of Eastern Europe, 1919–75*, vol. 1 (Oxford: Oxford University Press). The Balkans are examined in J. Lampe and M.R. Jackson (1982) *Balkan Economic History, 1550–1950* (Bloomington: Indiana University Press). Recently a number of texts on individual countries in the region have been published. They include: J. Lampe (1986) *The Bulgarian Economy in the Twentieth Century* (London: Routledge), T. Landau and J. Tomaszewsky (1988) *The Polish Economy in the Twentieth Century* (London: Routledge), A. Teichova (1988) *The Czechoslovak Economy, 1918–1980* (London: Routledge). All of these cover the post-war as well as inter-war years. On Austria there is the dated but valuable K.W. Rothschild (1947) *Austria's Economic Development between the Wars* (London: Muller), and on Albania a recent article, T. Hocevar (1987) 'The Albanian economy 1912–1944: a survey', *Journal of European Economic History*, **16**, pp. 561–568.

There are surprisingly few readily available references on Switzerland. J. Steinberg (1976) *Why Switzerland* (Cambridge: Cambridge University Press) has some economic material. J.F. Bergier (1984) *Histoire économique de la Suisse* (Lausanne: Payot) is a basic text available in German as well as French.

PART 4

The Second World War

12

The economy of the Second World War

12.1 Background to the war

In the 1930s, war became an increasing possibility. All powers were aware of the danger of war and continuously increased armament expenditure on the one hand, and on the other developed diplomatic measures to avoid conflict. Recourse to the discredited policy of appeasement by Britain and France was an elaborate exercise to avoid fighting. Although it cannot be claimed that the war had simply economic causes, there is little doubt that the unstable international economic environment, the economic rivalry of the 1930s, contributed to the coming conflict. It would, further, be difficult to argue that any nation in Europe, except for Germany, had anything to gain from war. Rearmament or increases in defence expenditures were expensive, with heavy drains on national treasuries and high opportunity costs for civilian production and consumption. Any stimulus to employment and demand coming from such government expenditure, given the under-utilised capacity in most parts of Europe, was likely to be limited in effect and almost certainly less than civilian expenditure. Added to this was the mutual inter-dependence of the major economic powers in Europe. Although the 1930s saw a slow recovery of international trade after the Depression, Britain, France and Germany remained significant trading partners. Even as late as 1938 Germany was Britain's fifth largest export market (in front of the USA) and particularly important for exports of textiles and coal – both depressed sectors in Britain.

France had no more interest than Britain in going to war. The slow recovery in France in the 1930s left her industrially weakened in comparison with Germany. France also had interests in eastern Europe

which were vulnerable to an extension of German influence. Appeasement was therefore also likely to result in economic losses for France.
Arguably Italy had some potential gains from war. However, her expansionist aspirations were much stronger than her ability to carry them out.
When war broke out in 1939 she remained neutral, initially, before
invading Greece in 1940. Throughout the war Italy was subordinate to,
and dependent upon, Germany.

Although their previous political behaviour had indicated great reluctance, Britain and France declared war on Germany in September 1939,
following the German invasion of Poland. This followed a steady expansion of German interests in preceding years: German troops reoccupied
the Rhineland in 1936; in the same year the Saar rejoined the Reich,
following a referendum. But these were German areas; a real territorial
expansion came in 1938, with the *Anschluss* with Austria. No action
from western powers followed, but France and Britain did increase arms
expenditures. Later, aggression in Czechoslovakia was not resisted by
the Great Powers and in early 1939 Bohemia and Moravia were incorporated into the Reich, with Slovakia notionally becoming an independent republic.

The intervening period of appeasement had allowed some further war
preparation in Britain and France but even before this time there had
been contingency. In 1934 British aircraft production was increased,
following an early perception of the potential threat from the air. This
had a twofold effect, an extension of the RAF and civilian aeroplane
construction and ground defences against aerial attack. These included
the mundane, air raid shelters and similar precautions, as well as the
more sophisticated development of radar. From 1939 the British government gave priority to aircraft production irrespective of cost.

'Shadow factories', industrial plants with potential military use, were
built alongside civilian works beginning in 1936. Seven such were built
alongside automobile factories; later Vickers Engineering and English
Electric had similar works. All this began before 1939; there was some
similarity to the USSR, where new industrial developments were sited
away from vulnerable borders. Tractor works were built with the designed intention of converting them to tank building in time of war. In
Britain, 29 new ordnance works were opened between 1936 and 1939.
Such preparations before the war enabled rapid expansion of armaments production during the war.

France had also made contingencies for war with Germany. The Maginot line was completed before 1936, by which time France had the
largest army in western Europe. Thereafter her relative economic weakness inhibited further military expenditures. Further rearmament
contributed to the fall of the Popular Front government, and the

conservative Daladier faced a general strike in 1938. The recovery effects of war preparations in France had been limited. There was some direct stimulus to sectors such as building, iron and steel and other metallurgical industries and engineering. It is generally accepted that arms expenditure had a counter-cyclical effect in much of Europe after 1937, when renewed recession threatened. On the other hand the multiplier effects of armaments were more limited than other areas of public expenditure. There were considerable opportunity costs. Imports of vital raw materials reduced the capacity to import consumer goods; expenditures had to be paid for through taxation or loans and they were very expensive.

Appeasement was thus an understandable policy, though one discredited by history. In the 1930s Britain and France could not negotiate from a position of strength, though it later became clear that they greatly over-estimated German military power. The emerging power in the east, the Soviet Union, was also an appeaser. Nazi Germany and the USSR signed a trade treaty and non-aggression pact in 1939 in advance of the invasion of Poland. Shortly after the German invasion Soviet troops moved west to secure frontiers and occupy the eastern third of Poland and annex the Baltic republics. There also followed a war with Finland and a further extension of Soviet borders.

It is evident that before 1939 there was a real and growing fear of war and of German military might in Europe. To what extent there was an economic cause of war is a contentious issue, but there is no doubt that there were some economic factors behind German expansion and, ultimately, war. With the collapse of the already fragile international economy in the 1930s all European nations were faced by economic difficulties. There was a desperate need to secure markets and sources of supply. While there was a rational mutual interest in international trade there was a widespread political pursuit of trade minimisation. Yet no nation could be perfectly self-sufficient. Britain needed to import a large proportion of foodstuffs and raw materials; even France was a net food importer and virtually dependent on imported energy. Germany and Italy, despite their efforts, remained dependent on a margin of food imports. High grade iron ore, bauxite, copper, tungsten, as well as oil, mineral fertilisers and hosts of other vital ingredients of a modern economy were imported from beyond Europe. In the inter-war years Britain and France between them 'controlled' almost a third of the world. As we have seen, imperial possessions and allies became increasingly important as trading partners in the 1930s. Germany had no such imperial allies. Many of her resources had been lost at Versailles. Similarly, Italy was a weak economy with few native resources for growth. There were specific and particular areas of conflict over resources such as oil.

Germany and Italy were particularly vulnerable in this respect. Britain and France had most influence in the Middle East; there was a fear that German expansion might cut off British and French supplies from that quarter. For Germany trading deals within Europe (especially the Balkans and the USSR) were essential to provide foodstuffs, raw materials and oil (from Romania and the USSR). This was also consistent with the revival of the *Mitteleuropa* concept, newly manifest in Hitler's imperial aims.

Britain and France sought to secure their economic interests in the Balkans before the Munich agreement. Both had large investments in this part of Europe. Britain bought all the Romanian oil that she could in early 1939 and both tried to secure continued trading arrangements with Greece and Romania. However, by this time Germany was able to offer better trading arrangements and British and French interests were gradually excluded. German trade domination in Hungary and Bulgaria was already complete.

There were various reasons for German expansion, commercial and military, into neighbouring states. But there was a real change in 1939 when Germany was prepared to risk a war. Why was this? This is a subject that has excited considerable attention for many years and continues to do so. Arguments vary from the substantially economic reasons of the urgent need for foodstuffs, living space and raw materials, to the political emphasis on long-term expansionism. Such a view would be supported by the declared aim of expanding the territory of the Reich – first to include the Volksdeutsche and then to take further living space in the east. This explanation, therefore, sees economic forces as being marshalled, through the four-year plan, for the political purpose of war. There is much to support such a view. Hitler's rambling objectives in *Mein Kampf*, written in the 1920s, outline such an aim. The expansion in the 1930s thus seems systematic and consistent with a long-term strategy.

Contrary arguments doubt the consistency of Hitler's thinking, however, seeing his behaviour as much more opportunistic and short-term, frequently irrational. There is general agreement that the economy was not well geared for war in 1939; emphasis on opportunism would cohere with this. On the other hand it is reasonable to deduce that Hitler did not really expect Britain and France to declare war. Such questions remain unresolved. Lack of war preparation might also point to relative economic weakness: that Hitler led Germany to war not because she had a powerful economic base but rather because she faced economic crisis.

The basis of this view is that from 1939 Germany faced inflationary pressures and growing consumption demand – overheating, in a modern phrase. There were real deficits in some food supplies, especially fats, and the four-year plan was behind schedule. Thus, the case goes, Germany was launched into expansion, even at the risk of war, because of domestic economic difficulty. Such a view, advanced particularly by Tim Mason, further puts forward the notion that Hitler was unsure of support among the now fully employed working class. The drive to the east would not only provide foodstuffs and living space but also unite the nation in a wave of patriotic fervour. However, as Hardach has pointed out, it is difficult to see the tyrannical forces of Nazi Germany, where there were extensive direct controls in the economy, including those over wages, being unduly anxious about unpopularity. Anyway, war was likely to be even more unpopular.

It is nonetheless true that Germany was militarily less prepared for war than she claimed (and others believed) at the time. Although, by 1939, Germany was spending more on arms than either Britain or France individually she was probably weaker militarily than the combined forces of her immediate enemies. Germany had superiority on the ground (105 divisions compared with 94 French, 40 Polish and 4 British in Europe), though there was a closer match with Britain in numbers of aircraft. Britain had overwhelming naval superiority. This in turn further heightened the need for expansion to the east in order to minimise seaborne imports. As it turned out Germany was far less vulnerable to naval blockade than had been anticipated (in either Britain or Germany). Britain was always dependent on seaborne trade and the threat to her supplies was always real.

It was not until the United States strategic bombing survey at the end of the war that a real perception of the relative lack of German economic commitment to war emerged. It thus fell into place that German plans in 1939 were not to commit economic resources for war so much as the reverse – to go to war to secure economic resources, regroup and move forward again for new gains. The military strategy of *Blitzkrieg* thus had a parallel economic basis, a *Blitzkrieg* economy. *Blitzkrieg* was the major and successful military strategy of the war years until the end of 1941. It depended on highly mobile ground forces with aerial support, which quickly enabled conquest of Poland, Denmark, Holland, Belgium and, by passing the Maginot line, France. The small British force sent as a token in response to the invasion of Poland (Britain and France could do nothing in reality to defend Poland) was driven into the sea and evacuated from Dunkirk.

Blitzkrieg was thus a successful policy, but was based on a land army. A naval and aerial invasion of Britain was called off after the Battle of Britain. In June 1941 German forces invaded the Soviet Union. By November of that year they had reached the suburbs of Moscow and were laying siege to Leningrad. From here *Blitzkrieg* as a military strategy was defeated in a long, drawn out war of attrition. What of the notion of a *Blitzkrieg* economy?

A strong consensus supports the idea of a *Blitzkrieg* economy in the early part of the war, though the concept is particularly associated with the writings of Alan Milward (1965, 1977). This suggests that the German economy was not converted to war needs in depth because it was not necessary. The fruits of conquest were used to provide the means for further conquest, though the long-term objectives were clear. These were essentially expansion in the east and the incorporation of the defeated territories into a larger economic system (*Grossraumwirtschaft*) under a New Order, somewhat similar to the nineteenth century notion of *Mitteleuropa*. In order to be able to expand to the east, it was first of all necessary to defeat France (in this scenario the defeat of Britain was not vital). France would not be expected to provide great value to the greater German economy; rather the major contribution would come from the Ukraine and the Balkans, in the form of food and raw materials. At the industrial heart would lie Germany, including Austria, and the industrial regions of Bohemia and Silesia. As it turned out this scheme was a long way from reality.

There is much to support the idea of a *Blitzkrieg* economy (many of the tanks used to invade France were made in Pilzen, formerly in Czechoslovakia, for instance). However, this view has been challenged by Richard Overy (1982, 1987, 1988). He stresses the long-term economic commitment to war and plans for a lengthy war (10–15 years) to run from 1942. That these plans were disturbed by the outbreak of war in 1939, before the plans were complete, makes them no less valid. Such matters of interpretation remain unresolved. We may safely conclude that in economic terms Germany was far from fully mobilised in 1939; that she had long-term expansionist objectives that could only be met by war at some point (though Hitler did not expect Britain and France to declare war in 1939). Thus war preparation was essential to the Nazi economy.

12.2 The war economy

Any consideration of the war economies in Europe is dominated by an examination of events in Germany. By the end of 1940 virtually the whole of continental Europe was allied to or occupied by Germany and thus directly influenced by the German war economy. The only exceptions were neutral states, Sweden, Switzerland, Spain and Portugal.

Britain, as has been suggested above, mobilised quickly for war and in some respects became more fully a war economy than Germany. A larger proportion of the civilian labour force was employed in war industries, for example, though Germany committed a higher proportion of national product to military expenditure. British output of nearly all military equipment exceeded German levels.

German economy at war

The economic history of Germany in the war years falls readily into three periods: the time of expansion and conquest through *Blitzkrieg* (to the winter of 1941/2); the period of prolonged war to mid-1944 and the final period to the collapse in May 1945, during which time there was maximum war effort in Germany.

In the *Blitzkrieg* period the effects of the war on the German economy were relatively minor. It remains a contentious issue how far this was a deliberate policy but it is generally agreed that the German economy was less fully geared for war than, for example, Britain. As has been stated above, the logic of *Blitzkrieg* was that there was little need for long-term productive plans. It is not always clear how far this was system or muddle, however. The lowest supply level of aluminium for German forces, for instance, was just at the time when the Red Army was preparing to counter-attack in the winter of 1941/2. German forces had invaded Russia in June 1941 inadequately equipped for winter fighting, because there seemed to have been an unrealistically optimistic assumption about the duration of the fighting. The further logic of *Blitzkrieg* was that conquered territories would provide resources. They would necessarily, therefore, need to be exploited in the short term. From the outset, therefore, there was a contradiction with the grandiose schemes for a New Order in Europe.

Within Germany the *Blitzkrieg* economy had only a small effect on consumption. The total output of consumer goods changed hardly at all, and consumer expenditure *in toto* in 1940 was higher than war expenditures. The British population were more directly affected by war than their German counterparts before 1941. Military production was varied to meet immediate demands: an emphasis on vehicles before the invasion of France; aeroplanes and ships before the Battle of Britain; general war supplies before the invasion of the USSR. The lack of commitment in depth provided the advantage of flexibility and adaptability.

As Milward (1965, 1977) has repeatedly stressed, *Blitzkrieg* reduced the need for control and planning. Government controls in all combatant nations were, in the short run, seen largely in terms of finance through taxation. In Germany personal tax rates were lower than in Britain, though real incomes had been lower than in Britain in 1939.

Germany also used occupation payments as an extraordinary source of taxation on those she conquered. As Britain was forced to run down her capital assets to finance the war (before the entry of the USA) Germany was rapidly expanding hers.

Germany, like the western Allies, was aware of the dangers of blockade. This had seriously weakened the economy of imperial Germany in the First World War. In one sense, therefore, German penetration into south-eastern Europe, and the incorporation of Austria and the Czech lands in the 1930s, had served to counteract such a danger. Further, the invasion of Poland itself provided Germany with increased access to coal and food supplies. Above all, the trade treaty with the USSR in 1939, immediately preceding the Polish invasion, had secured supplies of food, raw materials and fuels and so lessened any possible effect of systematic blockade. The war strategy of *Blitzkrieg* was a means to extend sources of further supplies as they arose.

The military strategy of *Blitzkrieg* came to an end on the vast expanses of European Russia. Germany's failure to defeat Soviet forces and the entry of the USA into the War in 1941 brought formal allies to Britain and her empire and military superiority to the opponents of the axis powers.

There were important changes in the German economy. More elaborate systems of control were introduced with a greater degree of commitment of resources to the war effort. Here again are areas of scholarly dispute over the extent or 'suddenness' of changes in the war economy. From an essentially expansionist position Germany was now required to fight a war of survival. Consumption was reduced as priority went to the needs of war; occupied territories were more fully exploited.

A central planning committee was established in February 1942 under the direction of Fritz Todt. His death quickly brought his deputy, Albert Speer, to the chair, a position of great responsibility. Many observers agree that it was Speer's organisational genius which enabled German resources to be marshalled for the long war effort – longer than was anticipated. Speer was able to oversee an increase in armaments by determining the distribution of raw materials. Greater war production was achieved through shifts in production rather than overall increases. Thus some, like Milward (1965, 1977), have doubted the extent and reality of planning as such, seeing the process much more as the control of resources and determination of priorities. Speer allowed industry much more leeway in the management of its own affairs. Control was limited also by conflict of interest and anomalies. The SS had their own economic empire, separated from the central planning body. It was only in 1942 that the Final Solution programme to exterminate Europe's Jews was introduced. Quite apart from the hideous brutality and inhumanity of this policy it involved a real and serious diversion of resources, especially of manpower and transport, to move and imprison such vast numbers. On the other hand, this inhumane policy was to be self-financing at no financial cost to the German taxpayer (there was always an opportunity cost, however). Thus the property and meagre belongings of the dispossessed Jews were used to pay for the means of their death.

Over the war years as a whole domestic resources were taken through taxation and borrowing to finance the war effort. Taxes paid for about a third of the cost, a fifth came from loans from institutions and war bonds and a third from bank credits. One eighth of the cost came from occupied territories. There was also a recourse to the printing press, in anticipation of further assets being secured through conquest. Even so, inflation in Germany in the war was kept under tighter control than elsewhere.

Labour

The constraint on the German economy was labour. Even before the war labour shortages had developed; in the war years, with conscription, they became serious. By the time Speer came to office six million men had been lost from the labour market – mostly under arms, some killed or wounded. The solution was to increase the employment of foreign labour, including prisoners of war, within and beyond Germany. Women were also employed on a significant scale in wartime Germany, especially as demands for labour increased. By 1944 female labour made up almost 52 per cent of the German total.

Foreign labour had been employed before the war as well, particularly migrant Polish and Italian workers. In wartime this increased substantially. Prisoners of war were, as a rule, forced to work (under the Geneva convention only officers were excused; German and Italian POWs in Britain were also required to work). Those from the east were subjected to the most brutal exploitation. In the short run, to 1941, Poles provided the majority of foreign workers; the proportion declined thereafter though the absolute numbers increased. In total 2.8 million Poles were forced to work in Germany. Initially, imprisoned Soviet soldiers were not allowed to work – they were considered racially inferior, though this did not prevent their being put to fight against their former comrades. In the initial onslaught on Russia some four million prisoners were taken; by February 1942 only 1.1 million were left alive. From April 1942 they were put to work, virtually as slaves, and casualties continued. The exploitation was not confined to men, nor to POWs. Half a million 'strong and healthy girls' were taken from the east to alleviate work for the German farmer and housewife. There is an interesting sidelight on racial policy: Russians, Poles and other Slavs were exploited, those in the former Baltic States were not. In part this was because they were not obviously enemies of Germany – their nations had been annexed by the USSR in 1940 and were arguably 'liberated' by the Germans after 1941. However, racial factors also played a part for Balts (the Jewish population apart) were considered as Aryan. They were never required to work for the Reich but instead were recruited to fight for the Reich against the Red Army. Those from Luxembourg were conscripted; the country was regarded as part of 'Greater Germany'.

Slave labour is inefficient, but of course cheap. IG Farben complained at the cost of slave labour, passed to the company by the SS, and at the low productivity. Other foreign labour was more productive. Altogether foreign workers increased in number from 4.2 million in 1942 to 6.3 million in 1943 and 7.1 million in 1944, the latter figure being equivalent to 20 per cent of the civilian labour force. About half were working in industry. The most productive, from the German point of view, were the French. By autumn 1942 there were 1.3 million French POWs and civilian workers in Greater Germany. Speer was greatly attracted by French workers; they were well educated and experienced in factory work, often highly skilled. Their productivity levels were close to that of German workers, and probably higher than of French workers in France. French labour made a great contribution to the German economy. Incentives were offered to recruit more French workers in Germany. A programme (known as *La Rélève*) to exchange French workers for released prisoners of war was instituted, with the enthusiastic endorsement of the Vichy regime. For every three workers who volunteered to go to Germany a prisoner would be released and sent home. It met with disappointing results, so that more German production was undertaken in France in the short run. As the war progressed more coercive measures were introduced. Altogether some 634 376 (civilian) workers left France to work in Germany. The figures exclude Pas-de-Calais and the Nord, which, added to those moving from Belgium, numbered 159 798. Polish workers were subject to effective conscription to work in Germany and sometimes to literal 'rounding up' on the streets. The French were never subject to such indignities. Another occupied territory, Norway, provided no labour for Germany, but it had a small population and even the need to 'import' labour from Denmark.

As well as using foreign labour under duress more effective use was made of German labour. Average labour productivity increased through extending working hours and, more especially, technological innovations. The major productivity improvements were in the armaments industry. However, German production never kept pace with the Allies. Curiously, standardisation was poor in German industry, though quality and reliability were of a high order. Workers were moved from service sectors to manufacturing, and from consumer goods into armaments. In these various ways Speer and the Planning Board were able to increase war production.

Such an increase, however, was indicative also of the slack in the German economy in the years before 1942. Throughout the war years, the Allies assumed that the German economy was stretched to full capacity. This mistaken notion, to be disabused only at the end of the war, formed the basis of the Allies' military strategy of systematic aerial bombardment. It was decided that bombing railways, industrial plants, shipyards and civilian areas would weaken the economy and the war effort by breaking the over-stretched chain of production and supply. This was a mistake. In economic terms aerial damage was minimal before 1944. Night raids by British bombers were more costly for the British, in weapons, machines and manpower, than for Germany.

It is also clear that there was yet more spare capacity in the German war economy. Round the clock shift work was less common than in Britain. Even in armaments production Germany was outperformed by the Allies – largely because of the American contribution. Although Speer was able to organise a threefold increase in arms production, the combined total of the Allies exceeded this. The USSR was able to exceed German production of tanks, military aircraft and guns. The major contribution came from the USA. In 1944 about 60 per cent of all the Allies' munitions were made in the USA. And it was not only in the supply of armaments that the USA was paramount. The most bulky and important shipments to Britain and the USSR under lend–lease were foodstuffs.

Britain also made generous provisions for her Soviet allies. These deliveries were grants, not loans (like lend–lease), and were made at great risk. Britain sent £308 million worth of military and £112 million non-military deliveries to the USSR. The USA sent $11.6 billion worth of supplies direct to the USSR, as well as constructing expensive transport facilities through Iran (Persia), and $30 000 million worth to Britain and the Empire.

German allies

The Axis powers were less co-ordinated economically than the western Allies. In particular Germany and Japan had virtually no contact at all, fighting separate wars. Within Europe Germany had closer links with her allied economies, which to a large extent had been built up before the war. Thus in 1940 the Balkan States, together with Greece and Hungary, were important trading partners. This was to continue. Such economies were important sources of raw materials and foodstuffs. As the war continued, however, Germany found herself having to support her allies economically.

The most dependent of all was Italy. The Italian economy had shown very little recovery in the 1930s. In the war years an inadequate tax system failed to finance military effort sufficiently. Inflation increased, a black market was rampant and total production declined. This was evident even when the war was going well; Italy was faced with complete ruin from 1942. By the end of the European war total production in Italy was no higher than it had been in 1900. Before her capitulation in 1943 Italy had become almost completely dependent on Germany. In 1941 and 1942 Germany took about 50 per cent of Italian exports and provided 61 per cent of imports. Italy was completely dependent on Germany for coal supplies, with the effect of some diversion from German war needs.

Occupied areas

As grand as the New Order for Europe had been, in reality it amounted to nothing. The occupied areas under German control were largely exploited for the German war effort. There was little co-ordination or integration with the economy of the Reich proper. Only in the long run was any attempt made to co-ordinate production in various areas. Further, the expectation that the eastern lands would be major sources of value to the Reich was not fulfilled.

Occupied areas were exploited for German war purposes in several ways. The provision of labour, which was one of the most important, has already been referred to. Beyond this was the payment of taxes, as occupation costs and bilateral trading deals, both of which were arranged to the advantage of the occupying power. In both cases also the arbitrary exchange rate was manipulated to German advantage. In addition there was direct plunder or looting and other consumption by occupying troops, which cannot easily be recorded. In all cases productive assets were run down.

Occupation costs (tax) were highest in *per capita* terms in Norway (and absolutely in France). In the first two years of the war they equalled 1842 krone per head. Payments from the Netherlands were close to this, those from France at about 42 per cent of this figure, from Denmark 31 per cent. Altogether occupation costs amounted to about one third of Norway's national income, though there are difficulties with making such an estimate. There had been grand plans for Norway, as a primary exporter of fish and minerals within the *Grossraumwirtschaft*. With the availability of cheap HEP and an established aluminium industry Norway was a further asset. Also the heavy water plant was developed in Norway. Otherwise industrial development was resisted by the occupiers.

But the value of the Norwegian economy was very limited. It was very small with no 'excess' labour for use in Germany. Norway had been heavily trade dependent, a primary producer but net importer of food and fuel before the war, much paid for by the merchant marine whose earnings were now negligible. Thus Germany had to supply Norway's needs so the country became more of an economic liability than an asset, with an import surplus from Germany. This is not to understate the hardships borne by the population. Norwegians were probably more harshly treated than the Danes who, like the Dutch, went without to feed the Reich. In Belgium German interests penetrated the well-established industrial bases, taking majority holdings of several industries. But, again, the results were not impressive for the German economy. Belgium was small, much of her capital was run down and was further exhausted in the war. The German market was dominant for the metallurgical and engineering sectors. But productivity was disappointing, sometimes declining through the use of outdated capital and passive resistance and sabotage by Belgian workers. Belgian resistance was one of the most effective in the war.

The most valuable occupied economy through the war was France. She provided much labour and the highest absolute level of occupation costs. In total French payments provided 42 per cent of German receipts from this source in the war. The country was divided into two, an unoccupied zone in the south east, and the rest under military occupation. The civilian government moved to Vichy in the unoccupied zone. The distinction disappeared in 1942 when all the country was occupied.

Occupation costs were initially set at 20 million RM per day. Although this was rarely met – the actual figure paid was nearer to 15 million – it was a severe strain on the French. It was made all the greater by the over-valuation of the mark, by 63 per cent compared with 1939 levels. (This was done elsewhere but to a lesser extent: 24 per cent for Croatia, 33 per cent for Polish General Government, 42 per cent for the Netherlands, 50 per cent for Belgium.) The tax was raised to 25 million RM in December 1942. French resources meanwhile were reduced with the annexation of Alsace-Lorraine and the separation of Flanders and eastern Burgundy.

The takeover of the French economy was piecemeal but became more extensive than elsewhere. Initially it amounted to looting or little more, taking copper, bauxite and other minerals as well as foodstuffs and transport equipment. However, this was not mere seizure. Formally supplies were purchased, through proper contracts, but the bargaining power always lay with the occupying forces. It was easier in the short run to gain access to iron ore, because the major mines were in the occupied zone, than bauxite, which was in the unoccupied zone. After 1942 the distinction disappeared.

As the German war economy came to depend more on all occupied areas after 1942, demands increased. More workers were recruited to work in Germany; more resources in France were used directly by Germany. France provided a ready made aircraft industry which was increasingly used for German military purposes. Gradually Speer tried to incorporate French industry into the German war economy rather than just take resources from it. This met with imperfect results as productivity declined because of inadequate capital replacement and poor domestic rations. But the increased exploitation of France in particular enabled the German war economy to survive for some time. Milward (1970) estimates that 40–50 per cent of the total non-agricultural production of France (in 1943) was for German consumption. There was a real contraction of French resources. Three-quarters of the iron ore, 60 per cent of iron and steel, 64 per cent of cars and bicycles, 34 per cent of chemicals were sent to Germany. Agricultural produce was vital also. By the end of the 1942–43 harvest year, Germany was taking 15 per cent of French agricultural output. The German bread ration depended on French grain.

All this added up to a decline of the French economy; falls in production, productivity and consumption. Real wages fell by at least 40 per cent as money incomes failed to keep pace with prices. Rations were reduced; consumption fell by more than in other western occupied countries. The inflation of the black market added to the real, if unrecorded, hardship for the French population.

Eastern territories

Under the theory of *Grossraumwirtschaft*, the eastern lands were expected to make a major contribution to the German economy, France a negligible or neutral one. As it turned out the opposite was the case. Early in the war there was systematic dispossession of Polish property in the zones incorporated into the Reich. The currency was replaced by the mark and Polish farmers were thrown off land which was taken over by German settlers, some 631 000 in total. These territories had, before the invasion, provided 100 per cent of Poland's coal, 97.5 per cent of her pig iron, 90 per cent of steel and 70 per cent of textiles and sugar. The remaining General Government of Poland was also looted. The objective seemed to be to turn Poland into an agrarian state and source of labour. Industrial equipment was dismantled and taken to Germany; high food procurements were imposed. Within nominally independent Poland (in reality the government was directly appointed by the Germans), Germans received larger food rations than native Poles; the Jews least of all. There were even some shops for the use of Germans only. The Poles suffered the greatest relative population loss in the war.

Bohemia and Moravia were annexed from Czechoslovakia and some areas of Yugoslavia, which were also dismembered and 'Germanised'. Czech industry was a major asset to Germany; Yugoslavia provided some vital raw materials such as chrome and bauxite. The Ukraine promised much, and for a while the occupying forces were welcomed as liberators from the Russians. However, the savagery of the occupation alienated the population and lost potential support. The population were treated as sub-human, as were the Poles, and subject to great cruelty, exceeded only by that meted out to the Jews. In May 1942 the Reich Commissar in the Ukraine ordered that all grain in private hands be surrendered save for 10 kg per head per month and 1.5 kg of fodder per day per head of cattle.

Apart from foodstuffs the occupied zones of the Soviet Union provided little for the Reich. Yet before the invasion these areas had been the industrial and agricultural heartland of the country. The Russians destroyed much themselves in retreat, flooding coal mines and destroying power plants and factories so that the invaders were never able to get them back into production. Partisan movements also served to disturb the German army. The only resource of any value to the economy was manganese. In more ways than one the war was won and lost on the plains of western Russia. The coal available was not adequate even for the occupying forces.

It is clear that war plans amounted to little. The New Order was not instituted because the territory could not provide a perfect or complete trading area. More importantly, the demands of war disturbed any such prospects. Racial and occupation policies destroyed whatever possibility there might have been. The German economy was not able to survive the drawn out demands of war after the expansion of *Blitzkrieg* faded out. She was able to delay the decline and defeat by passing on to the occupied areas the burdens of economic demands. The cost to the occupied areas was enormous and far greater in the east than the west. In all cases it involved a run down of productive capacity, so that it would have proved impossible to maintain a 'self-supporting' economic area. As the Germans retreated across western Russia through 1943 and 1944 they instituted their own 'scorched earth' policy and took with them food, livestock and movable property. Systematic destruction in defeat was used also in Finland (after 1944) and to a lesser extent Italy (after 1943), both former allies.

12.3   Neutral states

Neutral states did not avoid the war. The whole of Europe was subject to war in one way or another. Trade routes and markets were disrupted; transatlantic trade hazardous. Sweden was able to make some gains because Germany remained a major market; Sweden was the major source of supply of iron ore and high-quality industrial products like ball bearings. Switzerland faced some hardship in obtaining food imports.

Switzerland

When war broke out Switzerland mobilised her conscript army. This affected 10 per cent of the adult population – more than any other nation at the time. They were not required to fight, though they remained on alert in mountain locations. Hitler had not respected neutrality elsewhere. Ambitious plans were made to make the country self-sufficient in food as far as possible. This was striking as she had imported 45 per cent of all food (by calorific value) in 1938, when agriculture had provided only 9 per cent of national income. Western allies allowed food imports to the besieged economy, though Britain threatened to cut them off as a lever to limit Swiss trade with Germany. However, as Britain was also a customer of Switzerland she eased her attitude, allowing additional imports in 1943. For a time before then ships had been allowed to enter unoccupied French ports with food supplies for Switzerland. They bore the Swiss flag and were in effect a Swiss merchant navy.

In terms of foodstuffs, the Swiss response to war was more importantly to reduce consumption, from one of the highest pre-war levels, and increase home production. By 1944 imports were only one quarter of their 1937 level; the country had become self-sufficient in eggs, potatoes, three quarters of bread grains and half oil and fats. Industrially the country prospered by selling to both sides. Britain needed precision jewel bearings, for example, and made mountings for anti-aircraft guns under licence from Oerlikon. The vulnerability of geography made the Swiss beholden to Germany to an extent and they were forced by circumstance to sign clearing agreements in 1940 and 1941. Total trade fell in the war years but arms-related exports to Germany increased. At the end of the war her industries, like Sweden's, remained intact and she was therefore in a strong position to respond to demand in post-war Europe.

Sweden

Swedish neutrality in the war is generally regarded as having been beneficial to the economy. Like Switzerland she imposed rationing in the face of import difficulties; similarly, general mobilisation was introduced for fear of a German invasion. Unlike Switzerland, Sweden provided sanctuary for refugees, most famously almost the entire Jewish population from Denmark. But it is also true that Swedish industry profited from the German war economy. This was one reason why she was not invaded. Invasion and occupation would have meant resistance and probably therefore greater difficulty in obtaining the vital resources of iron and ball bearings and other goods. Being surrounded by Germany, her allies (Finland) or occupied states (Denmark and Norway), with the major export outlets through Narvik and the Baltic Sea under German control, Sweden had little option in trading with Germany. Germany became her largest market, taking 42 per cent of exports in 1941–44 compared with 17 per cent in 1936–38. Further, some Swedish merchant shipping effectively made up losses suffered by Germany. In return Germany sold fertilisers, coal and lignite, and synthetic rubber. The total volume of trade declined.

Swedish agriculture had been improved in the 1930s to a level close to basic self-sufficiency but there was still need for much seaborne trade. Further, the major paper and pulp industries needed export markets. Britain allowed Swedish merchant ships passage to non-belligerent markets and the import of such goods as coffee and rice. However, allied pressure was applied to reduce exports to Germany. SKF, the giant ball bearing manufacturer, reduced them for a while in 1943 before resuming former levels. Later, scarcely concealed threats from Britain and the USA to bomb the SKF factory led to a reduction in exported volume in 1944. Nonetheless these exports provided the company with substantial profits.

12.4   Further reading

The background to the Second World War has been extensively examined in recent years. An excellent general book is P. Bell (1986) *The Origins of the Second World War in Europe* (London: Longman). W.

Carr (1985) *Poland to Pearl Harbour. The Making of the Second World War* (London: Arnold) gives a more international picture, with greater emphasis on diplomatic affairs. Economic reorganisation for war by the major combatants has recently been surveyed by M. Harrison (1988) 'Resource mobilization for World War II: the U.S.A., U.K., U.S.S.R. and Germany, 1938–1945', *Economic History Review,* **41**, pp. 171–192. German objectives and preparations for war have been analysed in great detail. B. Klein (1959) *Germany's Economic Preparations for War* (Cambridge, Mass.: Harvard University Press) is a basic work. The idea of the '*Blitzkrieg* economy' is taken up and developed by A. Milward (1965) *The German Economy at War* (London: Athlone). Further major books by the same author develop the theme in relation to occupied territories: (1970) *The New Order and The French Economy* (Oxford: Oxford University Press) and (1972) *The Fascist Economy in Norway* (Oxford: Clarendon Press). He has also written a general work on the War (1977) *War, Economy and Society 1939–1945* (London: Allen Lane). Milward's ideas on German war preparation have been challenged by R.J. Overy in a number of articles: (1982) 'Hitler's war and the German economy: a reinterpretation', *Economic History Review,* **35**, pp. 272–291; (1987) 'Germany, Domestic Crisis and War in 1939', *Past and Present,* (contributors: T. Mason, R. Overy, D. Kaiser) **116**, pp. 138–168; (1988) 'Mobilization for Total War in Germany, 1939–41', *English Historical Review,* **53**, pp. 613–639. See also (1989) 'Debate: Germany, domestic crisis and war in 1939', *Past and Present,* **122**, pp. 200–240.

Postscript: Europe after World War Two

In contrast to the years following the First World War Europe after 1945 moved into a period of unprecedented growth and prosperity. This growth was accompanied by features missing from the inter-war years: secular inflation and international agreements to regulate exchange rates, payments and trade. International trade grew at a faster rate than total production and intra-European trade grew faster than the world total. Total trade turnover moved from $61 billion in 1950 to $312.7 billion in 1970 (in current prices). Of this total 21.6 per cent was intra-European in 1950, 39.5 per cent in 1970 (the 1938 figure was 29.2 per cent). Movements in total output in European countries are shown in Table P.1. On average the economies of western Europe grew at 1.5 per cent per annum between 1913 and 1938; from 1948 to 1958 the rate was 4.5 per cent per annum. Thus there are marked contrasts to the 1920s when recovery and growth was moderated by restrictions to international trade and exchange. However, there was no return, after 1945, to the liberal economic environment of the years before the First World War. Capital movements were restricted by exchange controls; the movement of labour was even more limited.

In the short run, however, the picture was far from favourable. The Second World War was far more destructive of life and property, and on a far wider scale, than the First. Aerial bombardment brought destruction to civilian areas unimagined a generation earlier. About 42 million people were killed in Europe in the war; of these 26 million were civilian. The greatest absolute losses were in the USSR (25 million), the greatest relative losses in Poland (4.5 million). An estimated 10 million dwellings were destroyed in Germany, four million in Britain, two million in France; losses in the east were of an even higher order. Capital

Table P.1   Index of total volume of output (GDP)

	1938	1948	1958	1968
Austria	100.0	82.0	170.8	269.7
Belgium	126.1	134.0	181.6	279.4
Denmark	160.5	189.7	268.7	429.1
Finland	197.5	219.5	334.3	545.7
France	120.8	125.8	205.0	347.8
Germany	168.8	124.9	322.8	529.1
Italy	148.0	146.1	262.3	462.8
Netherlands	171.6	221.4	337.9	567.7
Norway	208.1	271.1	371.2	593.7
Poland	145.3	195.8[3]	258.6	475.0
Spain	142.3[1]	113.7	203.6	368.0
Sweden	180.7	281.3	405.1	627.6
Switzerland	162.6	204.1	286.3	458.2
UK	132.5	150.2	192.8	265.8
Bulgaria	157.0	219.3[3]	355.1	714.3
Czechoslovakia	149.8[2]	156.3[3]	263.7	323.7
Hungary	134.3	127.8[3]	183.5	287.9
Yugoslavia	156.4	173.6	264.8	457.4

1913 = 100

[1] 1935
[2] 1937
[3] 1950

From B.R. Mitchell (1975) *European Historical Statistics*, (Cambridge: Cambridge University Press)

losses are difficult to calculate. The USSR probably lost the most (25 per cent of pre-war capital stock, though this was partly offset by territorial expansion). Britain lost 18 per cent, nearly all of which was in the form of overseas assets. Other losses in this sense amounted to 16 per cent for Austria, (West) Germany 12 per cent, France 10 per cent and Italy 7 per cent.

As in 1919 there were territorial changes. The USSR consolidated its territorial gains to incorporate the Baltic republics and much of eastern Poland, Karelia from Finland, Bessarabia (Moldavia) from Romania and border areas of Czechoslovakia. Germany ceded territory to Poland in the east. The political division of Europe between spheres of influence, east and west, was probably more important than territorial changes *per se*. Both contributed to the flood of refugees and displaced persons that appeared. It was estimated that there were eight million refugees in Berlin alone (mainly moving from east to west) after 1945. Urban starvation was reported in Germany, Hungary, Austria, Poland and the north of Italy. Even in 1947 rations in parts of Germany, which were low enough anyway (1550 calories per day), were often falling short; in the Ruhr they were as low as 800 calories.

Although there was no deliberately punishing peace treaty (in fact there was never any peace treaty between Germany and the western Allies), occupying forces did exact reparations from Germany for a period. Germany was occupied by the four major powers – Britain, France, the USA and the USSR – and its territory divided accordingly. As is well known the three western zones became the Federal Republic (the first elections were in 1949) and the Soviet zone the German Democratic Republic in 1950. In the short run, however, the occupying forces systematically removed resources from Germany. This was at its most extreme in the east, where Soviet forces picked the country clean and continued to make reparation demands until 1954. The western powers had put forward ideas to 'pastoralise' the German economy, completely removing its industrial potential. These were never implemented, though the Allies did set out to limit German industrial output to half the 1938 levels of production. British forces began dismantling machinery and equipment (the British occupied the major industrial regions as well as the Hamburg shipyards) with the aim of getting cheap capital for Britain and weakening a potential competitor. However, such a policy of destruction was quickly brought to an end (before the end of 1946) in the western zones. It was costly – local people had to be fed at allied, particularly American, expense, yet they were being denied the chance to work and earn a living. It was also increasingly evident that a greater perceived threat was in the east and that a revived and friendly Germany was a valuable ally and bastion. Thus a gradual shift towards encouraging production began. Probably the great turning point was the monetary reform in 1948. Price controls had failed to stem the force of inflation and shortages of consumer goods. At one stroke controls were lifted, rationing was ended and a new currency introduced (all adults receiving 40 DM).

Germany benefited very much from the 'recovery factor', whereby idle capacity could be brought back into production very rapidly with large returns but with little input. There was much available labour in Germany in the 1940s, much of it skilled. There were also cultural factors. The German people had nowhere to go but up. They displayed a readiness to work hard for little reward, both a function of an ingrained work ethic and the stark reality of having little choice. Italy was in a similar if less extreme position. Her economy was in virtual ruin in 1945 with the population facing starvation in some quarters. Direct short-term relief was needed to prevent social disaster, yet capital stock in industry and agriculture was little affected. There was cheaply financed recovery to 1949. However, in this and other cases the growth continued at a rapid rate thereafter.

France had a national plan for economic modernisation from 1946. This was to make up for the stagnation of the 1930s as much as the direct effects of war. The exiled governments of Belgium and Luxembourg agreed to form an economic union with the Netherlands as early as 1944. Sweden and Switzerland emerged from the war with their industrial plant intact and were thus in a good position to benefit from the general growth in demand. British recovery and growth was relatively weak. It is not easy to find reasons for such major developments but is clear that British relative decline had been proceeding for many years and was now accelerated or more sharply exposed by the experience of the war. As we have seen, Britain lost important assets in the war years; these had represented a major source of overseas income. For the first time Britain became a net debtor, owing five thousand million dollars in 1945 against assets of $3.5 billion – a high price for military victory.

There are two broad developments which influenced the pattern of post-war growth within and beyond Europe, and each began before the end of hostilities. These were the decisions made at Bretton Woods in New England and Yalta in the Crimea. The first agreed an international system of fixed exchange rates, the establishment of the International Monetary Fund and a commitment to liberalisation of international trade (though GATT was signed in 1947). The system created was imperfect but the very agreement suggested that there was common cause to avoid the nationalist and destructive policies of the 1930s. The second agreement (it was actually earlier in time than Bretton Woods) was the carving up of Europe into spheres of influence. This acknowledged the great power status of the Soviet Union and presaged the Cold War. At the same time it invited the USA to play an active part in fostering the development of post-war Europe, in contrast to the insularity she had displayed in the 1920s. Thus in subsequent years, the USA and the USSR in varying ways supported their client states in Europe.

Perhaps the major contrast with the years following the First World War was the substantial input of American aid through the Marshall Plan of 1947. The plan is often seen as a great turning point but was really a logical development of established policies of rehabilitation for western Europe. The economic effectiveness or relative importance of Marshall aid in bringing about recovery is subject to different judgements. But there is no doubt that the capital grants helped overcome bottlenecks to dollar imports in the short run. This was especially important as the USA was a vital source of supply for western Europe in the late 1940s. Under the European Recovery Programme, from April 1948 to June 1952, $22.5 billion were made available, $19.7 billion as grants. Britain was a major beneficiary but was not able to make as much economic progress as Germany, who received less; east European countries were unable to accept the offers of Marshall aid, yet they too showed rapid rates of growth. Thus the longer term effects of Marshall aid should not be exaggerated. Rather, Marshall aid was of short-term significance in helping to meet the demand for reconstruction capital; it did not provide a stimulus for reconstruction in itself.

The Marshall aid programme also encouraged European co-operation through the Organisation for European Economic Co-operation (OEEC) which implemented the European Recovery Programme. The OEEC included all the European states in receipt of Marshall aid. Of greater ultimate importance was the European Coal and Steel Community, in 1951, between West Germany, France, Benelux and Italy. This was a first step towards the European Economic Community (EEC) which was formed by the Treaty of Rome in 1957. Two years later an alternative trade area, the European Free Trade Association (EFTA), was formed. It is uncertain what real economic effects such institutions had on growth. Undoubtedly they extended markets, but in the short run might have produced a diversion of trade from other markets rather than trade creation. In the longer run it seems that they provided a real stimulus to international trade. It was particularly important for the relatively small trade-dependent economies to have secure access to the large markets of Europe – Germany and France in the EEC, Britain within EFTA. However, France and Germany themselves became more foreign trade-dependent, probably as a result of community membership. There was also the important political function of bringing French and German economic interests together, rather than being in conflict.

Moves towards intra-European co-operation, however modest, illustrate a degree of international political commitment that was lacking in the pre-war era. At the national level also, governments played a larger role in their economies than before. In western Europe the most extreme expression of this was the case of French planning, though other countries (such as the UK, Italy and even West Germany) took a number of industries into public ownership. More universally there was an increase in state expenditure on welfare and defence. There was also a widespread commitment to maintaining full employment. In order to fund this expenditure and maintain full employment governments had an interest in, and a need for, economic growth. It is far from certain, however, whether governments were effective in bringing about this growth.

The French use of indicative planning was apparently successful. It was backed up with a leading role (especially in regional development) being played by nationalised industries. On the other hand, countries without any such planning grew as fast as or faster than France. Italy had extensive state ownership, but little effective leadership; in West Germany there was no attempt at planning. Between 1948 and 1963 France achieved a compound growth rate of GDP of 4.6 per cent, Italy 6 per cent and West Germany 7.6 per cent. Scandinavia, Switzerland and the Benelux countries also achieved high growth rates but with little direct state intervention.

If a direct state role cannot fully explain post-war growth what of an indirect role? The political commitment to full employment has been widely associated with the implementation of Keynesian demand management policies. Here again empirical investigation has cast doubt on long held assumptions. There seems little to support the idea that Keynesian policies were effective in inducing growth. They were, anyway, never universally adopted as essential to economic policy – the economic powerhouse of West Germany did not follow such policies. Further, in the longer run, unemployment returned to the economies of western Europe. Overall it seems that governments have followed rather than instigated growth, with France being the outstanding exception. However, the political commitment to and expectation of a steadily growing economy contributed to a climate of expectation which in turn fostered optimistic investment decisions.

The real engine of growth in western Europe since the post-war recovery period has been the market and, in particular, that for consumer durables. Motor cars and household goods became leading sectors in the 1950s and beyond. Technological innovations in mass production and the use of relatively new materials on a mass scale (like alloys and plastics) reduced unit costs and enhanced the market; rising productivity and real wages added to demand; and investment, much coming into Europe from the USA, was buoyant to serve that demand. The European share of an expanding world trade increased. Between 1950 and 1960 world exports grew by 6.4 per cent per annum, west European exports by 7 per cent. Within Europe experience varied – British exports increased by a modest 1.9 per cent per annum, French by 7.2 per cent, Italian by 11.8 per cent and German by 13.8 per cent. And the growing German economy was an important source of demand within Europe.

As was to become clear with the first oil price shock of 1973 this was not an unbroken boom; there had been cyclical fluctuations throughout post-war years, but with a consistent upward secular trend until this time. In the 1970s unemployment and recession returned but the social and political effects were not to be as serious as in the 1930s.

In the east, the Soviet sphere of influence, the pattern of development was dictated very much by the Stalinist model of planning, based on Soviet experience. This produced growth led by the production of capital goods rather than a consumer-led boom. Also, foreign trade tended to lag, both because of the influence of the autarkic model of Stalin and because of the failure to establish a multilateral payments system akin to that in the capitalist world. Short-run recovery was limited by Soviet demands for reparations, though the effects of these were far from totally negative. Finland, for example, built up a capital goods industry to meet such demands, but at the cost of forgone consumption. She was never subject to Soviet style planning, however. In other cases there were clear economic distortions resulting from the orientation to the Soviet market and Soviet model. Industrially, Czechoslovakia was more developed than her Soviet master; the trade of this country and Hungary, as well as others, was more properly directed to the west. But political factors prevented the operation of market relations.

To some extent politics have been more directly influential in shaping the economies of Europe since the Second World War than in earlier years. The nature and extent of the part played by government nationally or by international agreement is subject to debate. The long held positive view of the role of the Bretton Woods system has been questioned, as has the effectiveness of Keynesian policies of demand management. However, one general proposition remains true. Whereas after the First World War governments sought to recreate the old, to re-establish the liberal international system of pre-war years, after the Second World War there was no such nostalgia. Nobody wanted to recreate the 1930s but rather to introduce a radically new economic regime.

Index